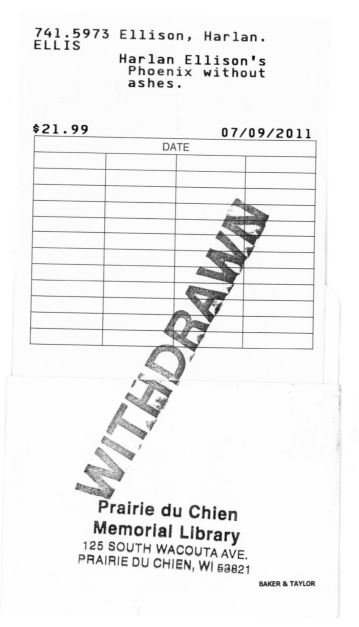

HARLAN ELLISON'S
PHOENIX WITHOUT ASHES

An EDGEWORKS Offering
ABBEY

in association with
IDW PUBLISHING | SAN DIEGO

IDW

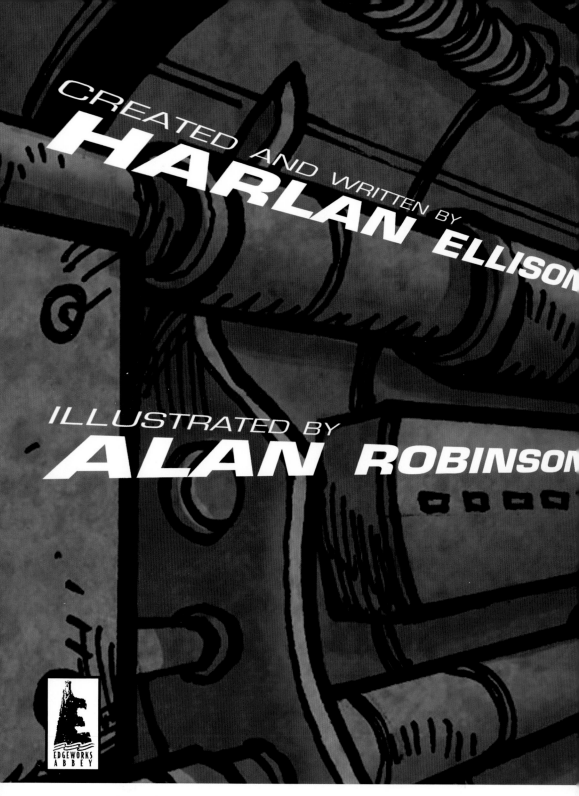

CREATED AND WRITTEN BY **HARLAN ELLISON**

ILLUSTRATED BY **ALAN ROBINSON**

EDGEWORKS
ABBEY

Special thanks to Ed Bryant for his invaluable assistance.

www.IDWPUBLISHING.com

Regular Edition ISBN: 978-1-60010-800-6   14 13 12 11   1 2 3 4
S/N Edition ISBN: 978-1-60010-932-4   14 13 12 11   1 2 3 4

IDW™ IDW Publishing is: Operations: Ted Adams, CEO & Publisher • Greg Goldstein, Chief Operating Officer • Matthew Ruzicka, CPA, Chief Financial Officer • Alan Payne, VP of Sales • Lorelei Bunjes, Director of Digital Services • Jeff Webber, Director of ePublishing • AnnaMaria White, Dir., Marketing and Public Relations • Dirk Wood, Dir., Retail Marketing • Marci Hubbard, Executive Assistant • Alonzo Simon, Shipping Manager • Angela Loggins, Staff Accountant • Cherrie Go, Assistant Web Designer • Editorial: Chris Ryall, Chief Creative Officer, Editor-In-Chief • Scott Dunbier, Senior Editor, Special Projects • Andy Schmidt, Senior Editor • Justin Eisinger, Senior Editor, Books • Kris Oprisko, Editor/Foreign Lic. • Denton J. Tipton, Editor • Tom Waltz, Editor • Mariah Huehner, Editor • Carlos Guzman, Assistant Editor • Bobby Curnow, Assistant Editor • Design: Robbie Robbins, EVP/Sr. Graphic Artist • Neil Uyetake, Senior Art Director • Chris Mowry, Senior Graphic Artist • Amauri Osorio, Graphic Artist • Gilberto Lazcano, Production Assistant • Shawn Lee, Graphic Artist

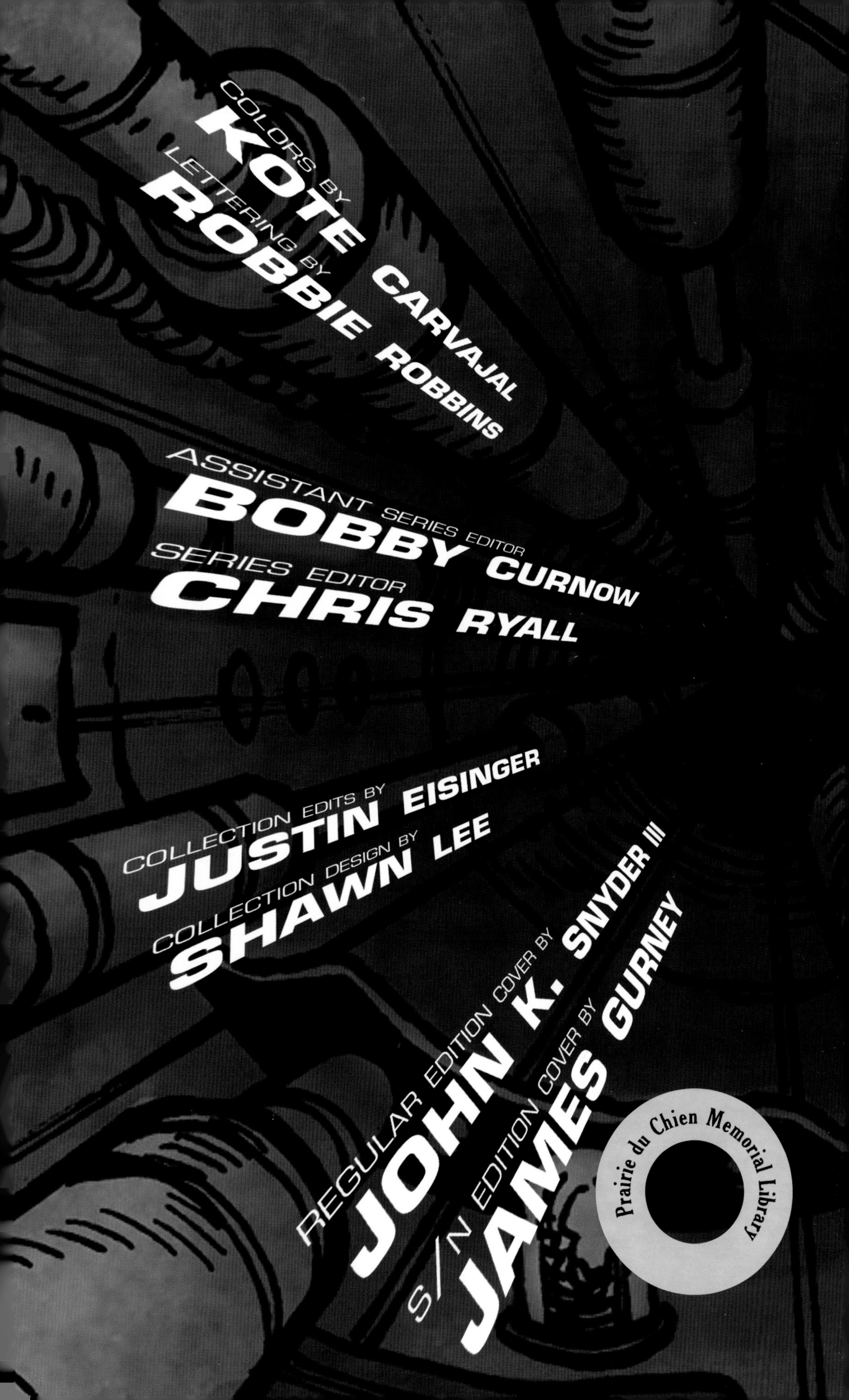

COLORS BY
KOTE CARVAJAL

LETTERING BY
ROBBIE ROBBINS

ASSISTANT SERIES EDITOR
BOBBY CURNOW

SERIES EDITOR
CHRIS RYALL

COLLECTION EDITS BY
JUSTIN EISINGER

COLLECTION DESIGN BY
SHAWN LEE

REGULAR EDITION COVER BY
JOHN K. SNYDER III

S/N EDITION COVER BY
JAMES GURNEY

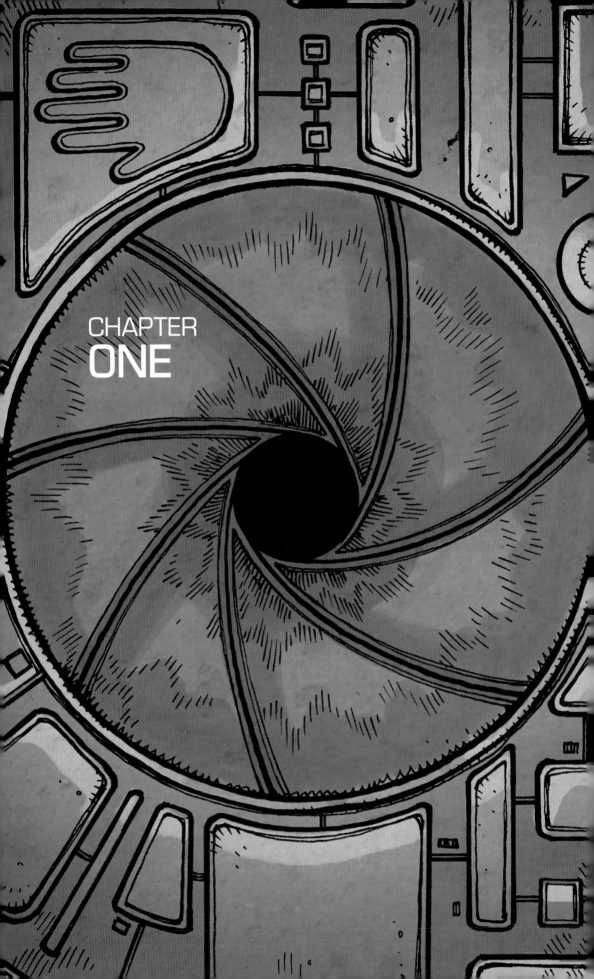

CHAPTER
ONE

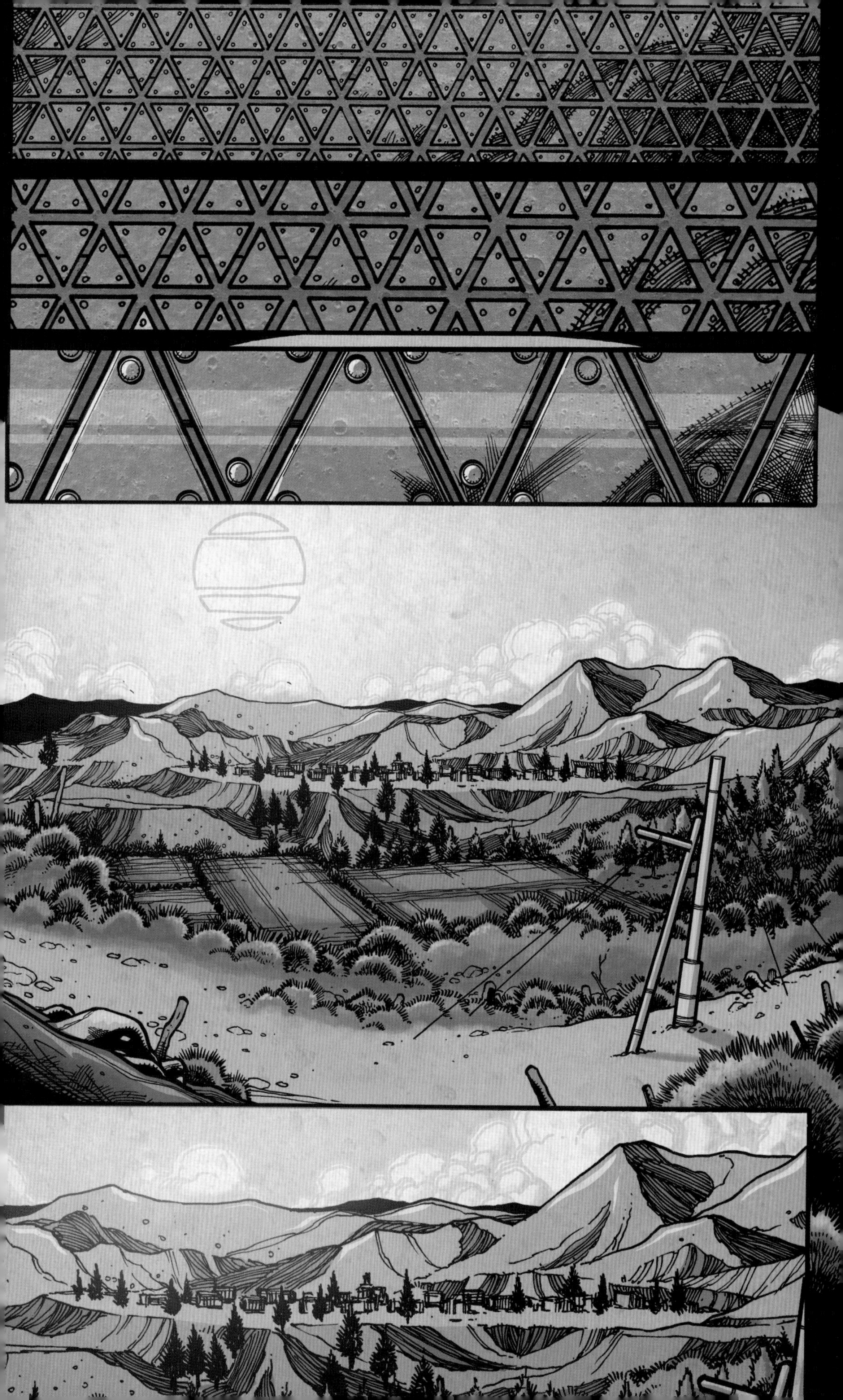

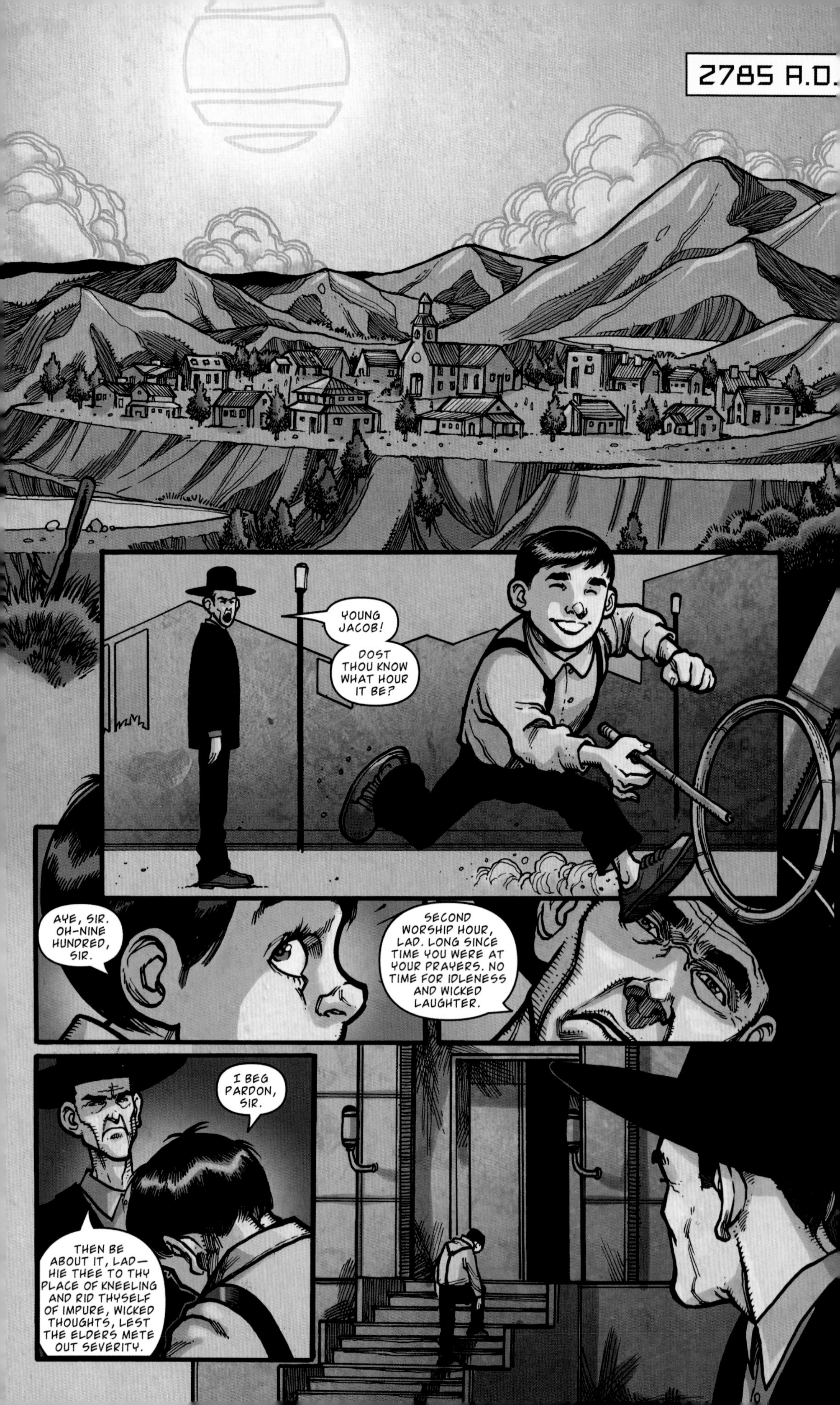
2785 A.D.
YOUNG JACOB!
DOST THOU KNOW WHAT HOUR IT BE?
AYE, SIR. OH-NINE HUNDRED, SIR.
SECOND WORSHIP HOUR, LAD. LONG SINCE TIME YOU WERE AT YOUR PRAYERS. NO TIME FOR IDLENESS AND WICKED LAUGHTER.
I BEG PARDON, SIR.
THEN BE ABOUT IT, LAD— HIE THEE TO THY PLACE OF KNEELING AND RID THYSELF OF IMPURE, WICKED THOUGHTS, LEST THE ELDERS METE OUT SEVERITY.

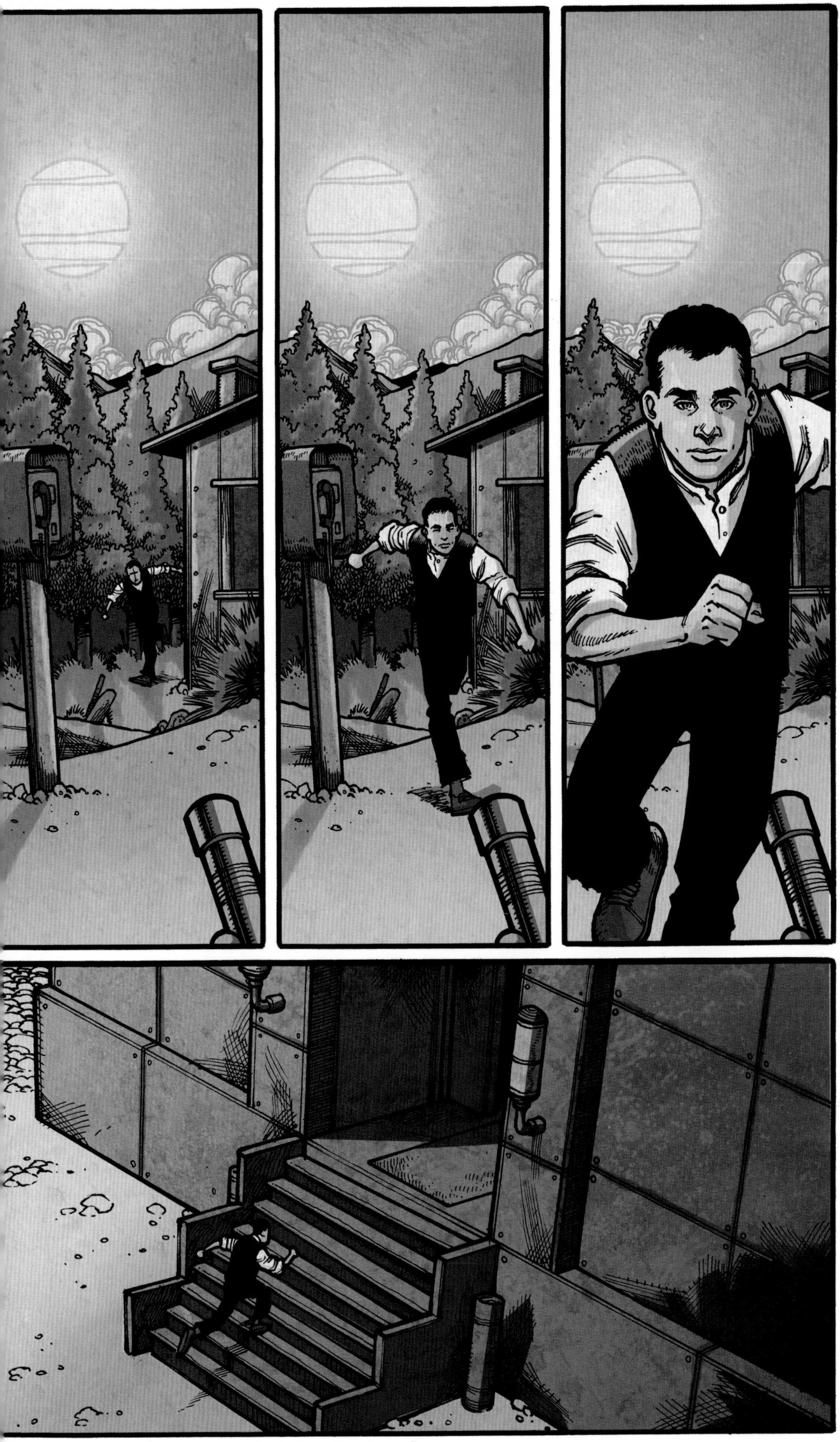

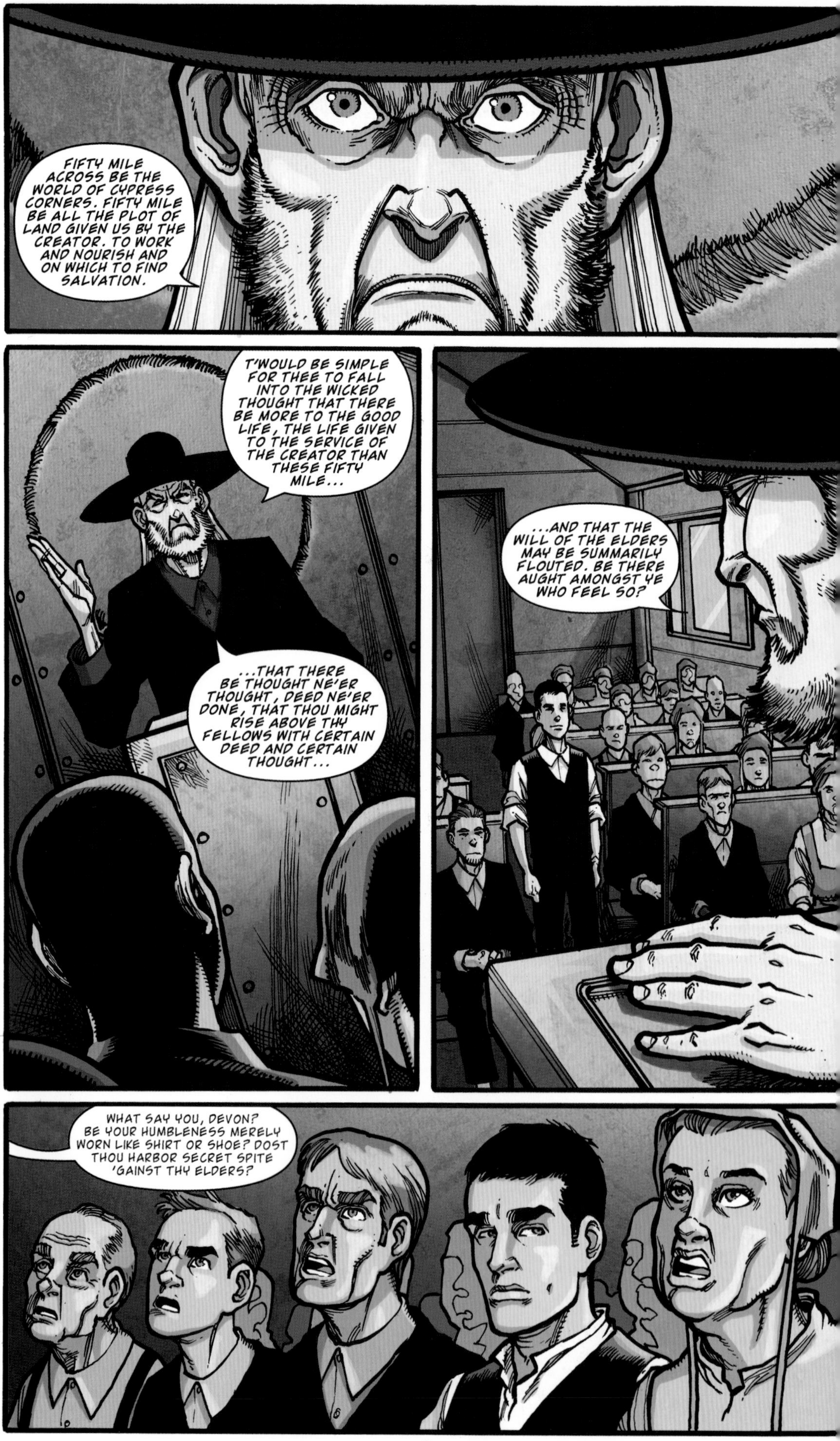
FIFTY MILE ACROSS BE THE WORLD OF CYPRESS CORNERS. FIFTY MILE BE ALL THE PLOT OF LAND GIVEN US BY THE CREATOR. TO WORK AND NOURISH AND ON WHICH TO FIND SALVATION.
T'WOULD BE SIMPLE FOR THEE TO FALL INTO THE WICKED THOUGHT THAT THERE BE MORE TO THE GOOD LIFE, THE LIFE GIVEN TO THE SERVICE OF THE CREATOR THAN THESE FIFTY MILE...
...THAT THERE BE THOUGHT NE'ER THOUGHT, DEED NE'ER DONE, THAT THOU MIGHT RISE ABOVE THY FELLOWS WITH CERTAIN DEED AND CERTAIN THOUGHT...
...AND THAT THE WILL OF THE ELDERS MAY BE SUMMARILY FLOUTED. BE THERE AUGHT AMONGST YE WHO FEEL SO?
WHAT SAY YOU, DEVON? BE YOUR HUMBLENESS MERELY WORN LIKE SHIRT OR SHOE? DOST THOU HARBOR SECRET SPITE 'GAINST THY ELDERS?

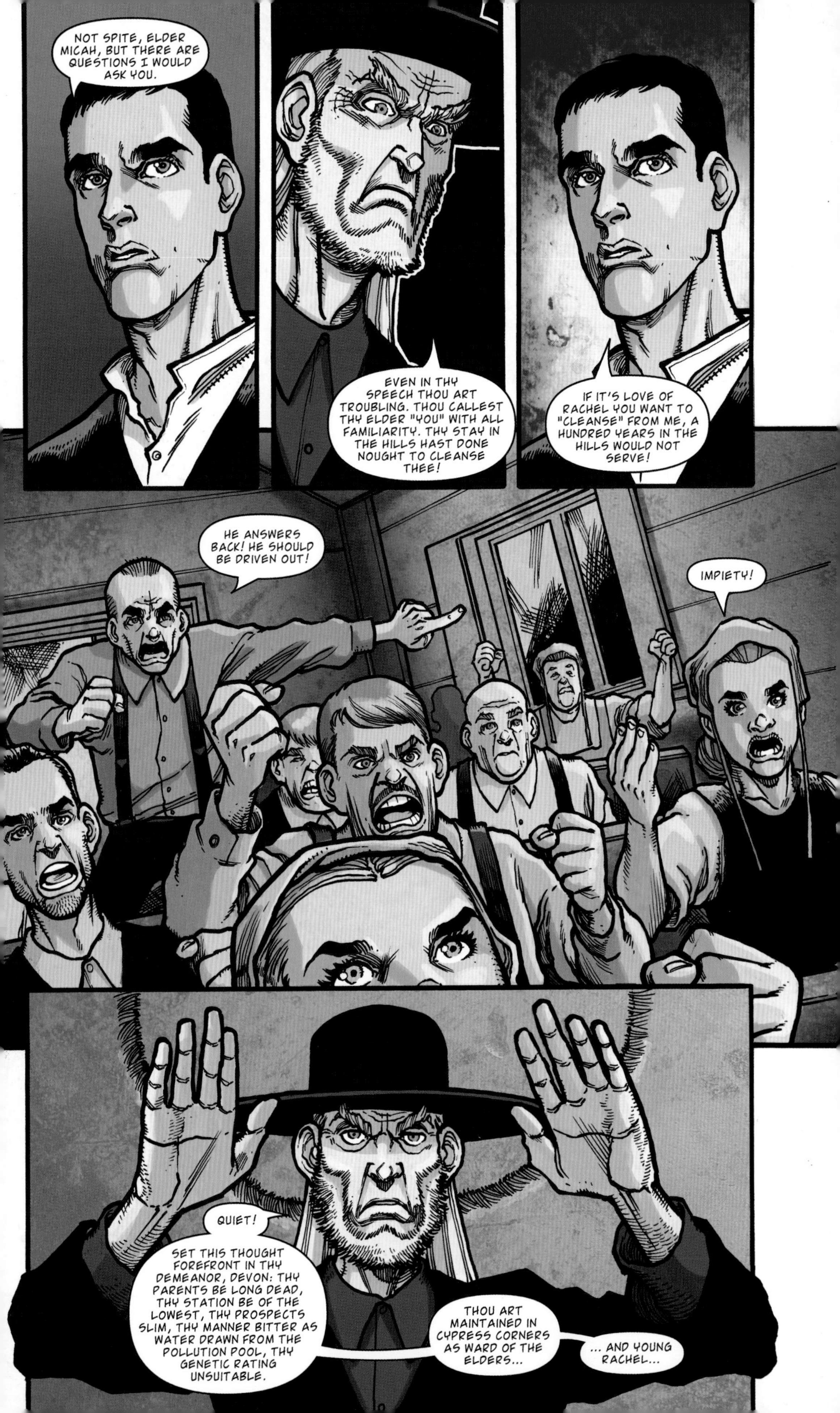
NOT SPITE, ELDER MICAH, BUT THERE ARE QUESTIONS I WOULD ASK YOU.
EVEN IN THY SPEECH THOU ART TROUBLING. THOU CALLEST THY ELDER "YOU" WITH ALL FAMILIARITY. THY STAY IN THE HILLS HAST DONE NOUGHT TO CLEANSE THEE!
IF IT'S LOVE OF RACHEL YOU WANT TO "CLEANSE" FROM ME, A HUNDRED YEARS IN THE HILLS WOULD NOT SERVE!
HE ANSWERS BACK! HE SHOULD BE DRIVEN OUT!
IMPIETY!
QUIET!
SET THIS THOUGHT FOREFRONT IN THY DEMEANOR, DEVON: THY PARENTS BE LONG DEAD, THY STATION BE OF THE LOWEST, THY PROSPECTS SLIM, THY MANNER BITTER AS WATER DRAWN FROM THE POLLUTION POOL, THY GENETIC RATING UNSUITABLE.
THOU ART MAINTAINED IN CYPRESS CORNERS AS WARD OF THE ELDERS...
... AND YOUNG RACHEL...

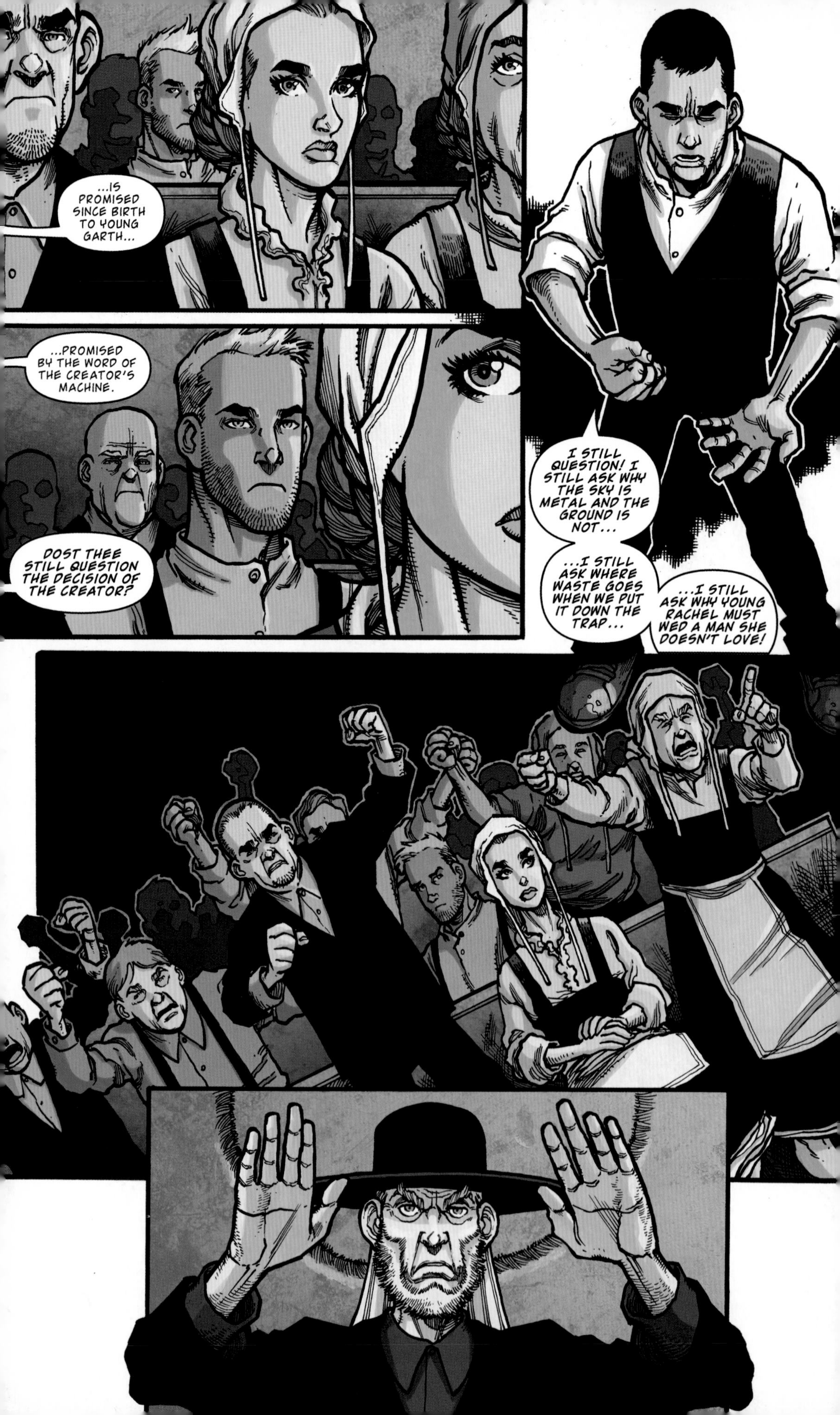
...IS PROMISED SINCE BIRTH TO YOUNG GARTH...
...PROMISED BY THE WORD OF THE CREATOR'S MACHINE.
DOST THEE STILL QUESTION THE DECISION OF THE CREATOR?
I STILL QUESTION! I STILL ASK WHY THE SKY IS METAL AND THE GROUND IS NOT...
...I STILL ASK WHERE WASTE GOES WHEN WE PUT IT DOWN THE TRAP...
...I STILL ASK WHY YOUNG RACHEL MUST WED A MAN SHE DOESN'T LOVE!

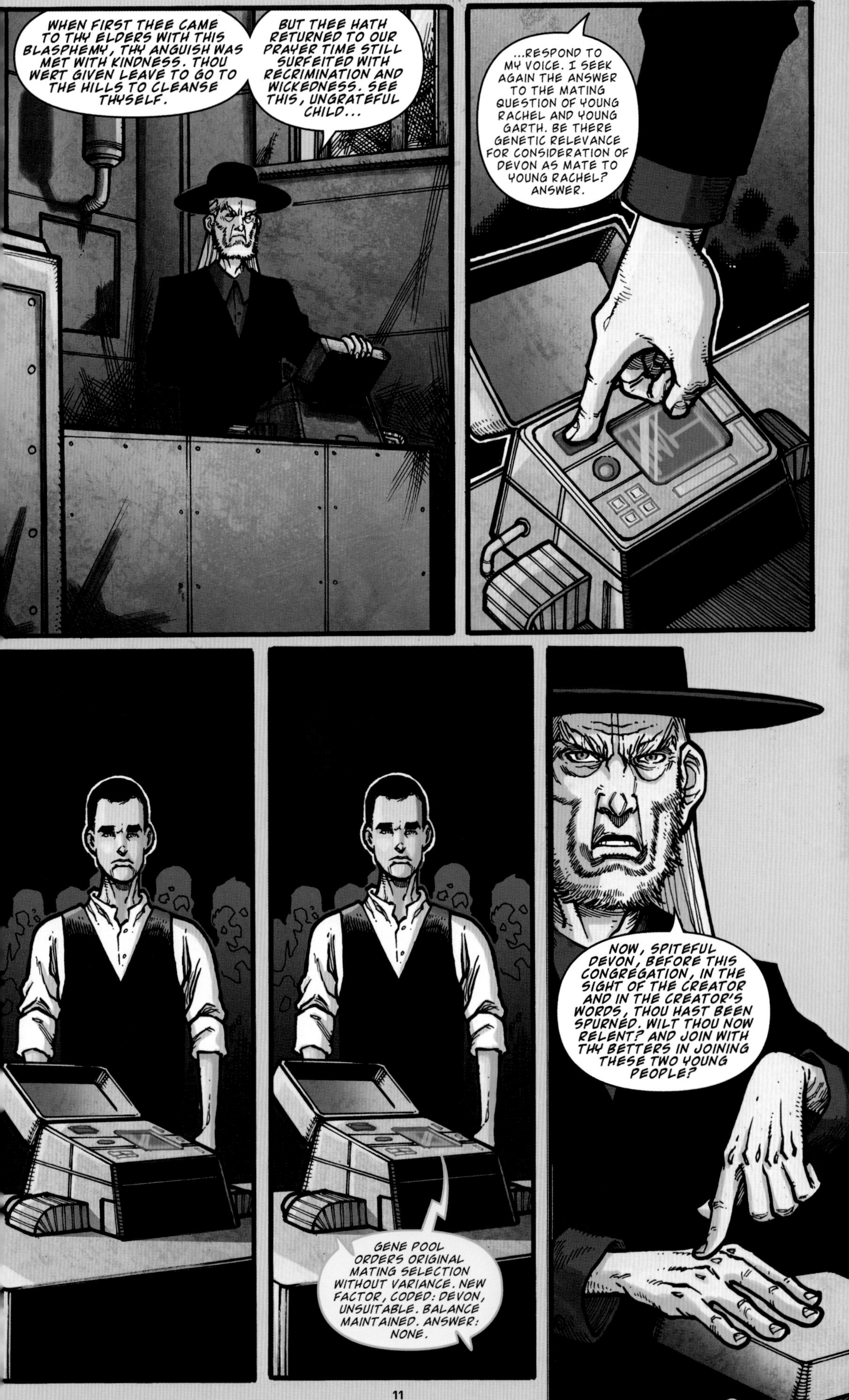
WHEN FIRST THEE CAME TO THY ELDERS WITH THIS BLASPHEMY, THY ANGUISH WAS MET WITH KINDNESS. THOU WERT GIVEN LEAVE TO GO TO THE HILLS TO CLEANSE THYSELF.
BUT THEE HATH RETURNED TO OUR PRAYER TIME STILL SURFEITED WITH RECRIMINATION AND WICKEDNESS. SEE THIS, UNGRATEFUL CHILD...
...RESPOND TO MY VOICE. I SEEK AGAIN THE ANSWER TO THE MATING QUESTION OF YOUNG RACHEL AND YOUNG GARTH. BE THERE GENETIC RELEVANCE FOR CONSIDERATION OF DEVON AS MATE TO YOUNG RACHEL? ANSWER.
GENE POOL ORDERS ORIGINAL MATING SELECTION WITHOUT VARIANCE. NEW FACTOR, CODED: DEVON, UNSUITABLE. BALANCE MAINTAINED. ANSWER: NONE.
NOW, SPITEFUL DEVON, BEFORE THIS CONGREGATION, IN THE SIGHT OF THE CREATOR AND IN THE CREATOR'S WORDS, THOU HAST BEEN SPURNED. WILT THOU NOW RELENT? AND JOIN WITH THY BETTERS IN JOINING THESE TWO YOUNG PEOPLE?

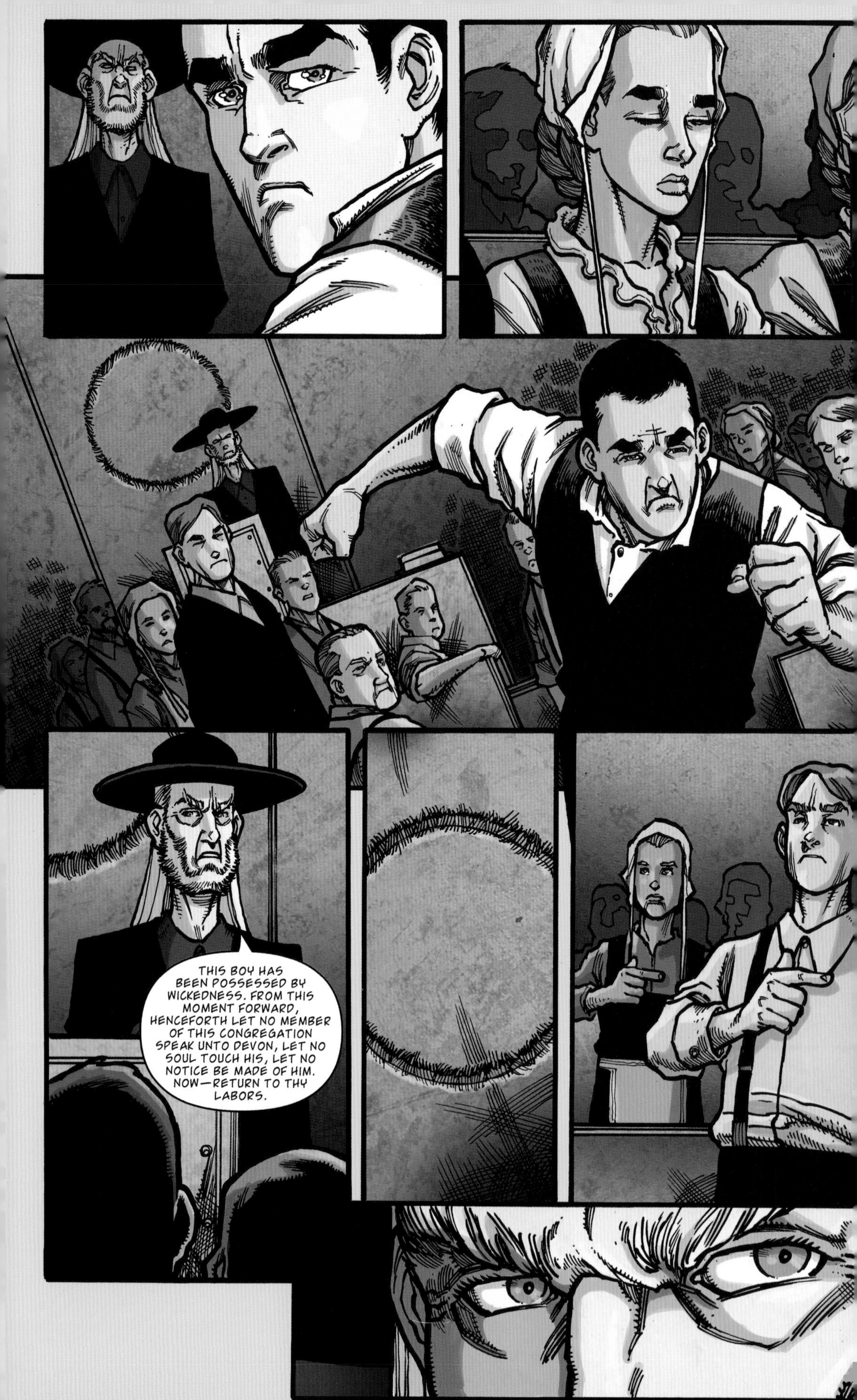
THIS BOY HAS BEEN POSSESSED BY WICKEDNESS. FROM THIS MOMENT FORWARD, HENCEFORTH LET NO MEMBER OF THIS CONGREGATION SPEAK UNTO DEVON, LET NO SOUL TOUCH HIS, LET NO NOTICE BE MADE OF HIM. NOW—RETURN TO THY LABORS.

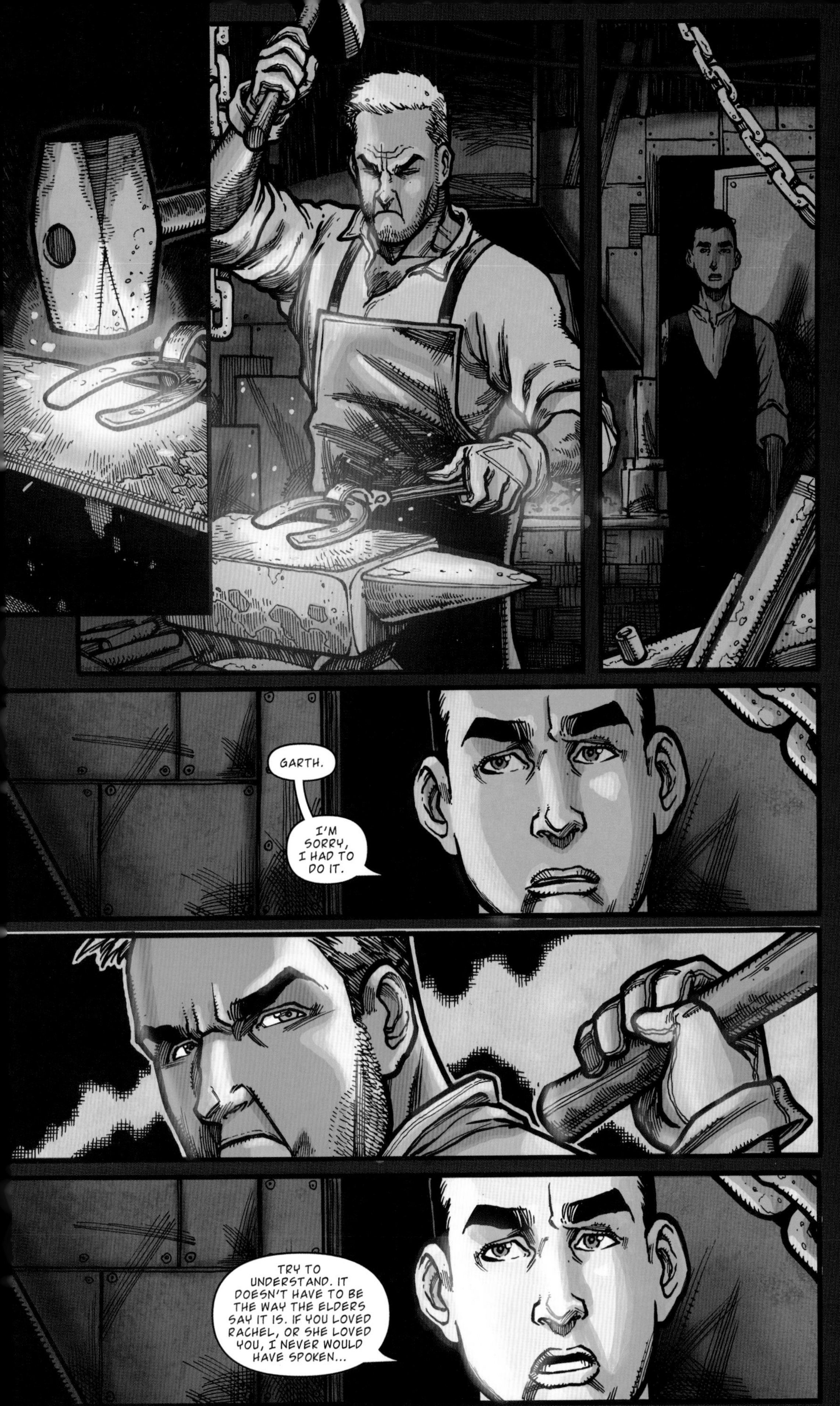

GARTH.
I'M SORRY, I HAD TO DO IT.
TRY TO UNDERSTAND. IT DOESN'T HAVE TO BE THE WAY THE ELDERS SAY IT IS. IF YOU LOVED RACHEL, OR SHE LOVED YOU, I NEVER WOULD HAVE SPOKEN...

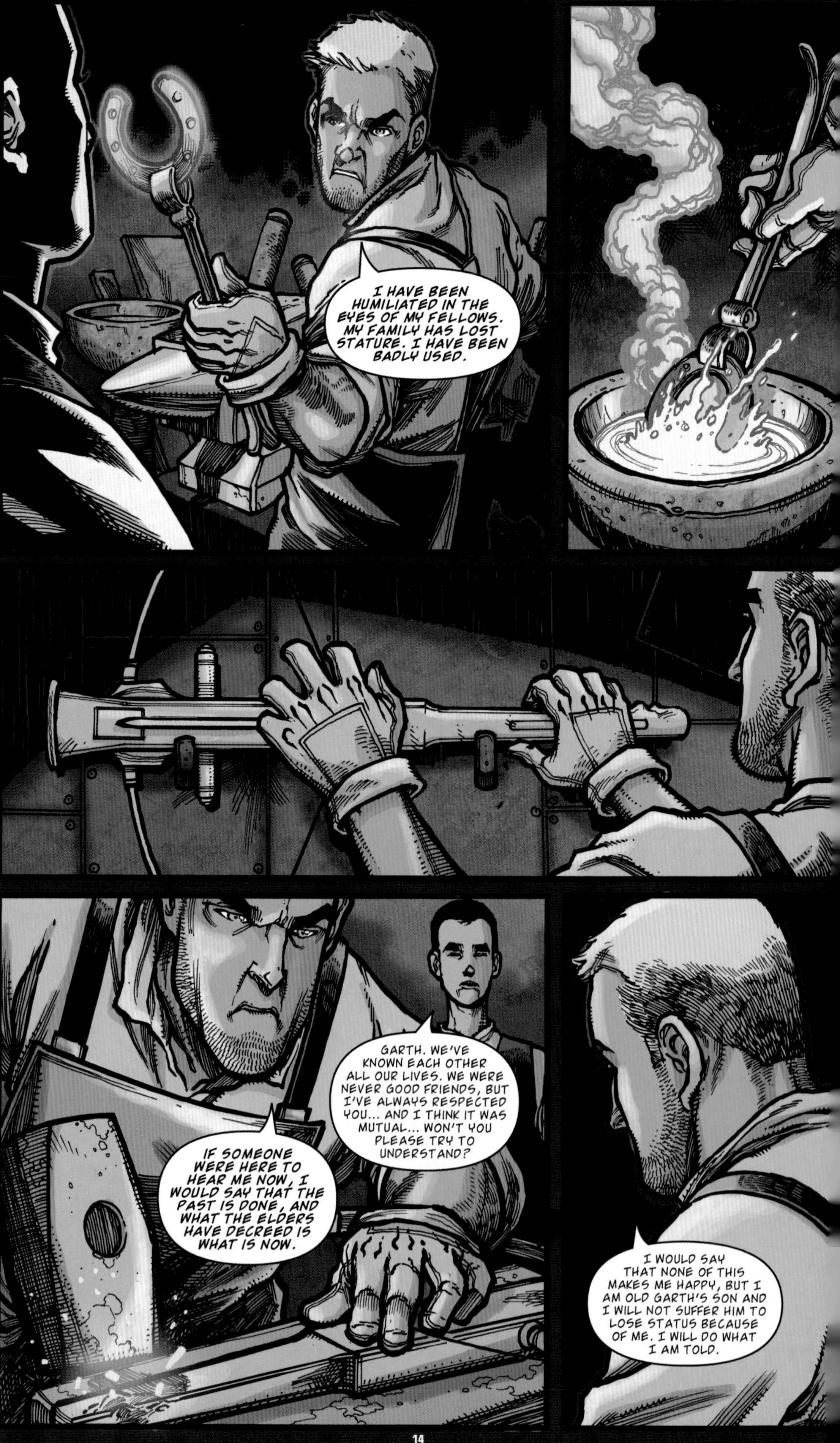
I HAVE BEEN HUMILIATED IN THE EYES OF MY FELLOWS. MY FAMILY HAS LOST STATURE. I HAVE BEEN BADLY USED.
GARTH. WE'VE KNOWN EACH OTHER ALL OUR LIVES. WE WERE NEVER GOOD FRIENDS, BUT I'VE ALWAYS RESPECTED YOU... AND I THINK IT WAS MUTUAL... WON'T YOU PLEASE TRY TO UNDERSTAND?
IF SOMEONE WERE HERE TO HEAR ME NOW, I WOULD SAY THAT THE PAST IS DONE, AND WHAT THE ELDERS HAVE DECREED IS WHAT IS NOW.
I WOULD SAY THAT NONE OF THIS MAKES ME HAPPY, BUT I AM OLD GARTH'S SON AND I WILL NOT SUFFER HIM TO LOSE STATUS BECAUSE OF ME. I WILL DO WHAT I AM TOLD.

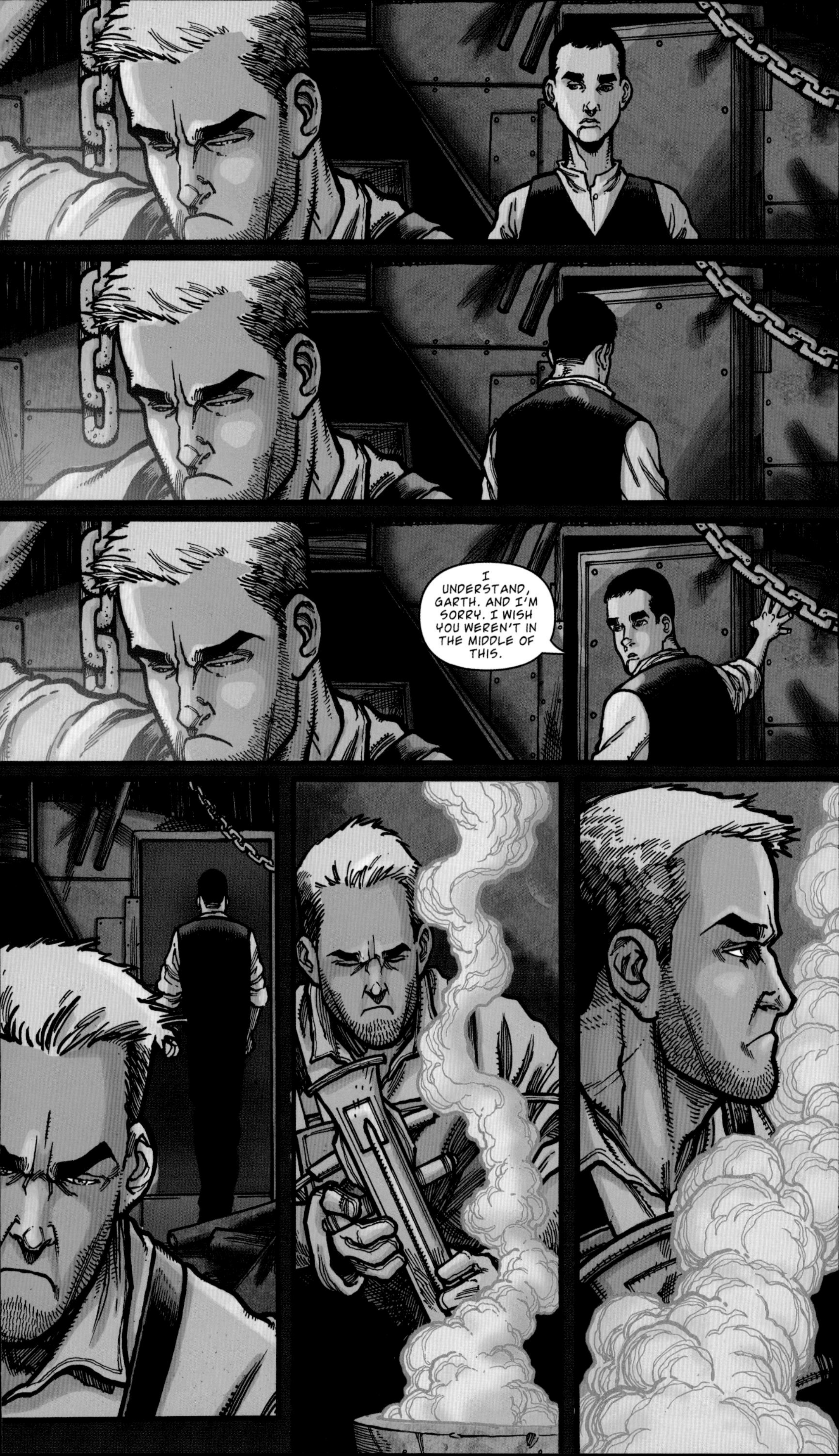
I UNDERSTAND, GARTH. AND I'M SORRY. I WISH YOU WEREN'T IN THE MIDDLE OF THIS.

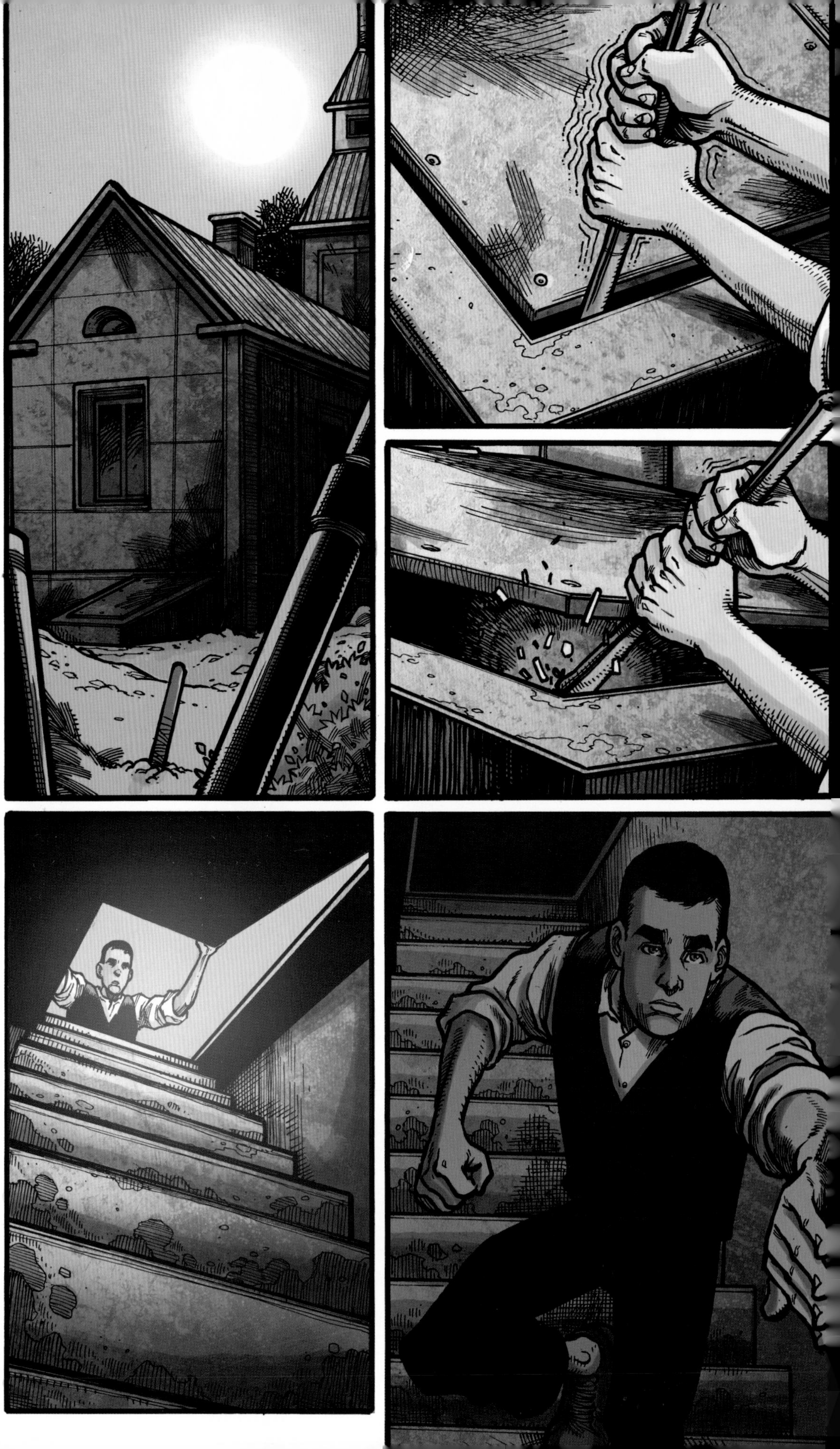

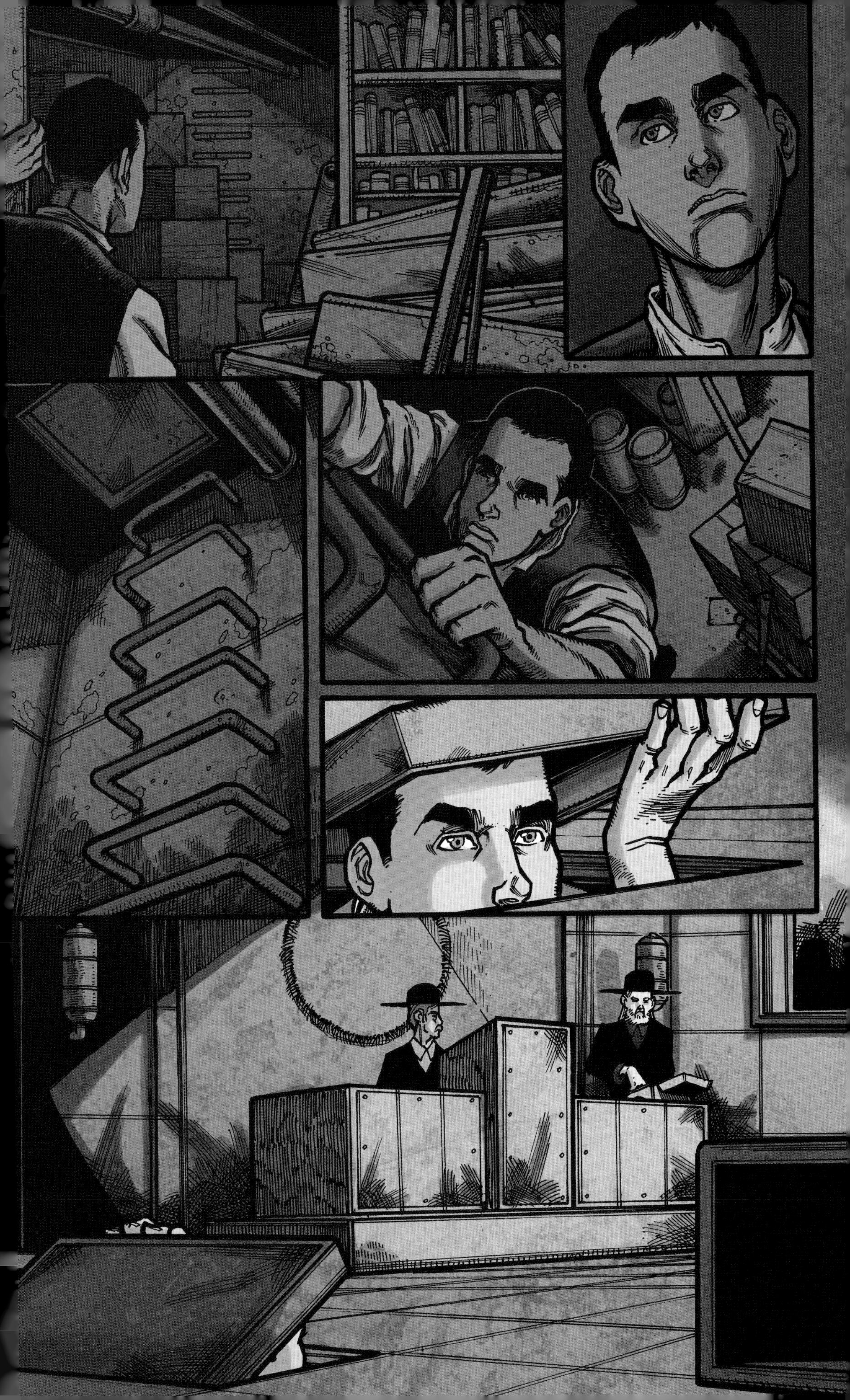

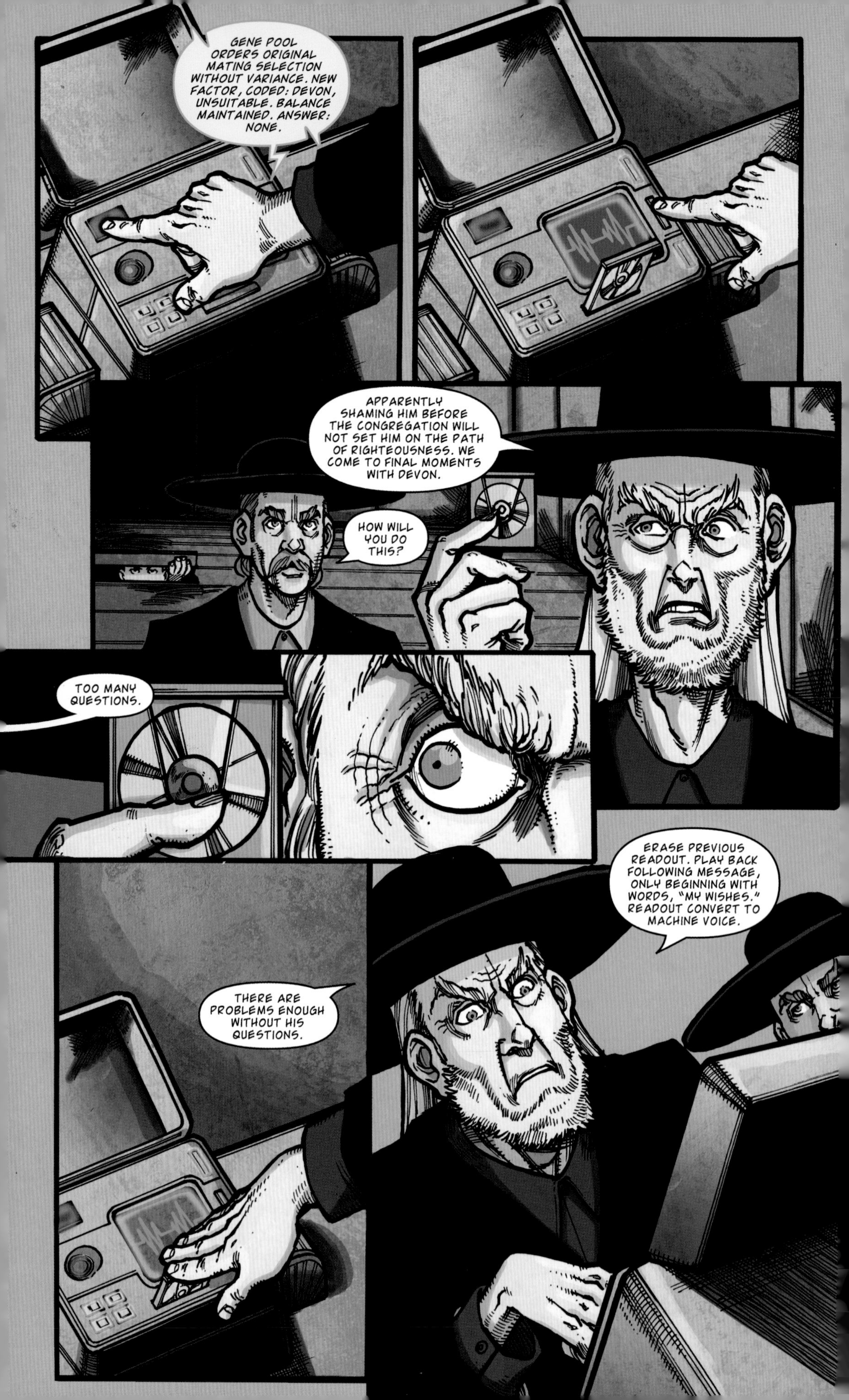
GENE POOL ORDERS ORIGINAL MATING SELECTION WITHOUT VARIANCE. NEW FACTOR, CODED: DEVON, UNSUITABLE. BALANCE MAINTAINED. ANSWER: NONE.
APPARENTLY SHAMING HIM BEFORE THE CONGREGATION WILL NOT SET HIM ON THE PATH OF RIGHTEOUSNESS. WE COME TO FINAL MOMENTS WITH DEVON.
HOW WILL YOU DO THIS?
TOO MANY QUESTIONS.
THERE ARE PROBLEMS ENOUGH WITHOUT HIS QUESTIONS.
ERASE PREVIOUS READOUT. PLAY BACK FOLLOWING MESSAGE, ONLY BEGINNING WITH WORDS, "MY WISHES." READOUT CONVERT TO MACHINE VOICE.

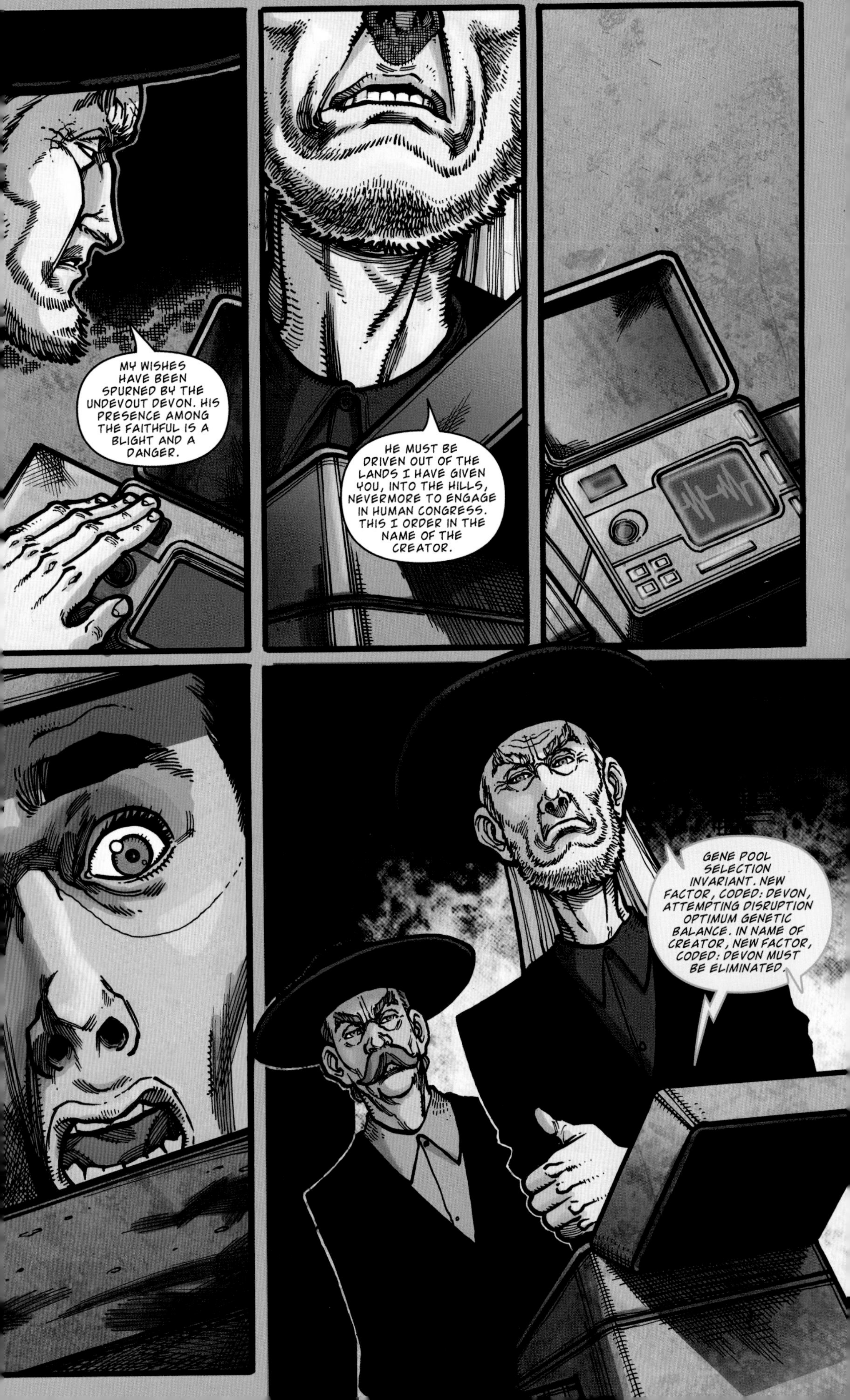

MY WISHES HAVE BEEN SPURNED BY THE UNDEVOUT DEVON. HIS PRESENCE AMONG THE FAITHFUL IS A BLIGHT AND A DANGER.
HE MUST BE DRIVEN OUT OF THE LANDS I HAVE GIVEN YOU, INTO THE HILLS, NEVERMORE TO ENGAGE IN HUMAN CONGRESS. THIS I ORDER IN THE NAME OF THE CREATOR.
GENE POOL SELECTION INVARIANT. NEW FACTOR, CODED: DEVON, ATTEMPTING DISRUPTION OPTIMUM GENETIC BALANCE. IN NAME OF CREATOR, NEW FACTOR, CODED: DEVON MUST BE ELIMINATED.

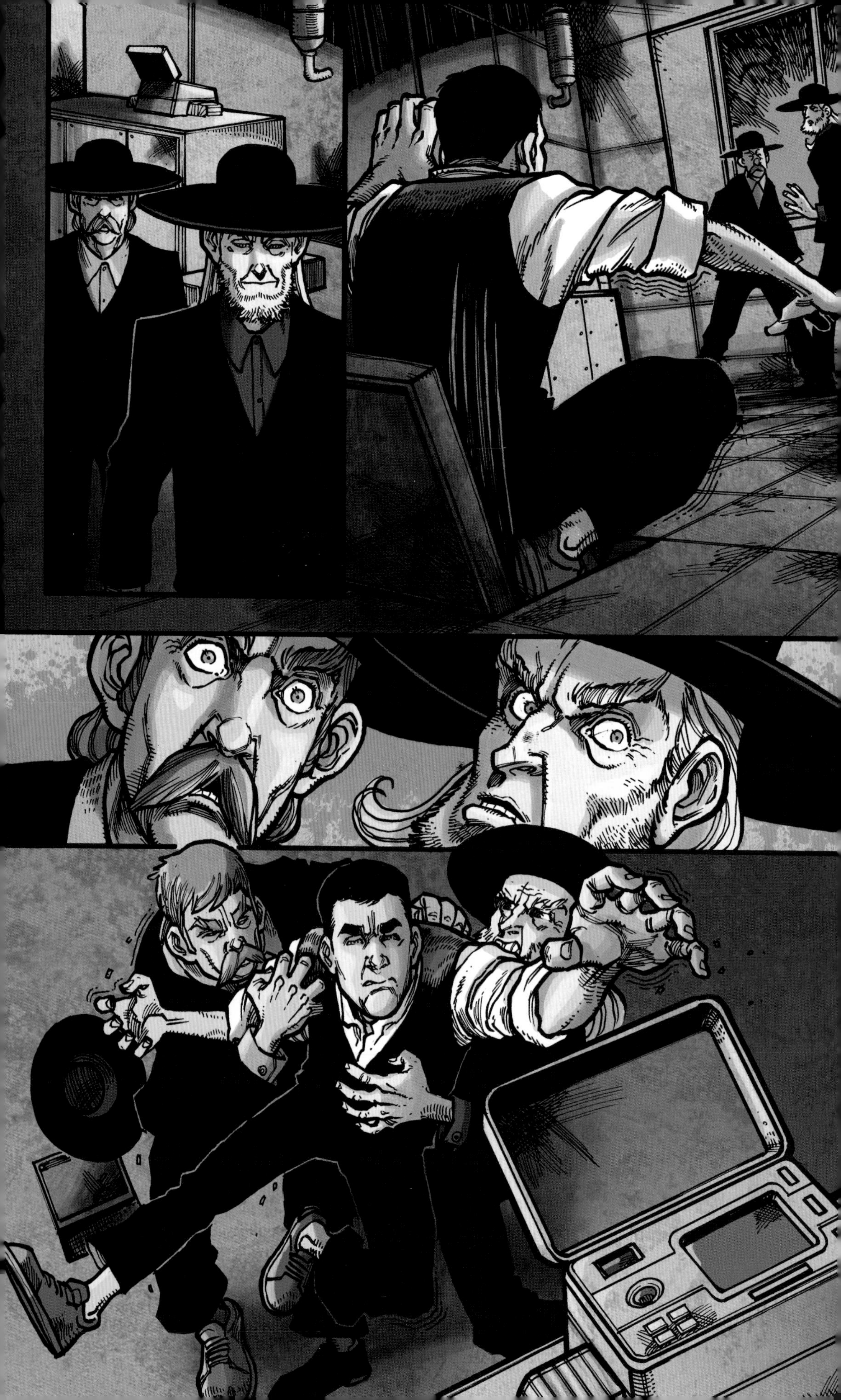

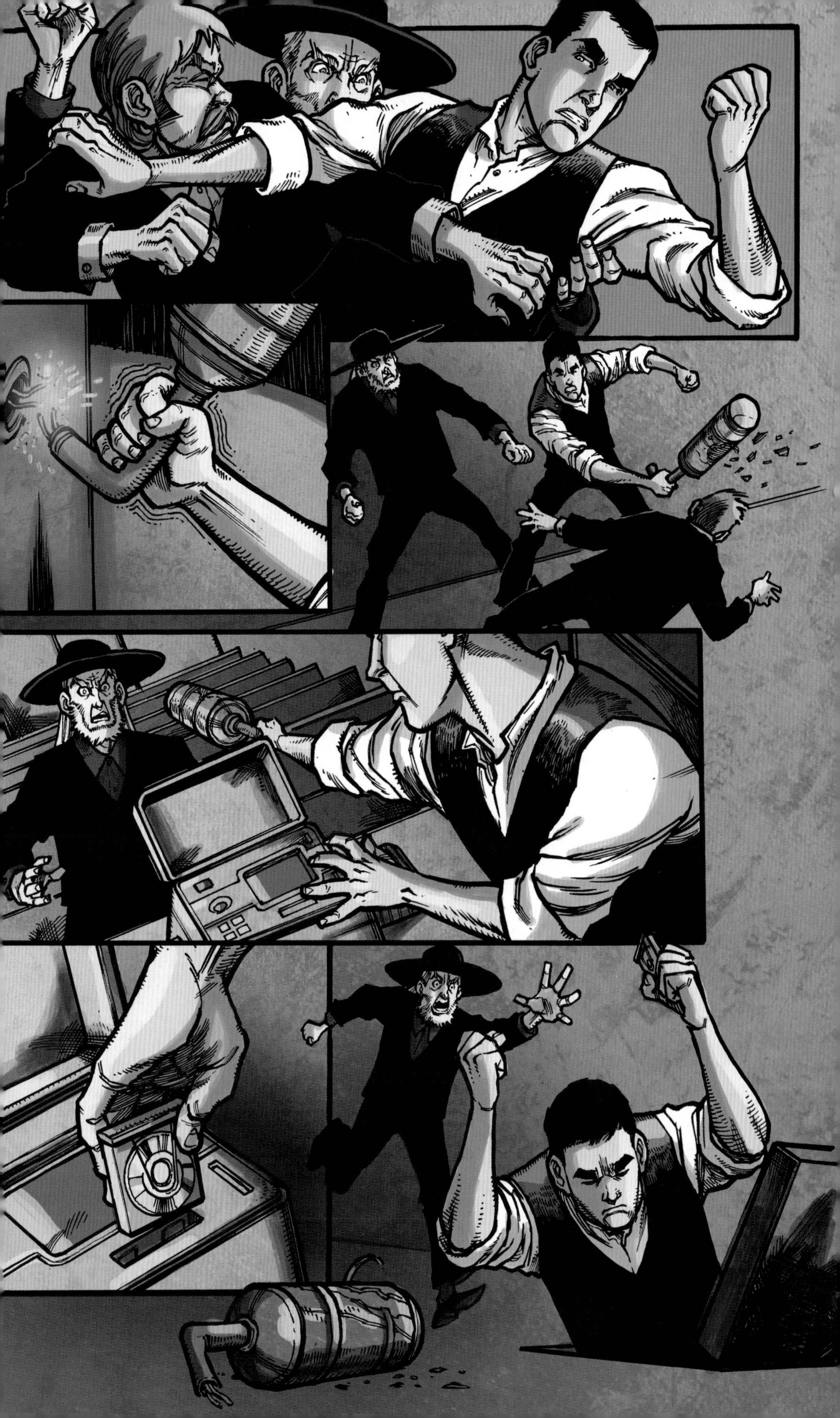

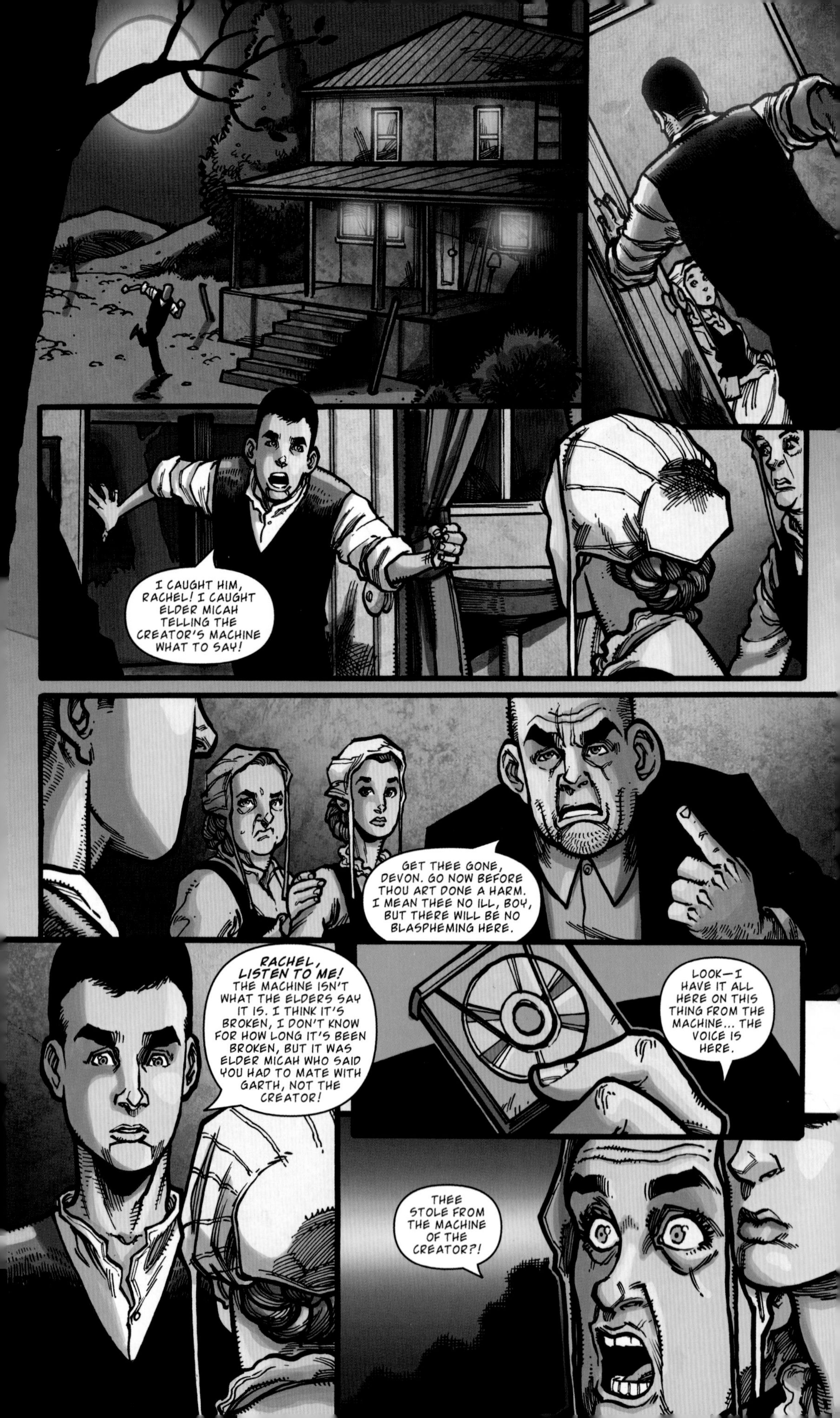
I CAUGHT HIM, RACHEL! I CAUGHT ELDER MICAH TELLING THE CREATOR'S MACHINE WHAT TO SAY!
GET THEE GONE, DEVON. GO NOW BEFORE THOU ART DONE A HARM. I MEAN THEE NO ILL, BOY, BUT THERE WILL BE NO BLASPHEMING HERE.
RACHEL, LISTEN TO ME! THE MACHINE ISN'T WHAT THE ELDERS SAY IT IS. I THINK IT'S BROKEN, I DON'T KNOW FOR HOW LONG IT'S BEEN BROKEN, BUT IT WAS ELDER MICAH WHO SAID YOU HAD TO MATE WITH GARTH, NOT THE CREATOR!
LOOK—I HAVE IT ALL HERE ON THIS THING FROM THE MACHINE... THE VOICE IS HERE.
THEE STOLE FROM THE MACHINE OF THE CREATOR?!

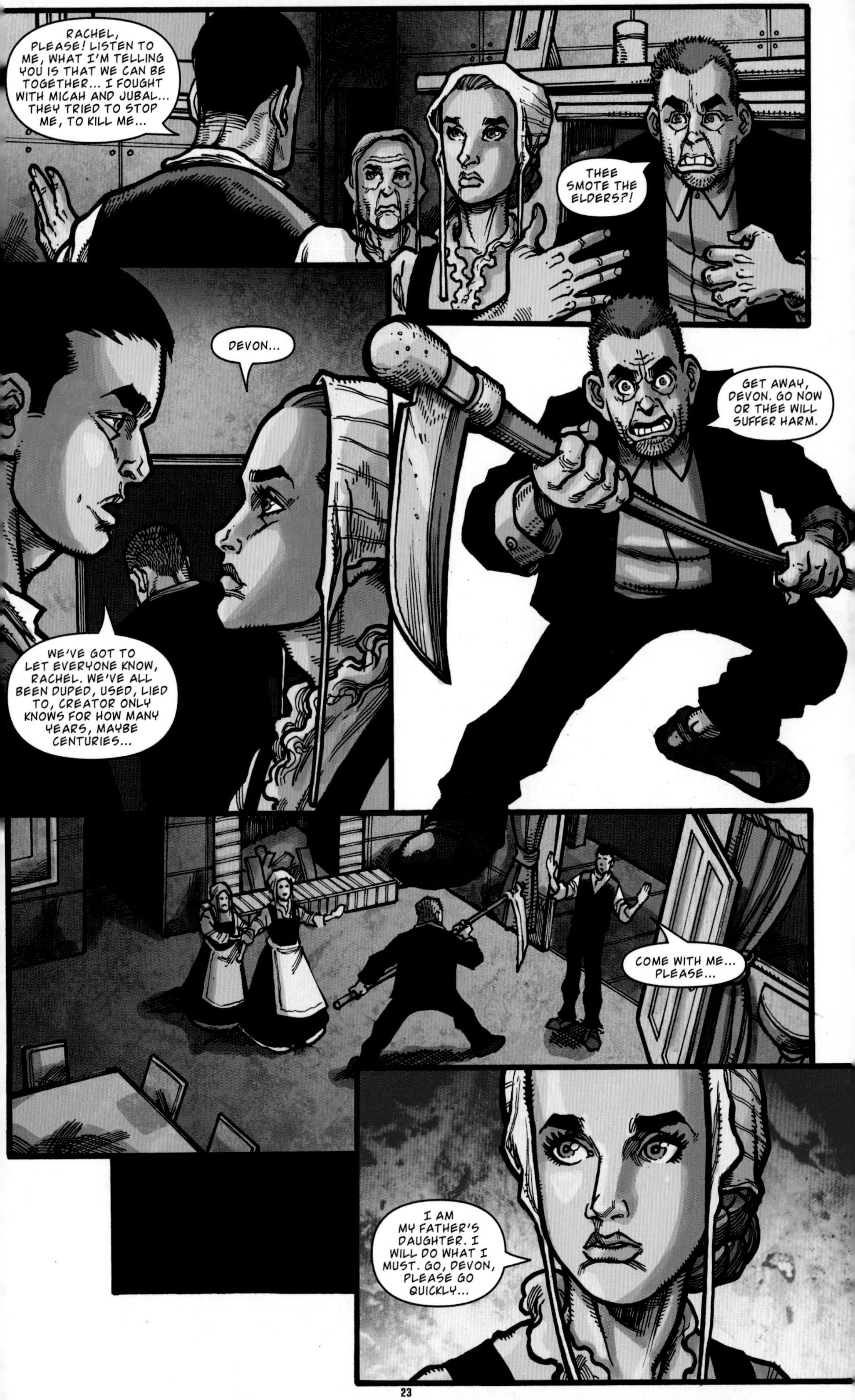
RACHEL, PLEASE! LISTEN TO ME, WHAT I'M TELLING YOU IS THAT WE CAN BE TOGETHER... I FOUGHT WITH MICAH AND JUBAL... THEY TRIED TO STOP ME, TO KILL ME...
THEE SMOTE THE ELDERS?!
DEVON...
WE'VE GOT TO LET EVERYONE KNOW, RACHEL. WE'VE ALL BEEN DUPED, USED, LIED TO, CREATOR ONLY KNOWS FOR HOW MANY YEARS, MAYBE CENTURIES...
GET AWAY, DEVON. GO NOW OR THEE WILL SUFFER HARM.
COME WITH ME... PLEASE...
I AM MY FATHER'S DAUGHTER. I WILL DO WHAT I MUST. GO, DEVON, PLEASE GO QUICKLY...

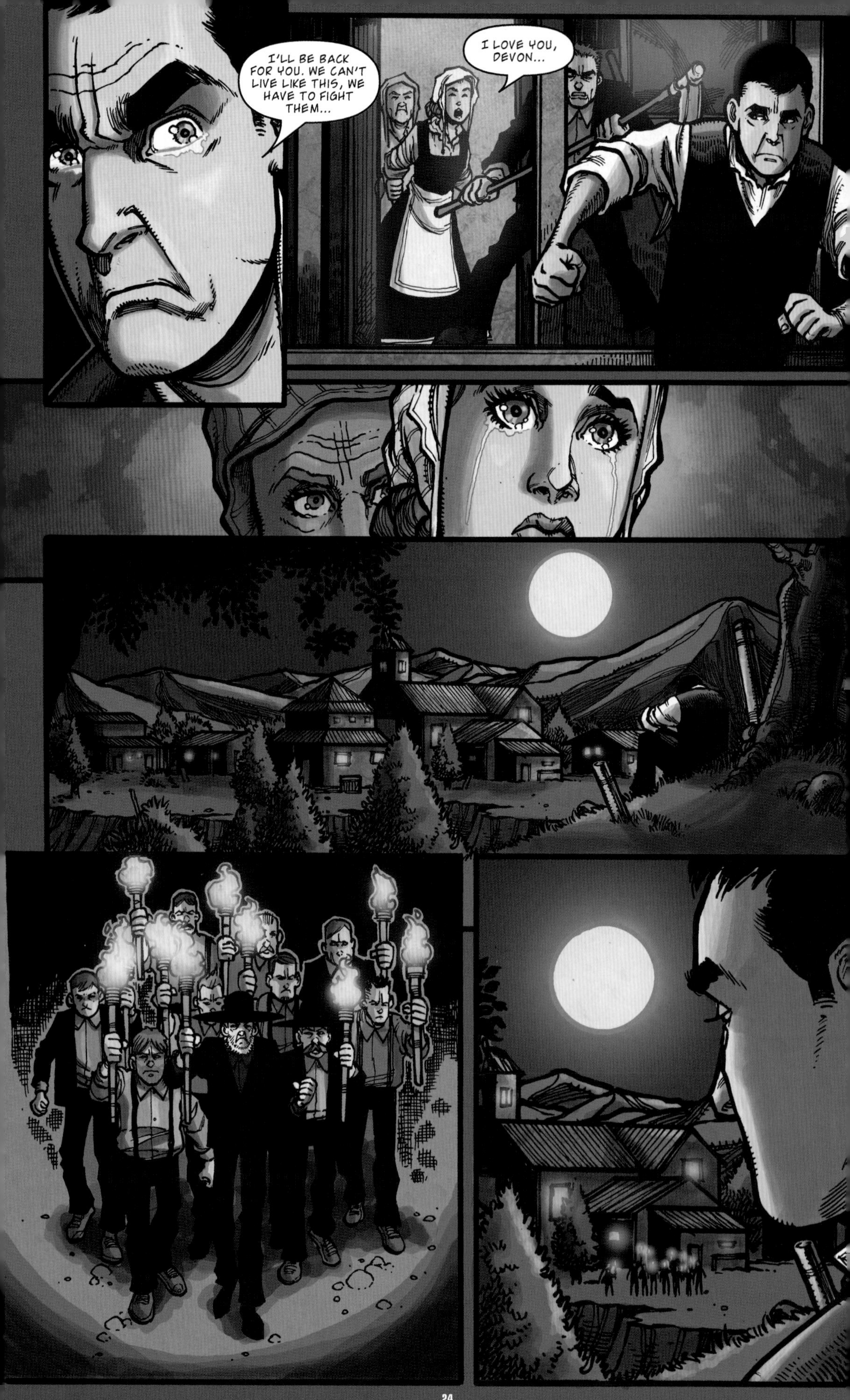

I'LL BE BACK FOR YOU. WE CAN'T LIVE LIKE THIS, WE HAVE TO FIGHT THEM...
I LOVE YOU, DEVON...

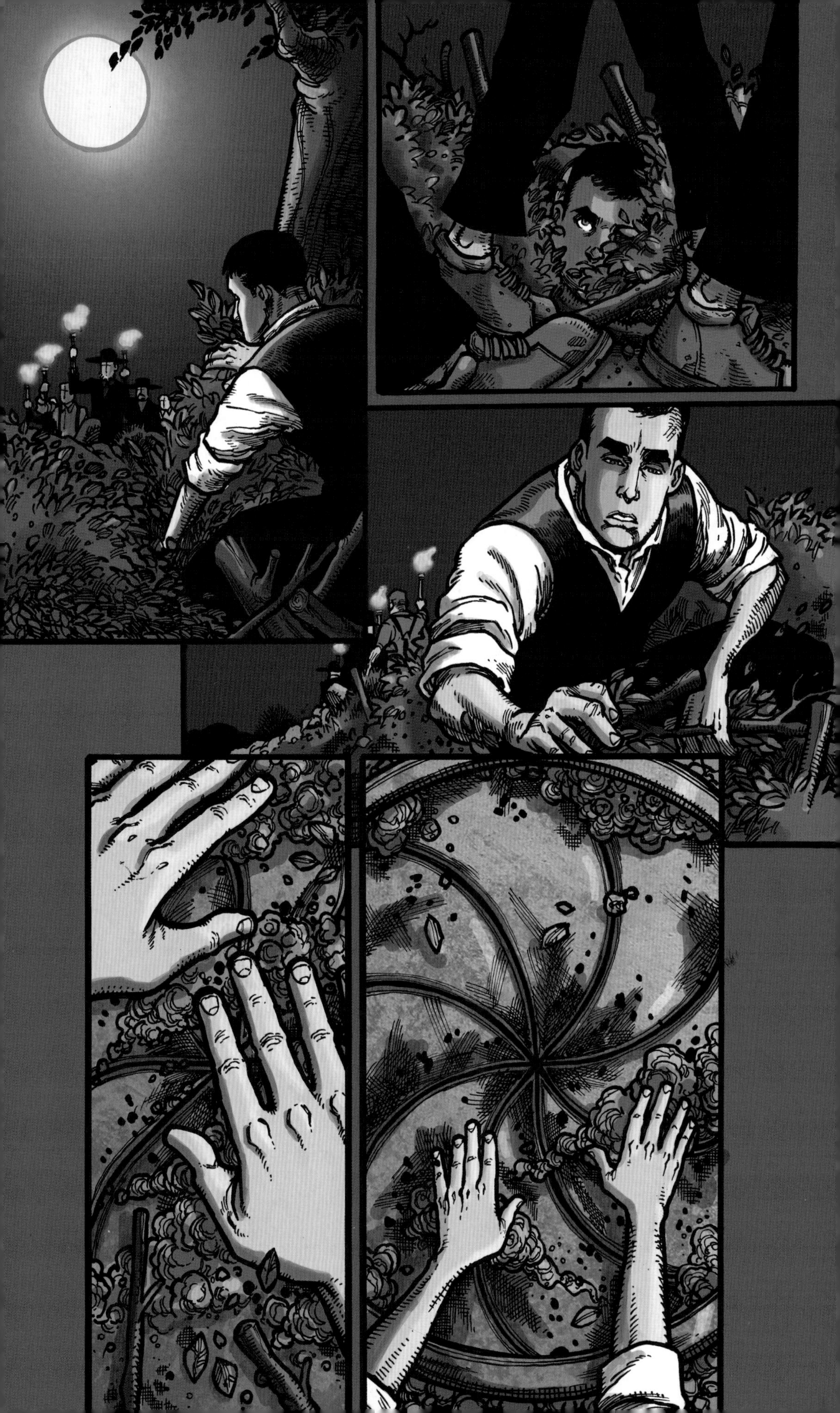

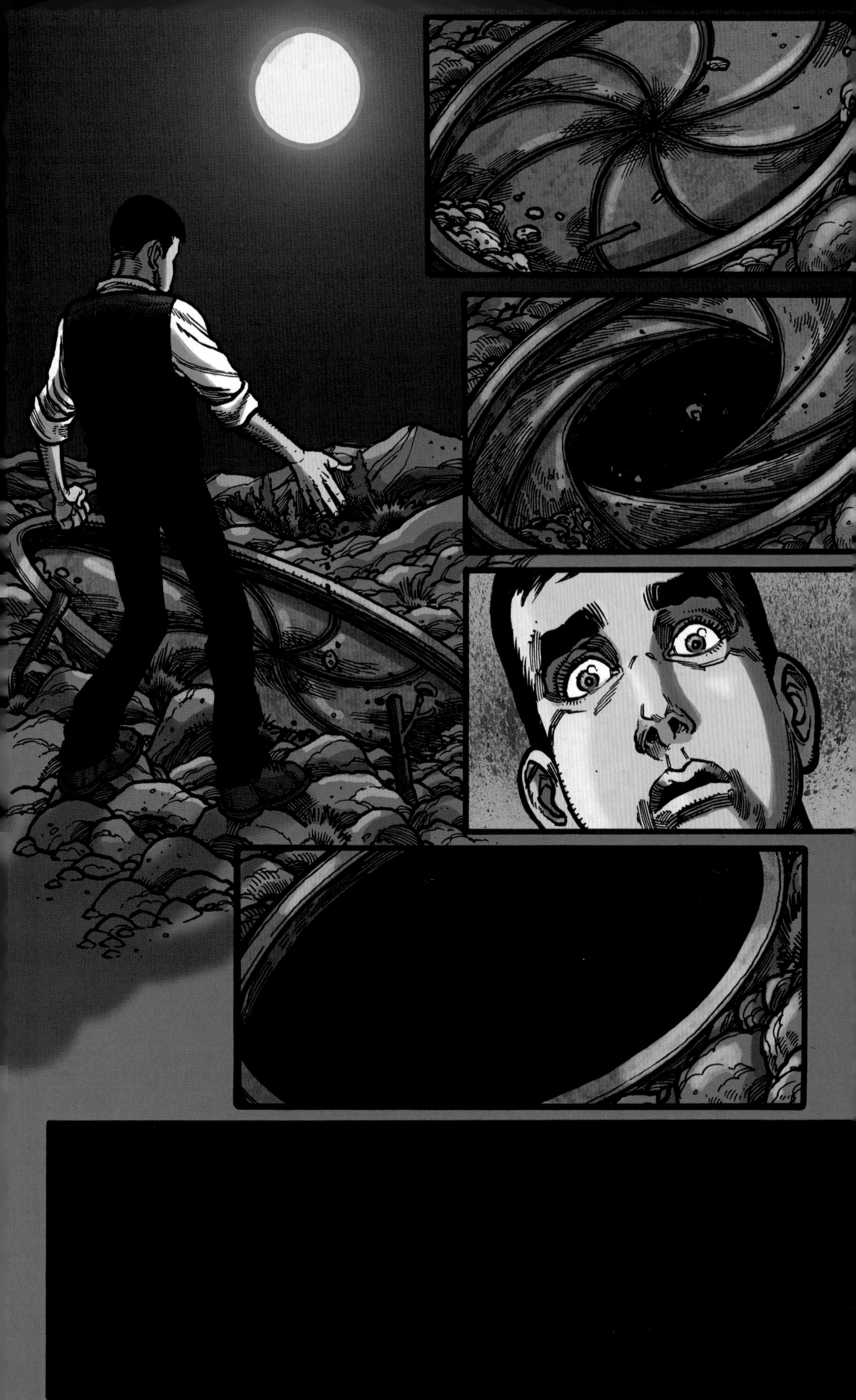

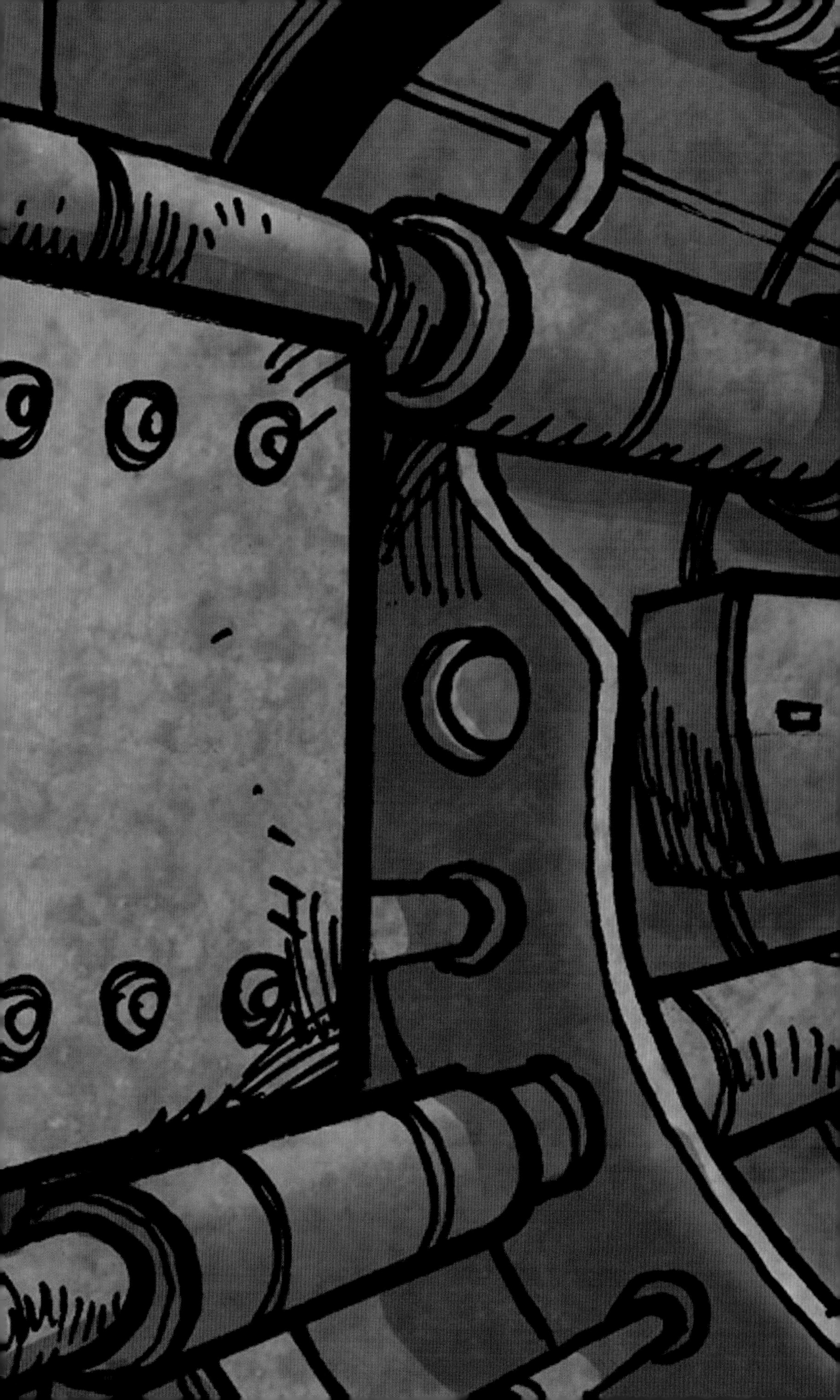

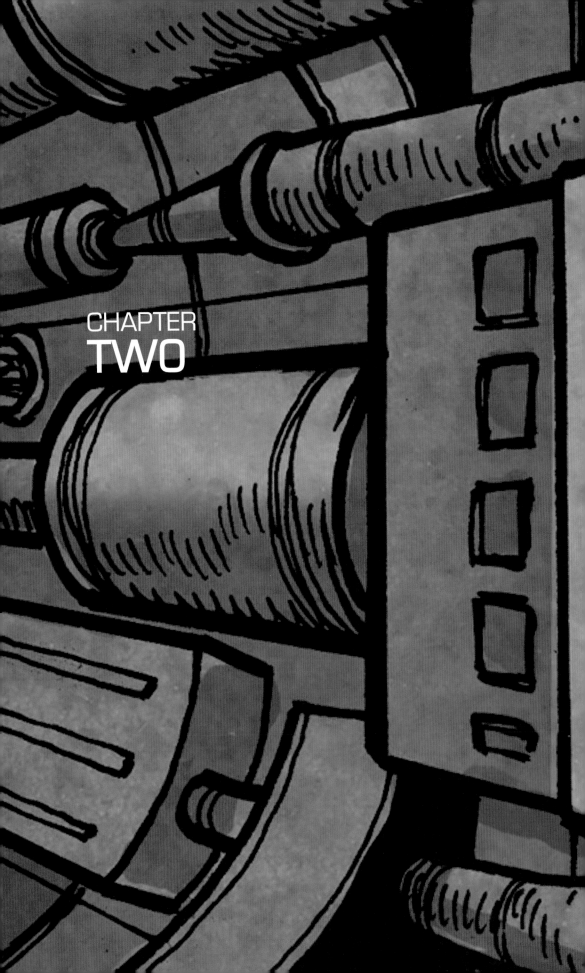

CHAPTER
TWO

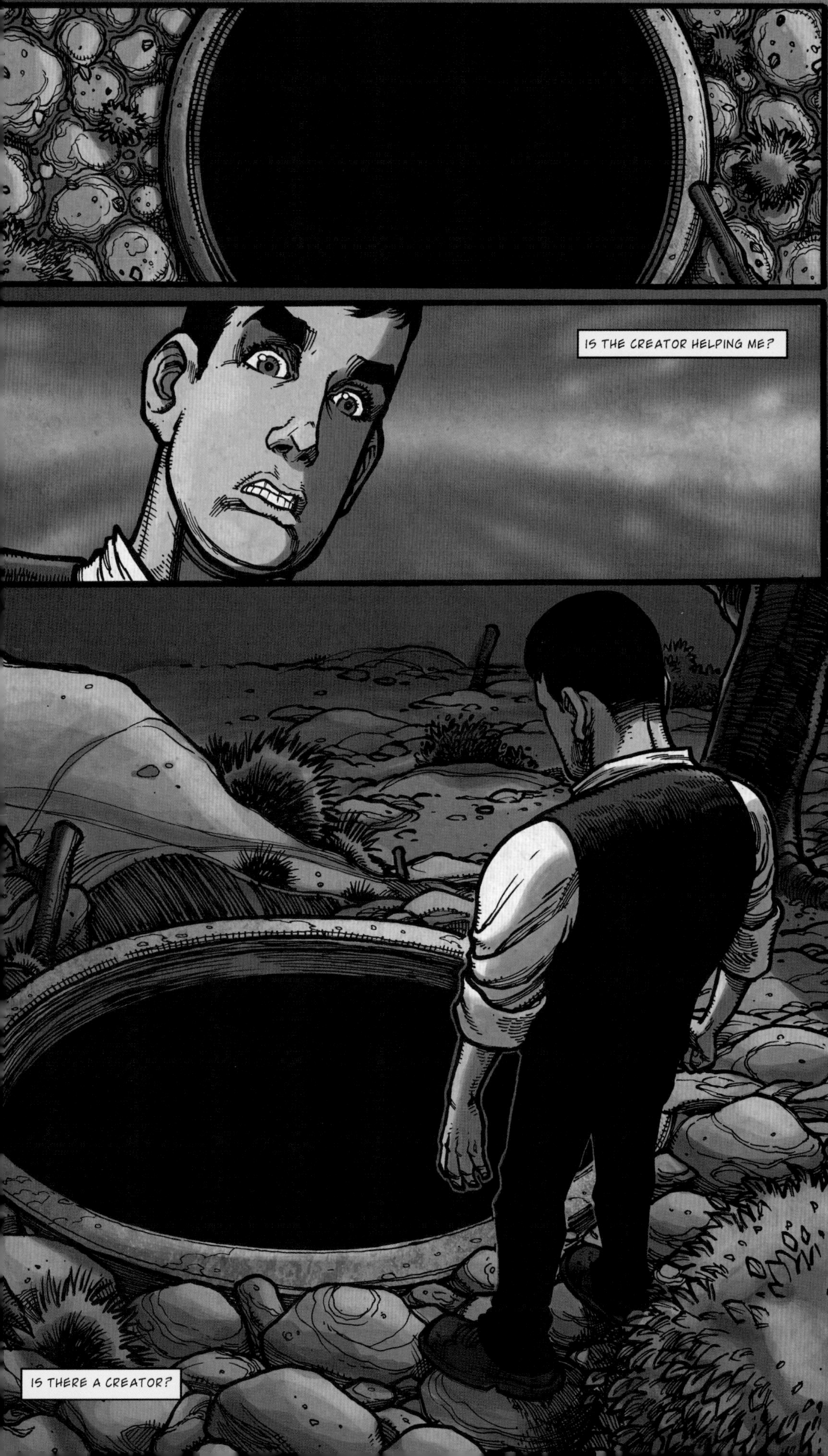
IS THE CREATOR HELPING ME?
IS THERE A CREATOR?

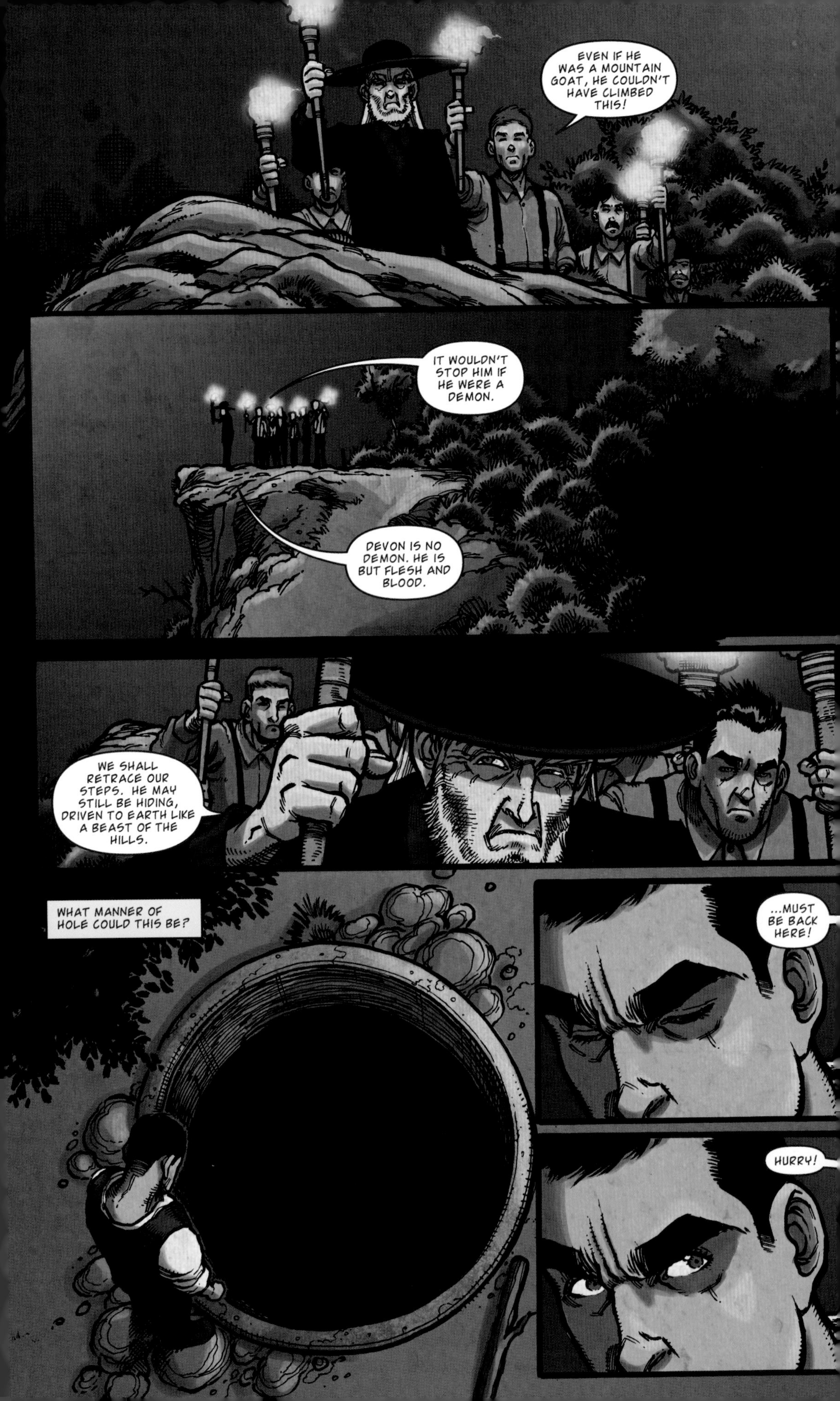
EVEN IF HE WAS A MOUNTAIN GOAT, HE COULDN'T HAVE CLIMBED THIS!
IT WOULDN'T STOP HIM IF HE WERE A DEMON.
DEVON IS NO DEMON. HE IS BUT FLESH AND BLOOD.
WE SHALL RETRACE OUR STEPS. HE MAY STILL BE HIDING, DRIVEN TO EARTH LIKE A BEAST OF THE HILLS.
WHAT MANNER OF HOLE COULD THIS BE?
...MUST BE BACK HERE!
HURRY!

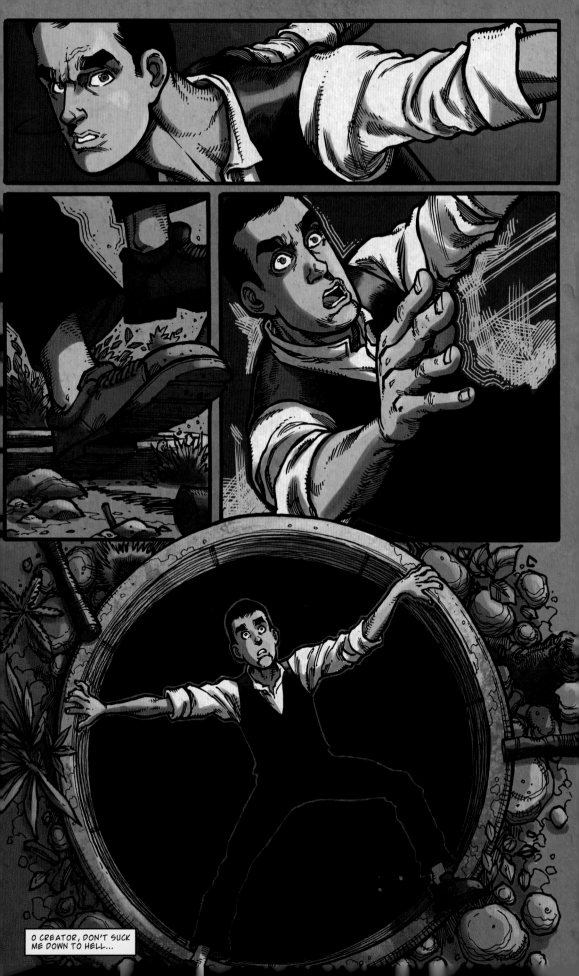

O CREATOR, DON'T SUCK ME DOWN TO HELL...

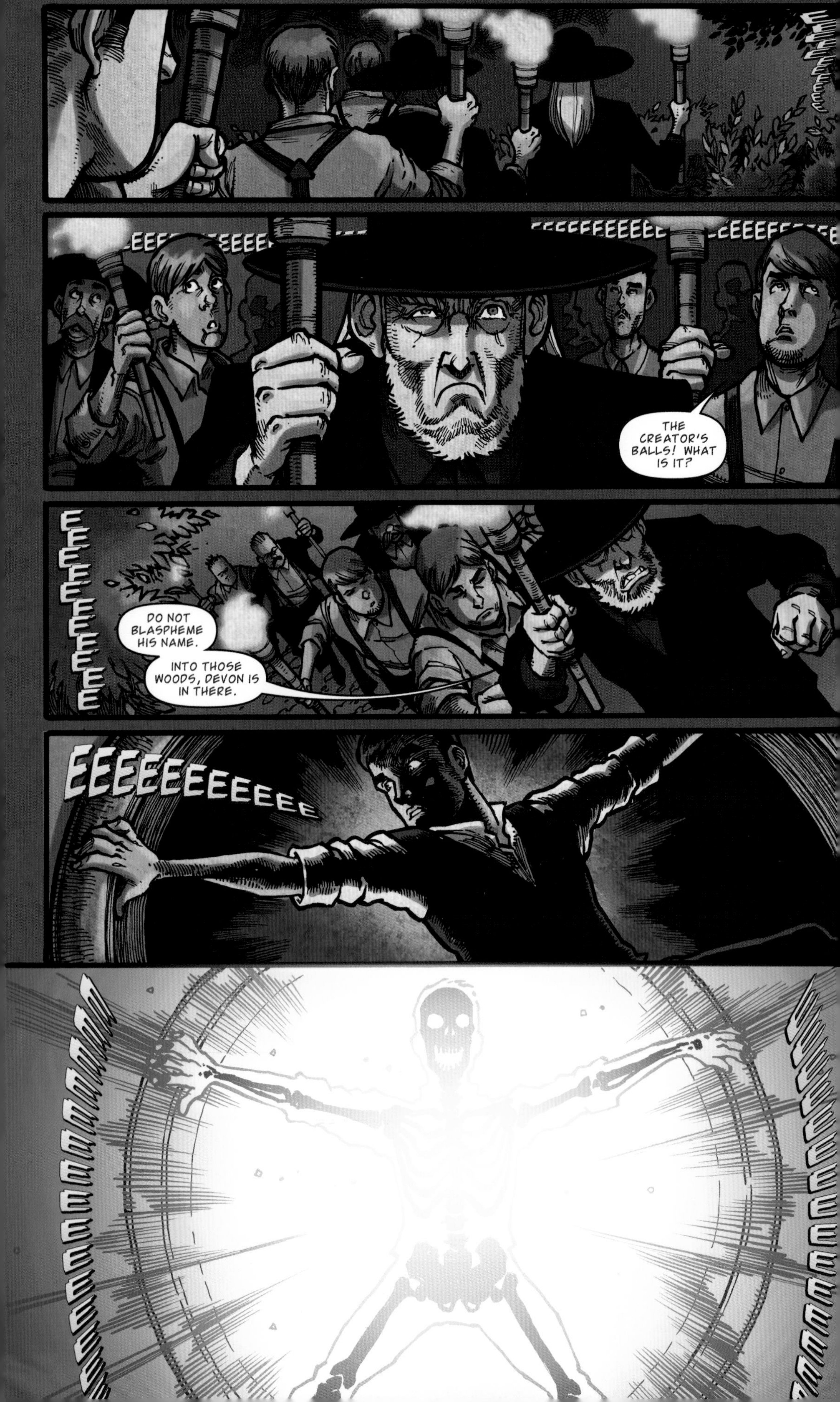
THE CREATOR'S BALLS! WHAT IS IT?
DO NOT BLASPHEME HIS NAME.
INTO THOSE WOODS, DEVON IS IN THERE.

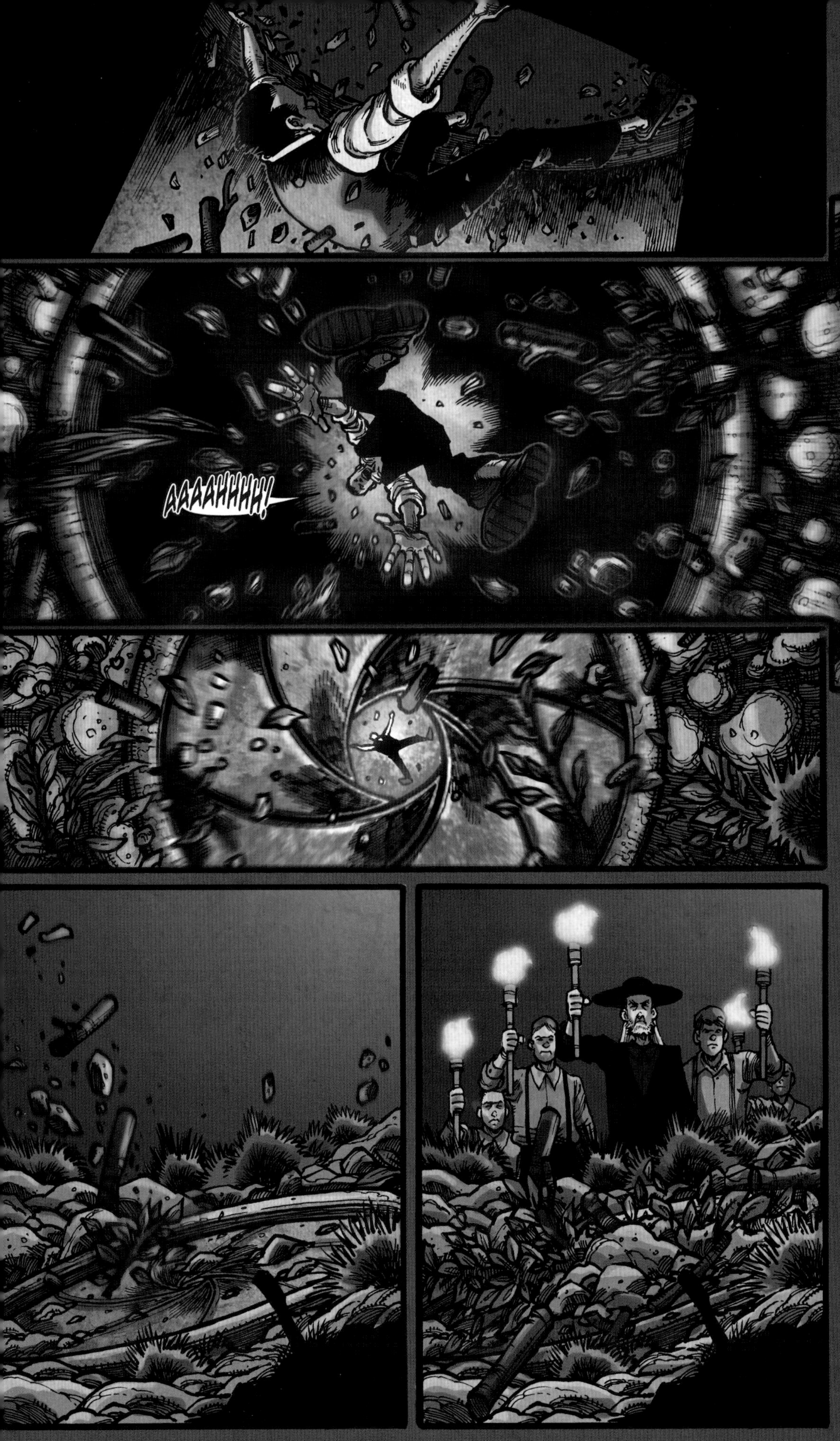
AAAAHHHH!

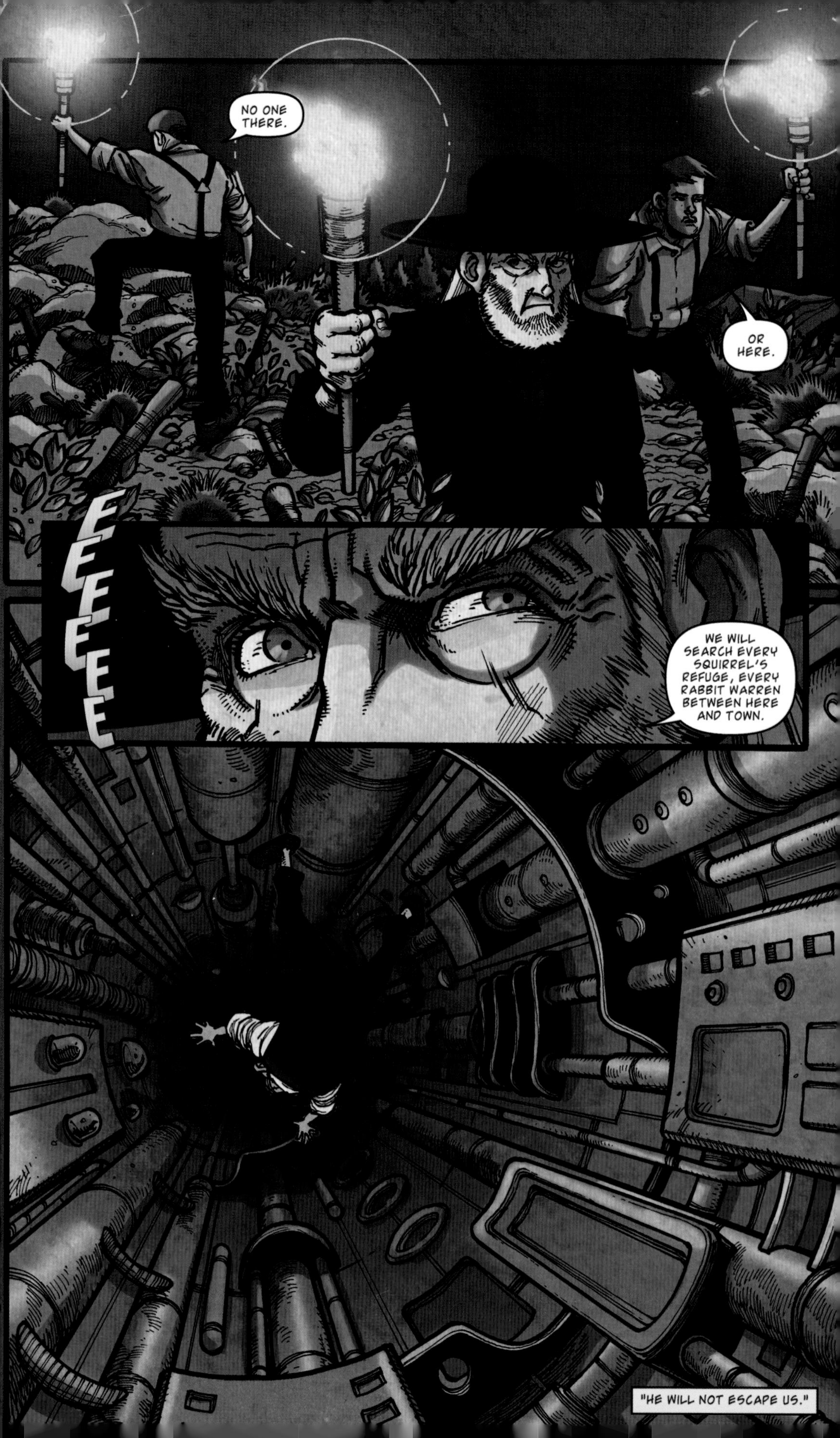
NO ONE THERE.
OR HERE.
EEEEEEE
WE WILL SEARCH EVERY SQUIRREL'S REFUGE, EVERY RABBIT WARREN BETWEEN HERE AND TOWN.
"HE WILL NOT ESCAPE US."

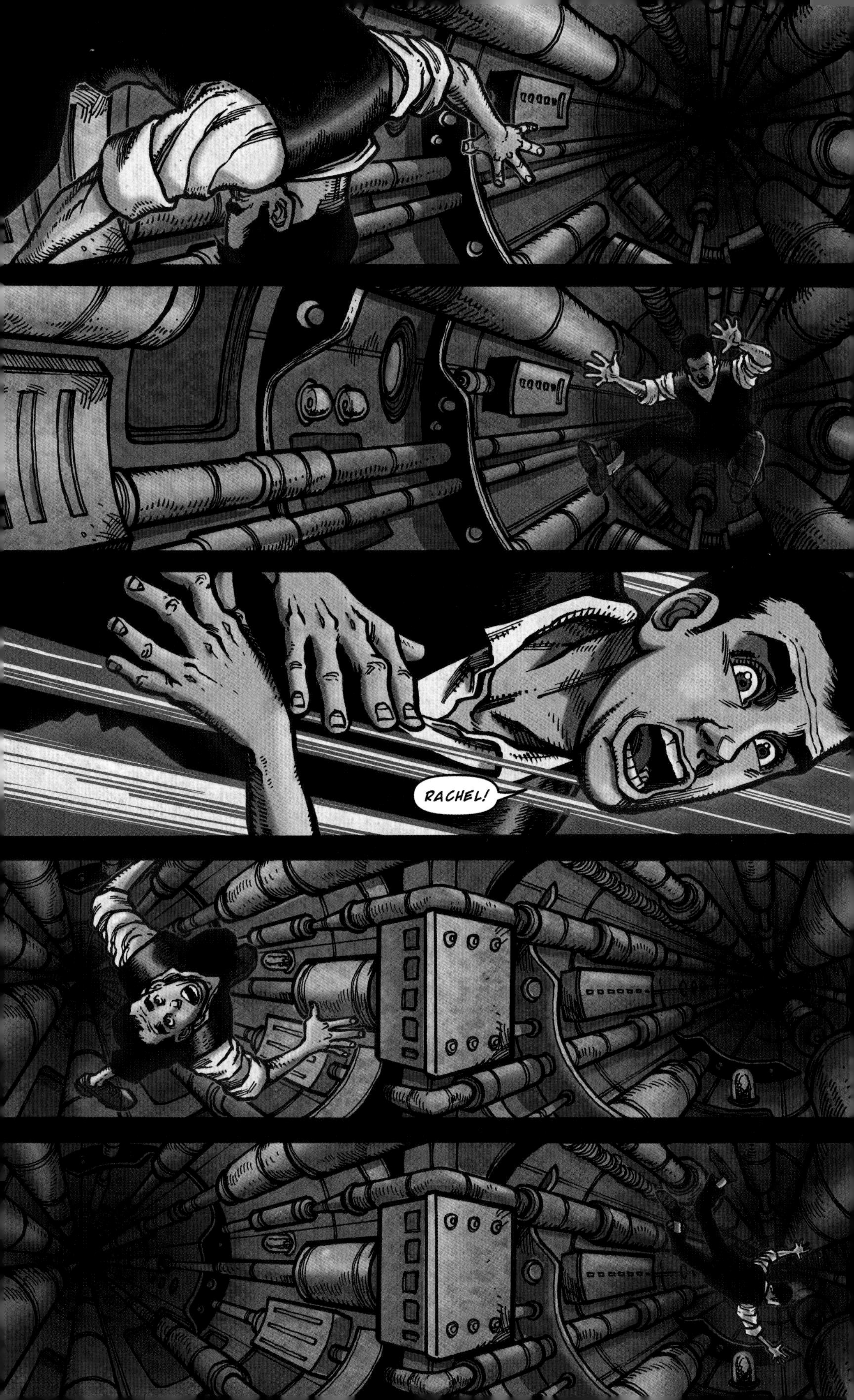
RACHEL!

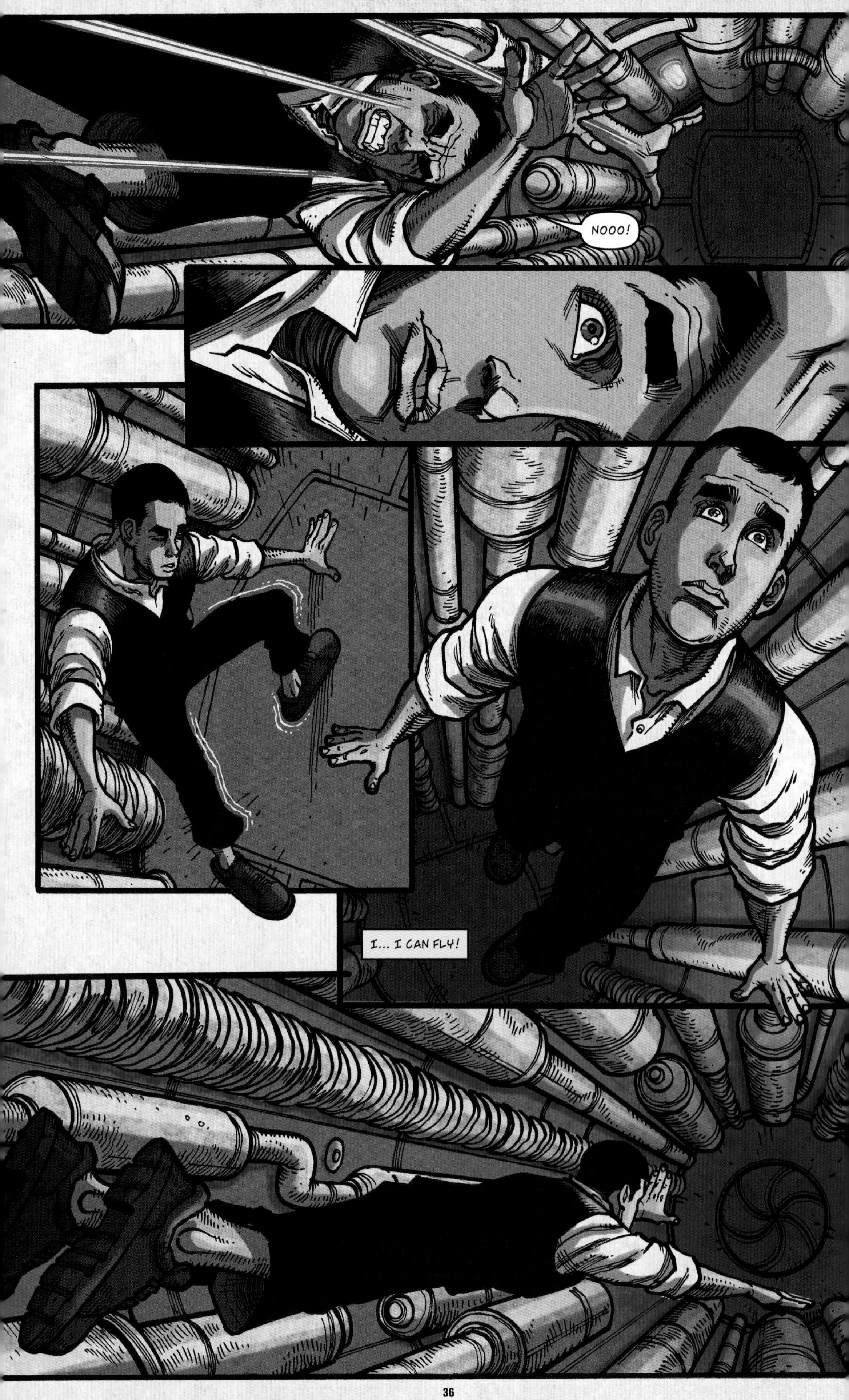
NOOO!
I... I CAN FLY!

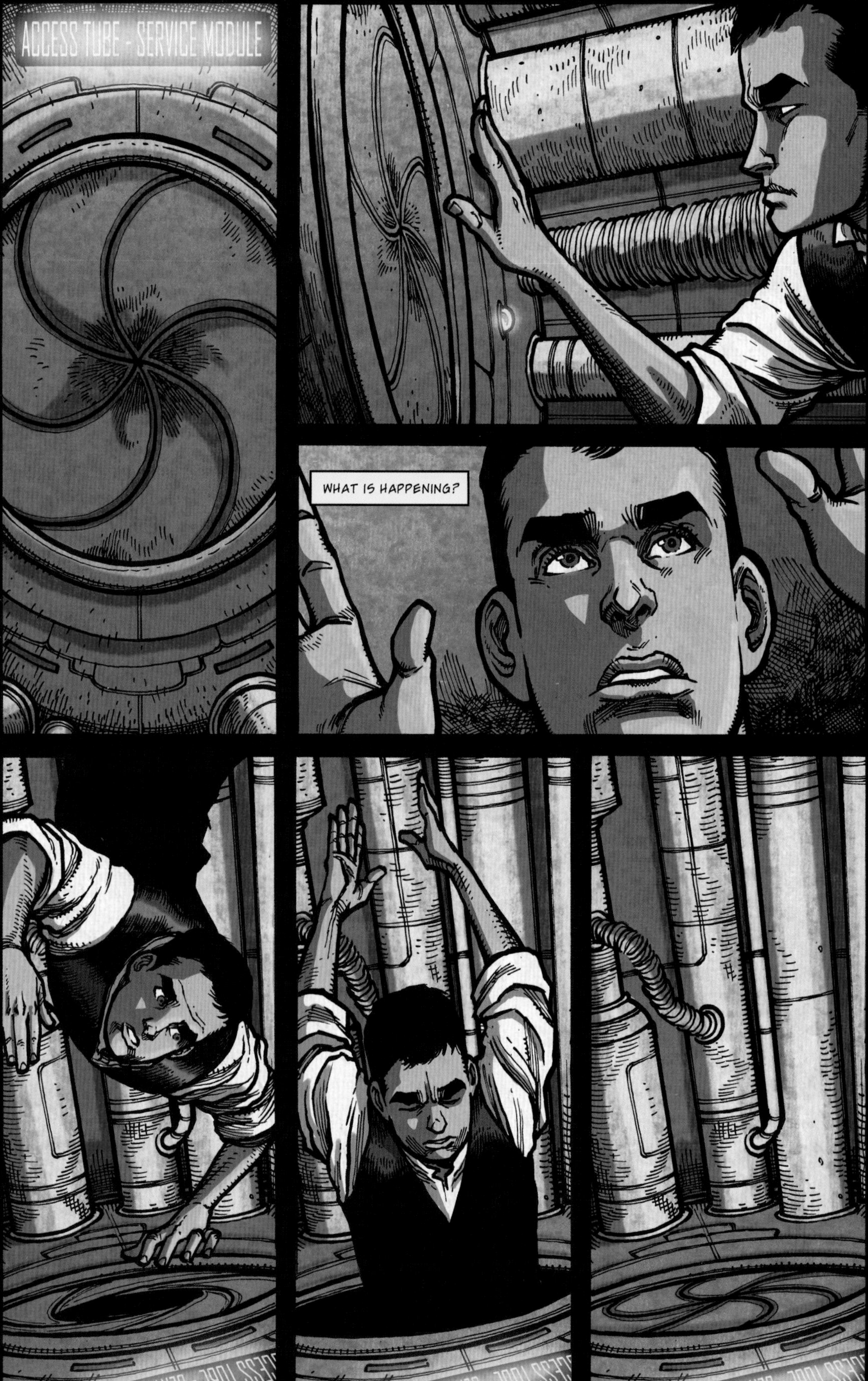

ACCESS TUBE - SERVICE MODULE
WHAT IS HAPPENING?

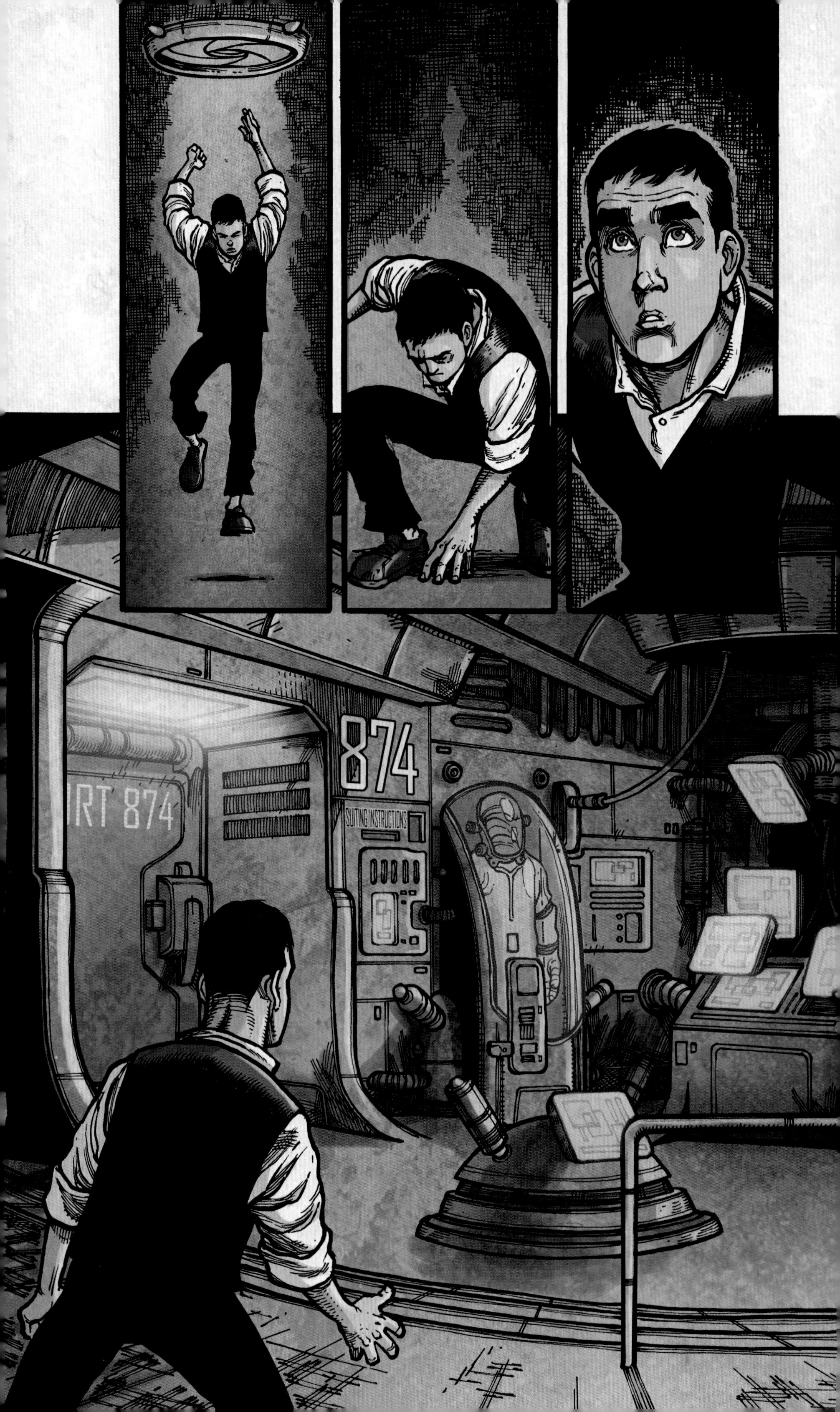
874
RT 874
SUITING INSTRUCTIONS

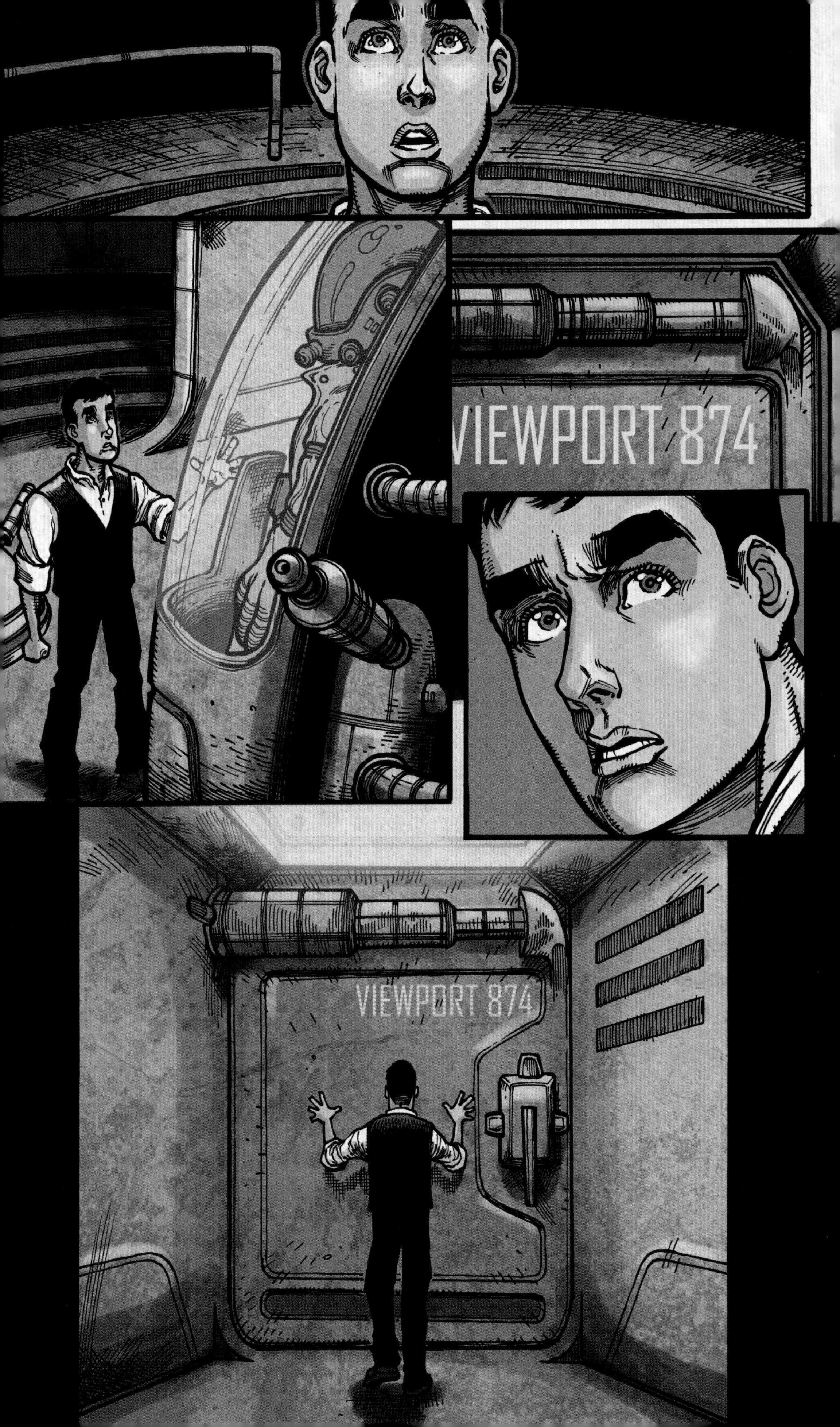
VIEWPORT 874
VIEWPORT 874

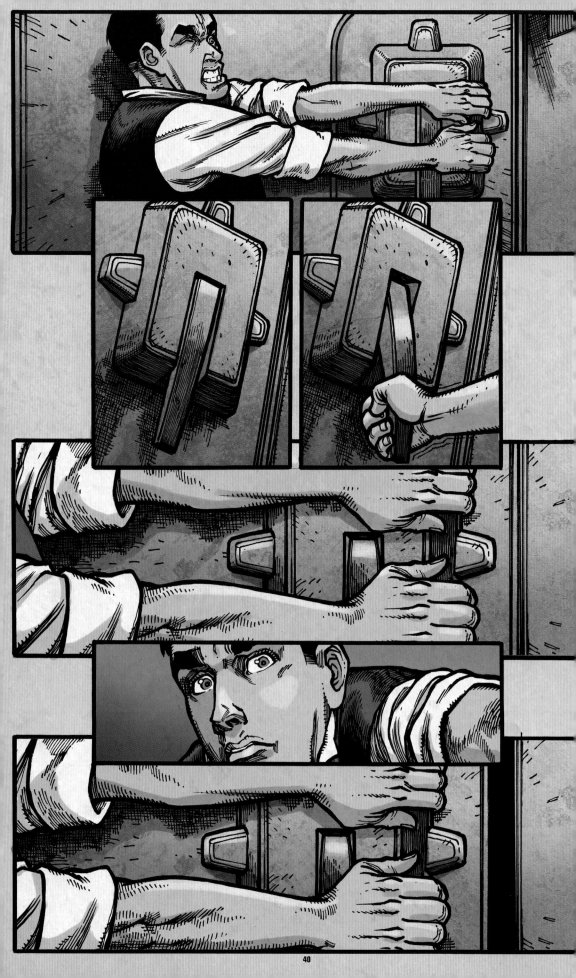

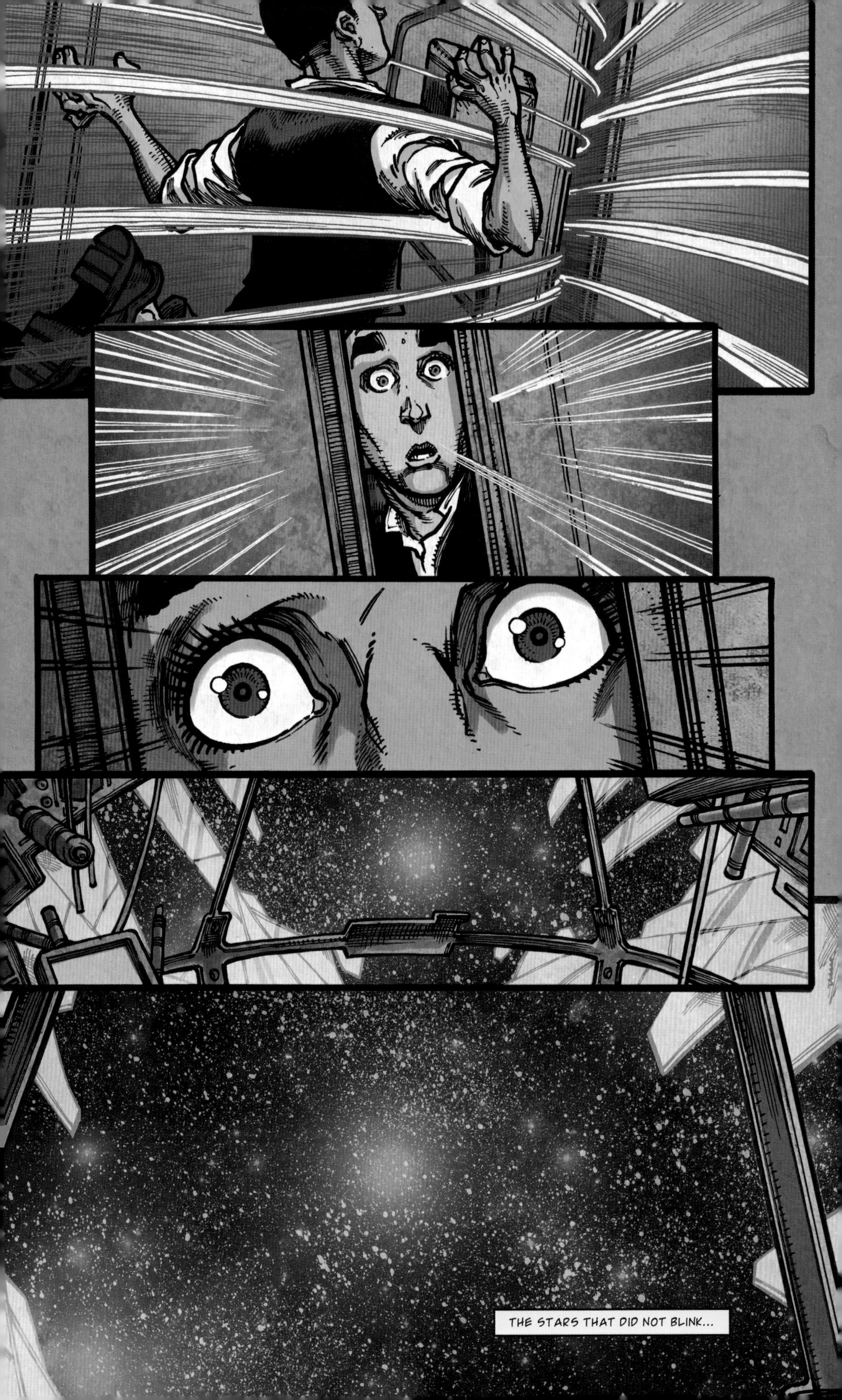
THE STARS THAT DID NOT BLINK...

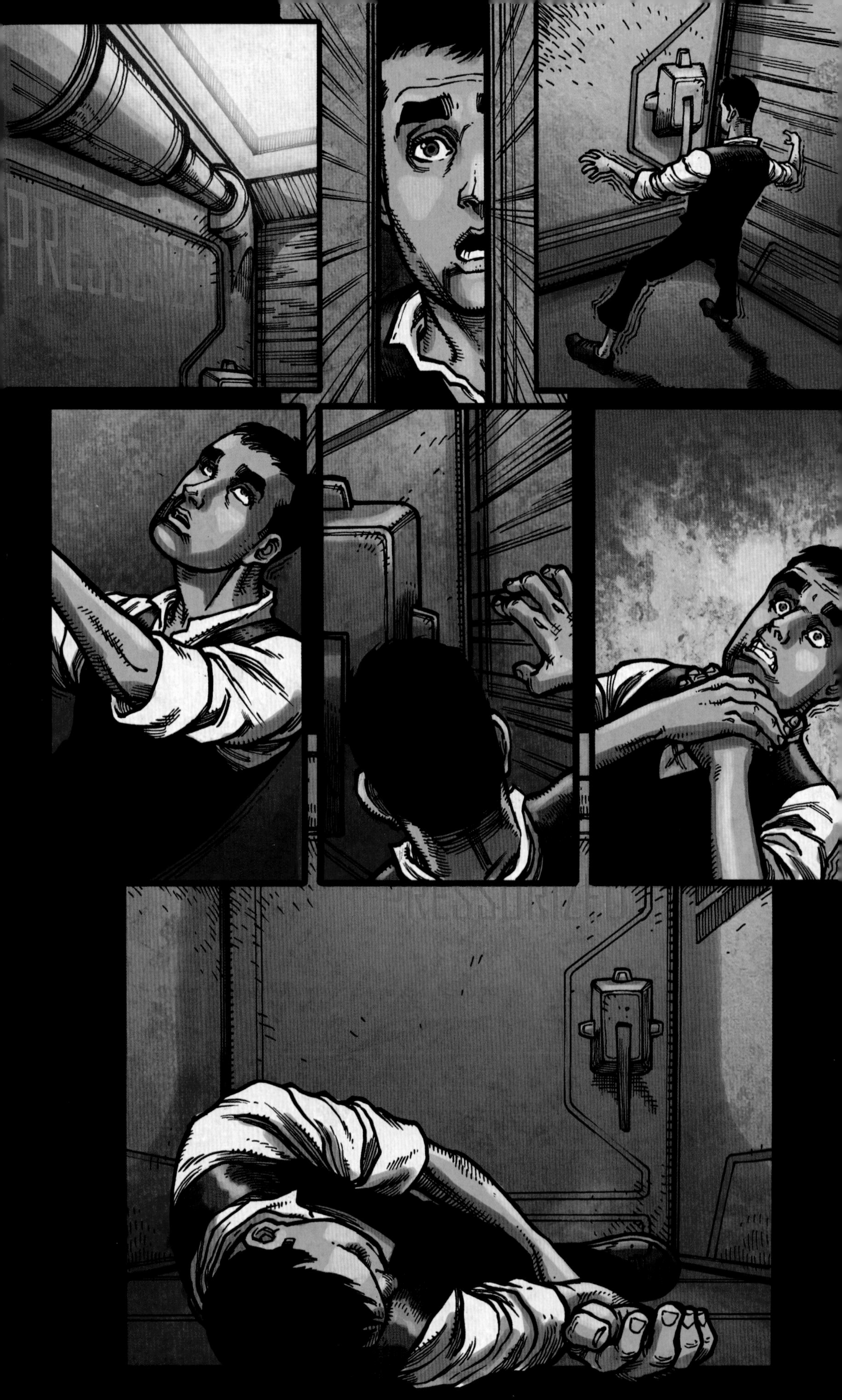

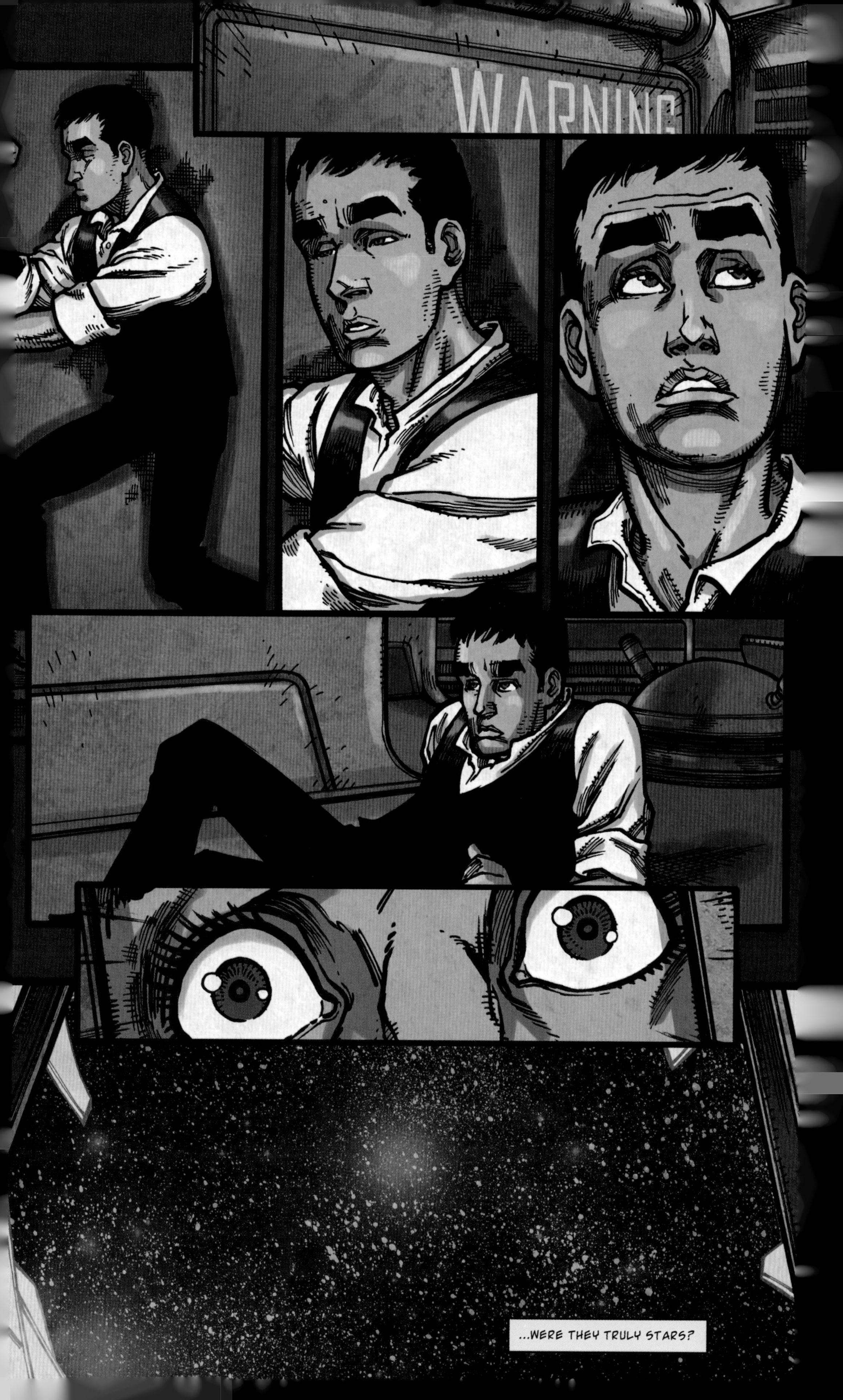
WARNING
...WERE THEY TRULY STARS?

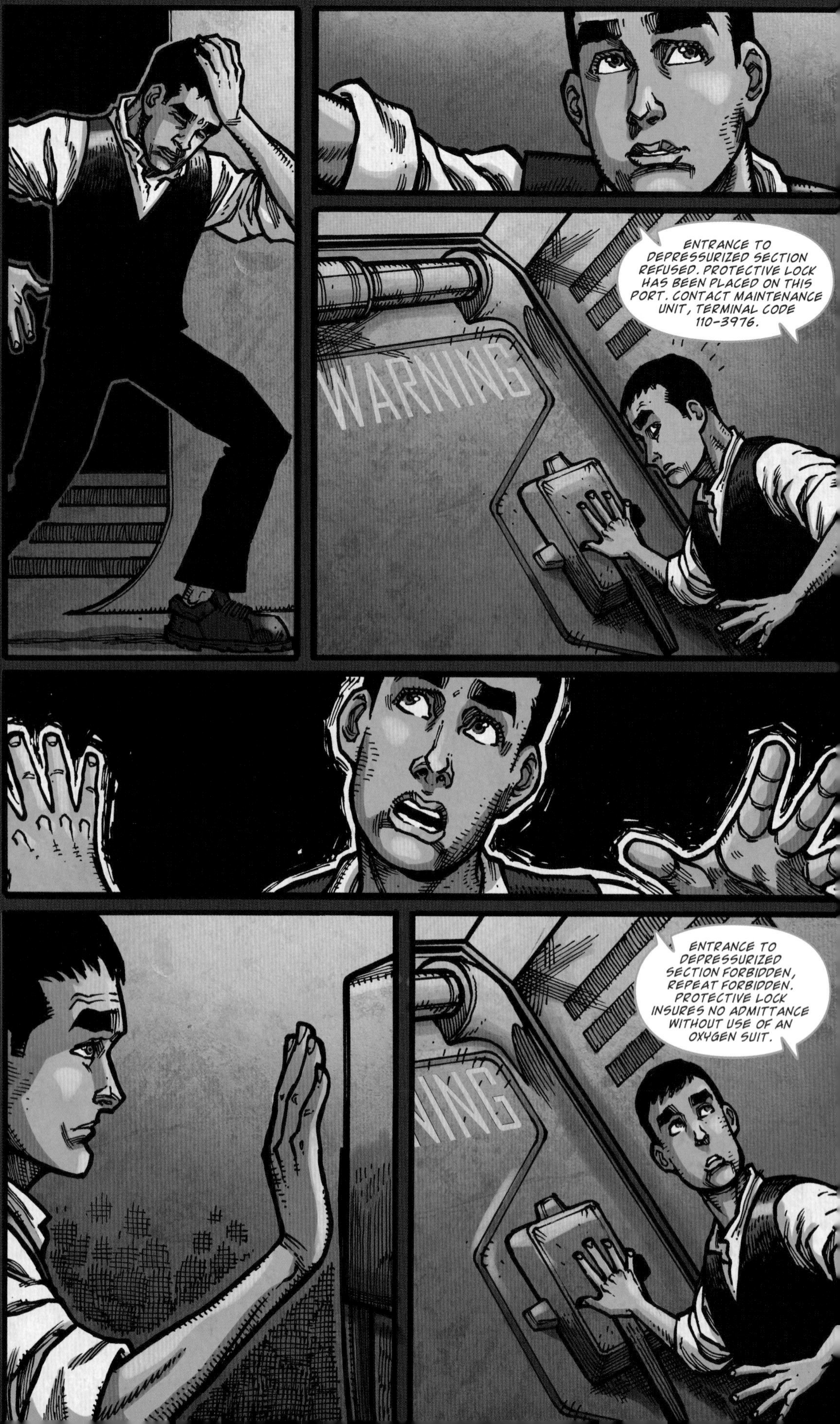
WARNING
ENTRANCE TO DEPRESSURIZED SECTION REFUSED. PROTECTIVE LOCK HAS BEEN PLACED ON THIS PORT. CONTACT MAINTENANCE UNIT, TERMINAL CODE 110-3976.
ENTRANCE TO DEPRESSURIZED SECTION FORBIDDEN, REPEAT FORBIDDEN. PROTECTIVE LOCK INSURES NO ADMITTANCE WITHOUT USE OF AN OXYGEN SUIT.

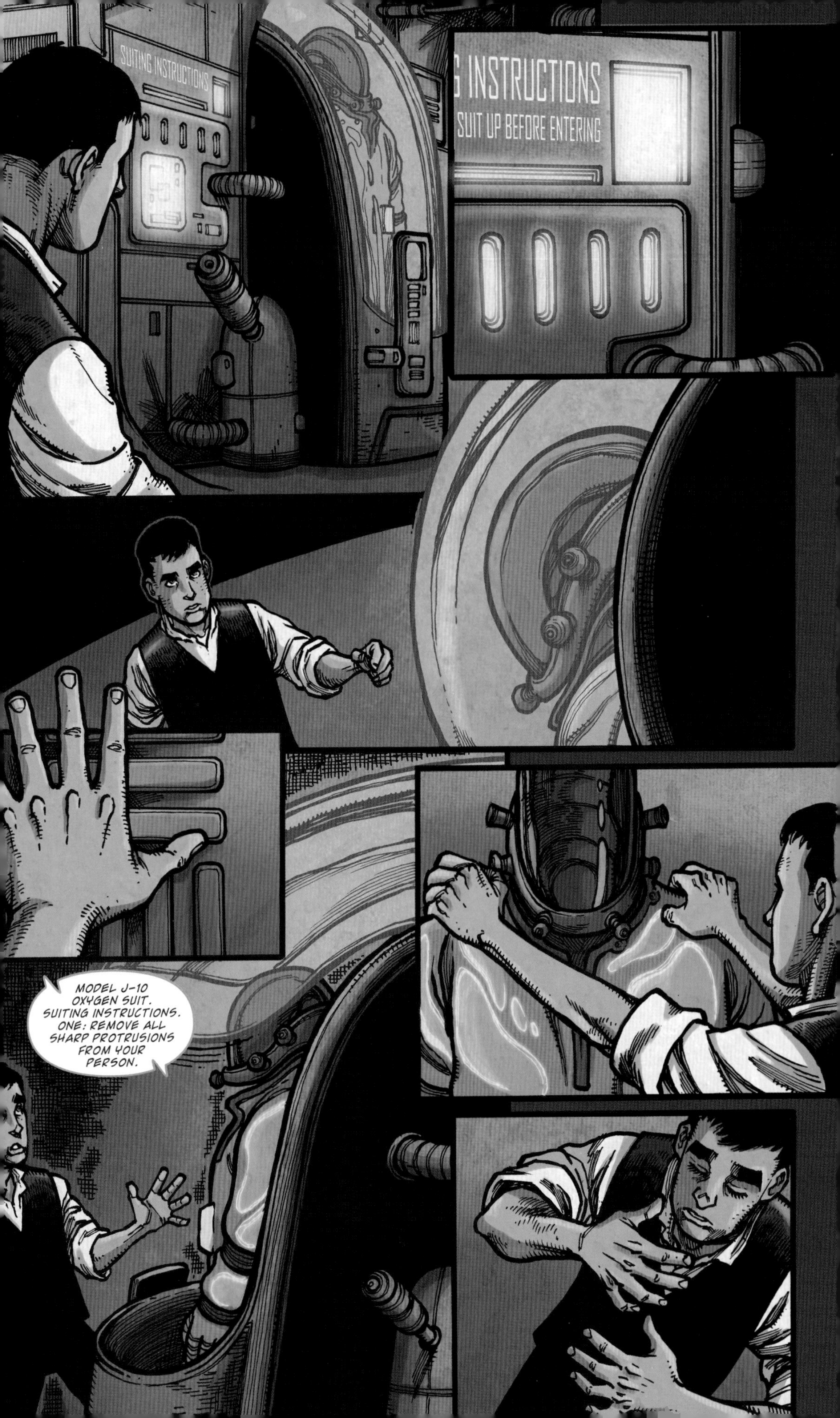
SUITING INSTRUCTIONS
G INSTRUCTIONS
SUIT UP BEFORE ENTERING
MODEL J-10 OXYGEN SUIT. SUITING INSTRUCTIONS. ONE: REMOVE ALL SHARP PROTRUSIONS FROM YOUR PERSON.

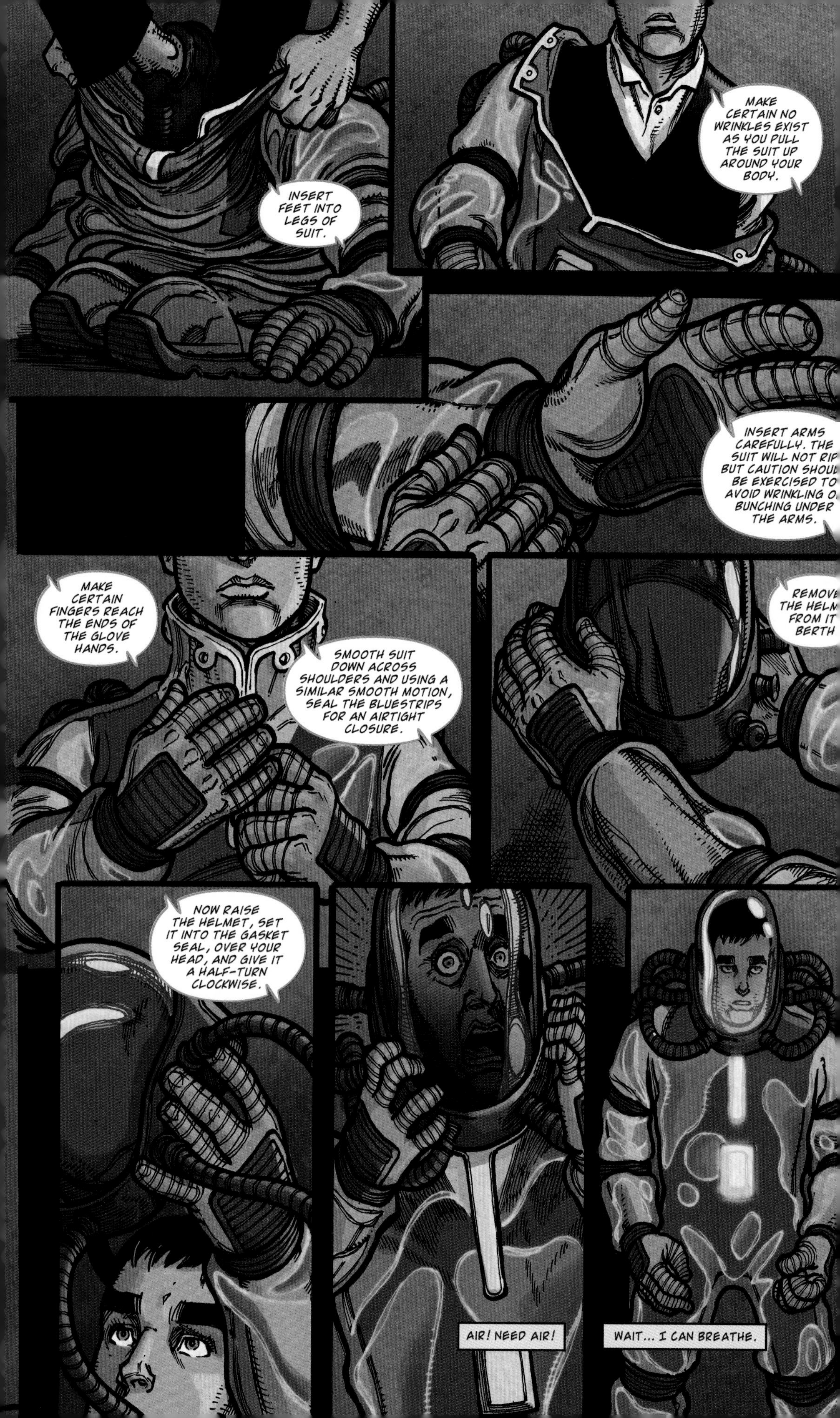
INSERT FEET INTO LEGS OF SUIT.
MAKE CERTAIN NO WRINKLES EXIST AS YOU PULL THE SUIT UP AROUND YOUR BODY.
INSERT ARMS CAREFULLY. THE SUIT WILL NOT RIP BUT CAUTION SHOUL BE EXERCISED TO AVOID WRINKLING O BUNCHING UNDER THE ARMS.
MAKE CERTAIN FINGERS REACH THE ENDS OF THE GLOVE HANDS.
SMOOTH SUIT DOWN ACROSS SHOULDERS AND USING A SIMILAR SMOOTH MOTION, SEAL THE BLUESTRIPS FOR AN AIRTIGHT CLOSURE.
REMOVE THE HELM FROM IT BERTH
NOW RAISE THE HELMET, SET IT INTO THE GASKET SEAL, OVER YOUR HEAD, AND GIVE IT A HALF-TURN CLOCKWISE.
AIR! NEED AIR!
WAIT... I CAN BREATHE.

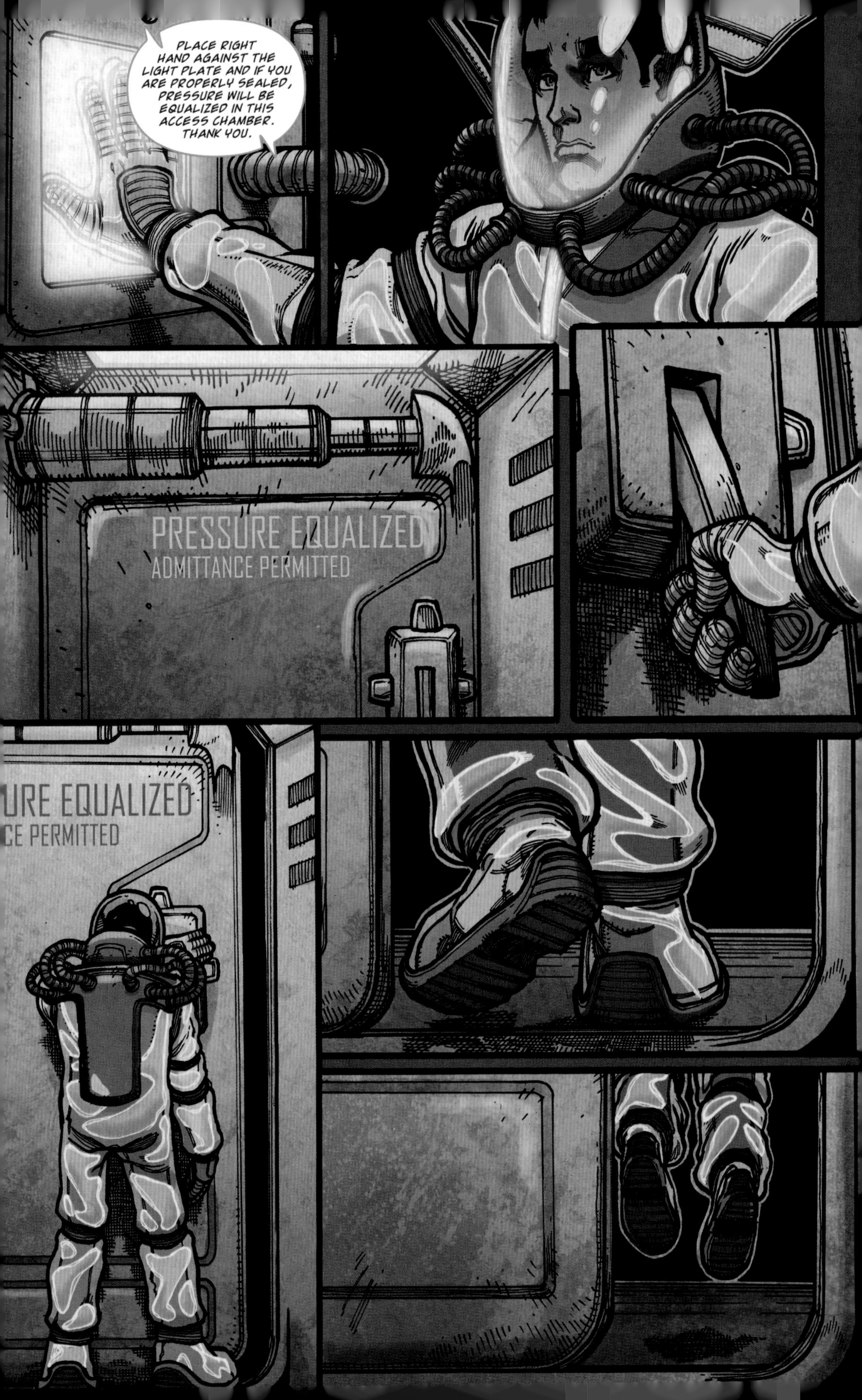
PLACE RIGHT HAND AGAINST THE LIGHT PLATE AND IF YOU ARE PROPERLY SEALED, PRESSURE WILL BE EQUALIZED IN THIS ACCESS CHAMBER. THANK YOU.
PRESSURE EQUALIZED
ADMITTANCE PERMITTED

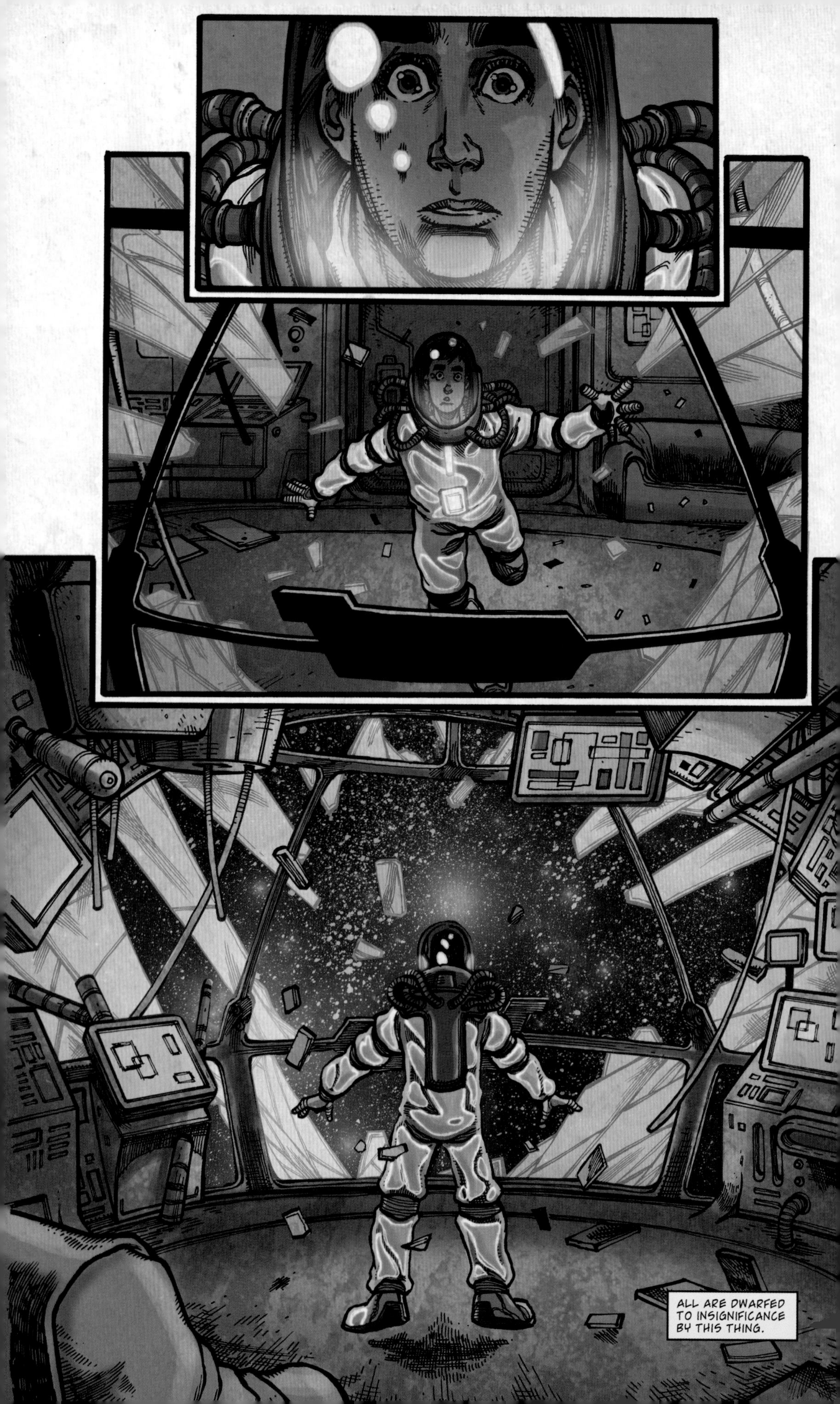
ALL ARE DWARFED TO INSIGNIFICANCE BY THIS THING.

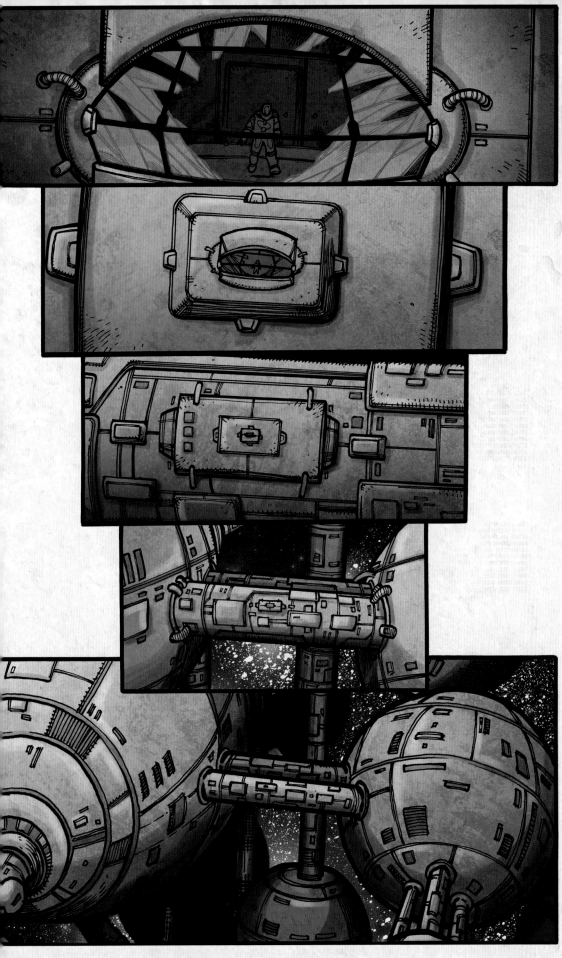

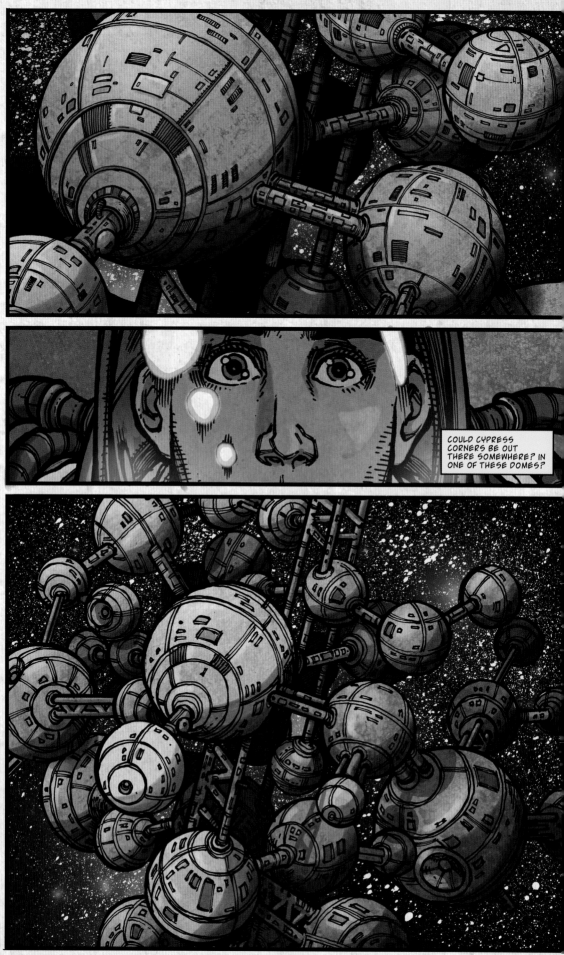

COULD CYPRESS CORNERS BE OUT THERE SOMEWHERE? IN ONE OF THESE DOMES?

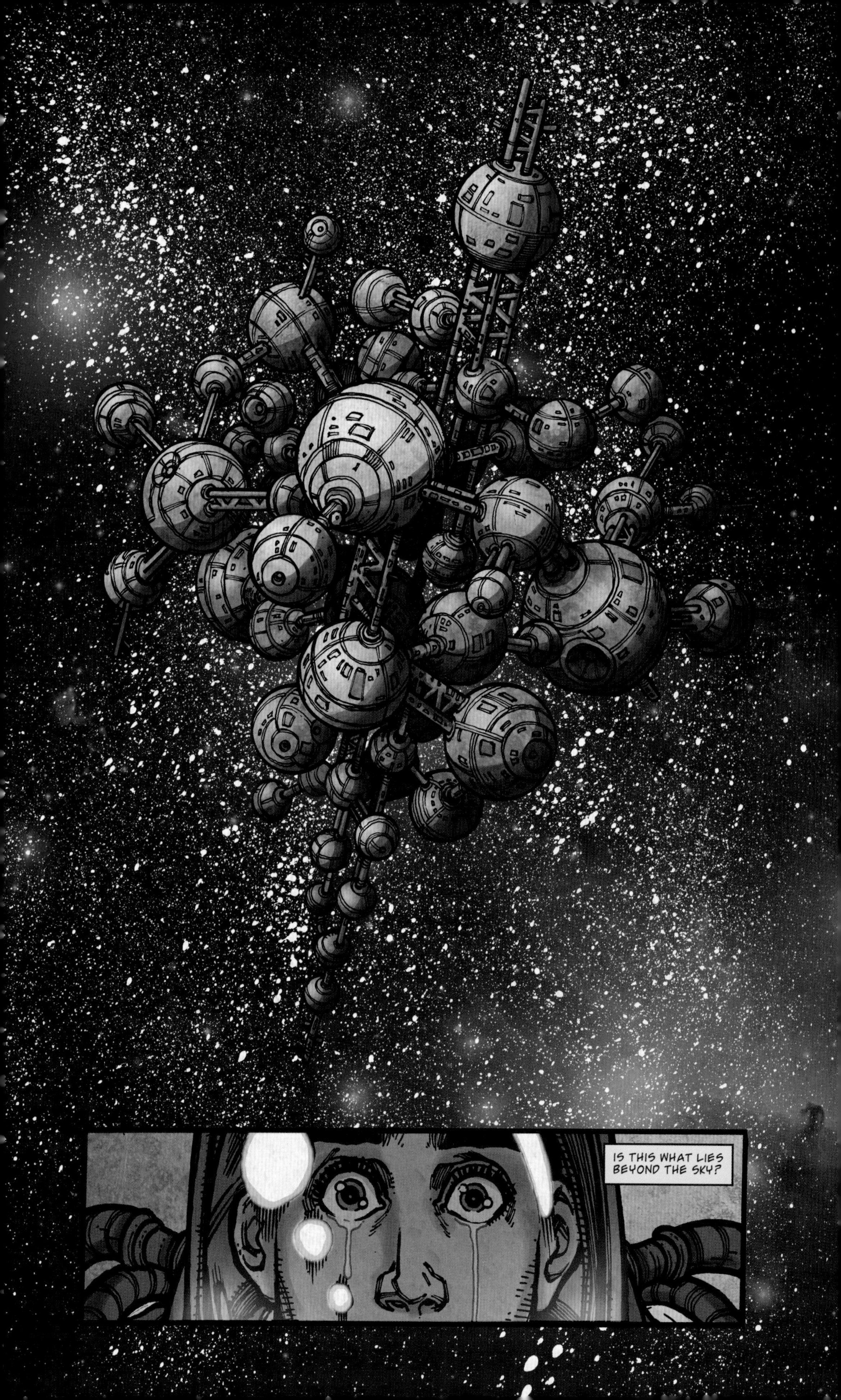
IS THIS WHAT LIES
BEYOND THE SKY?

CHAPTER THREE

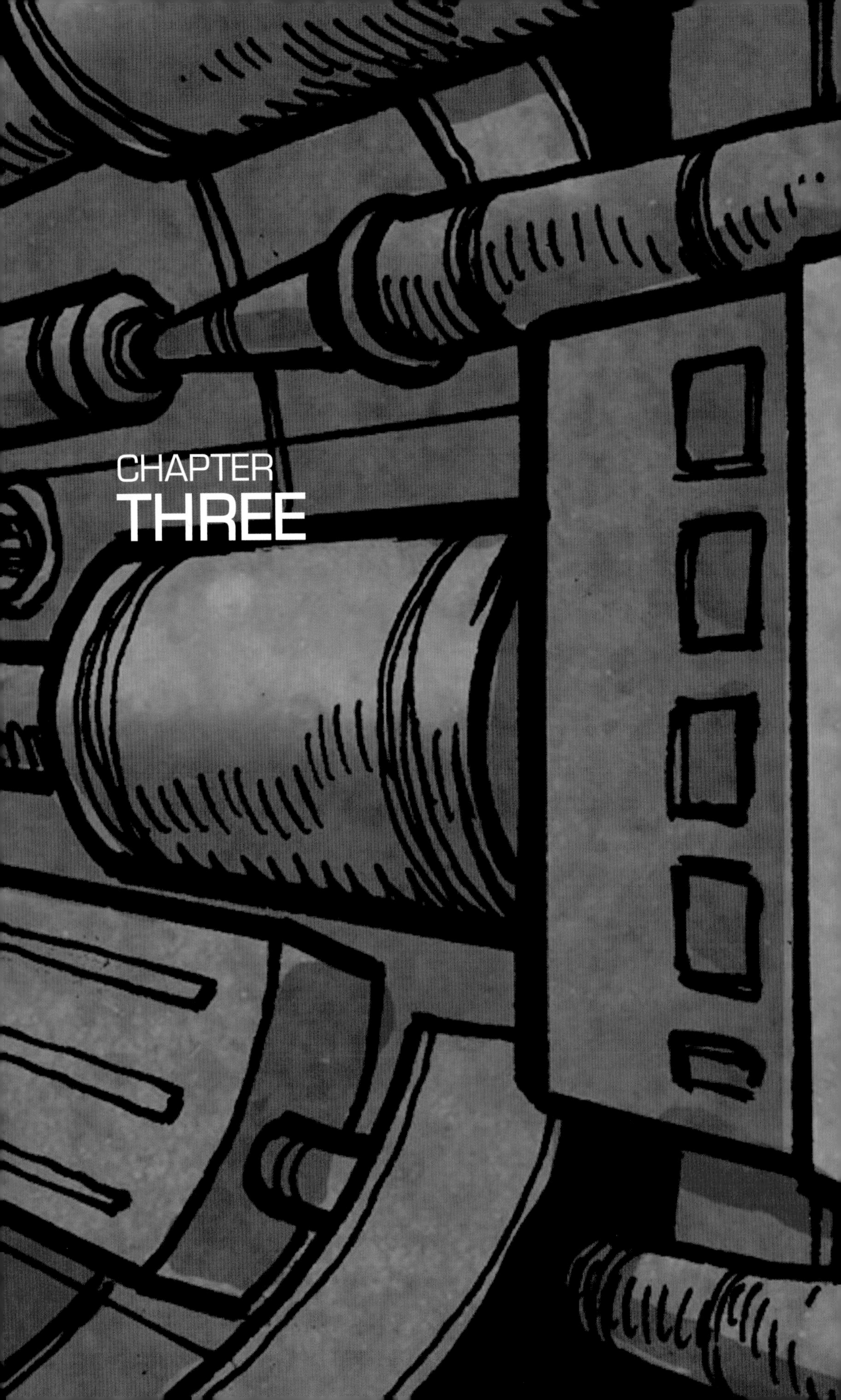

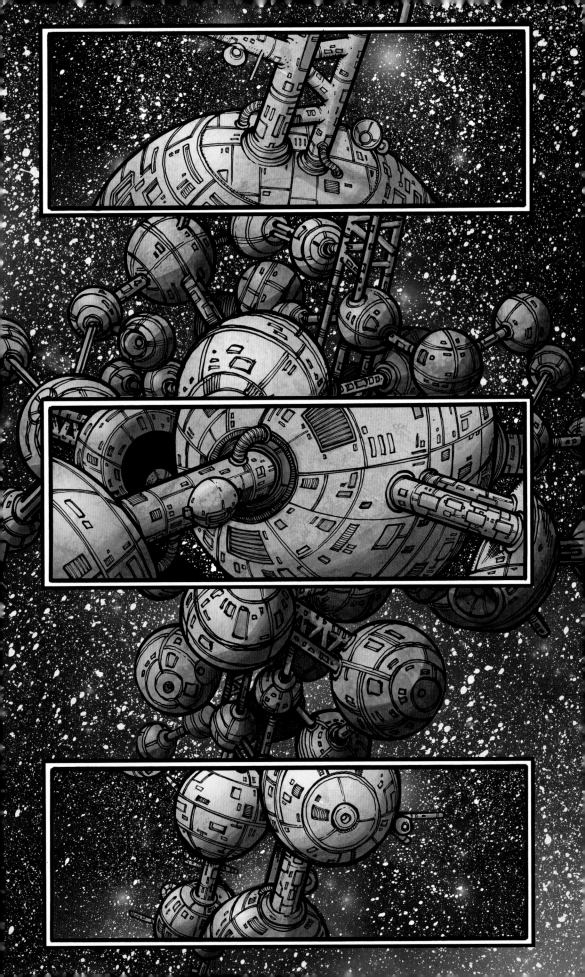

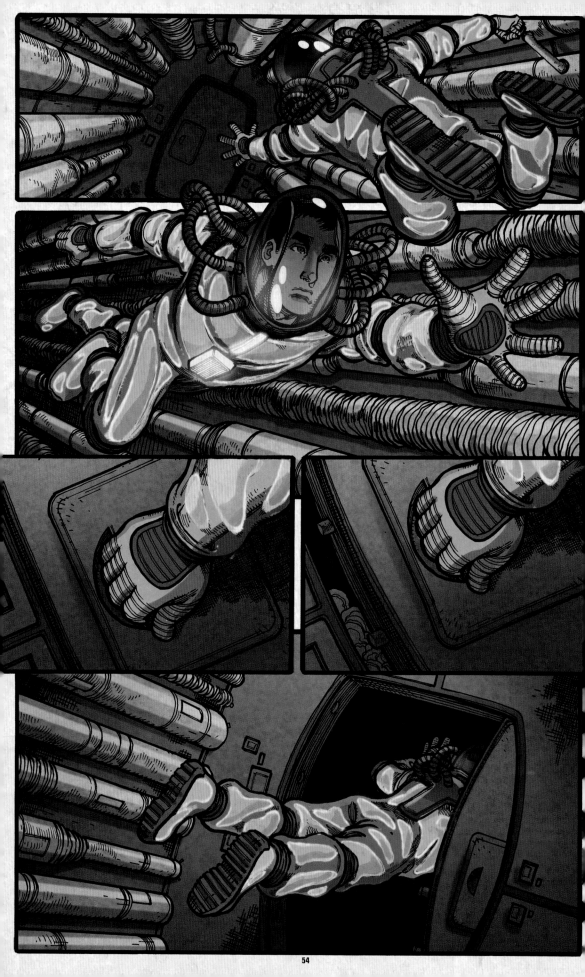

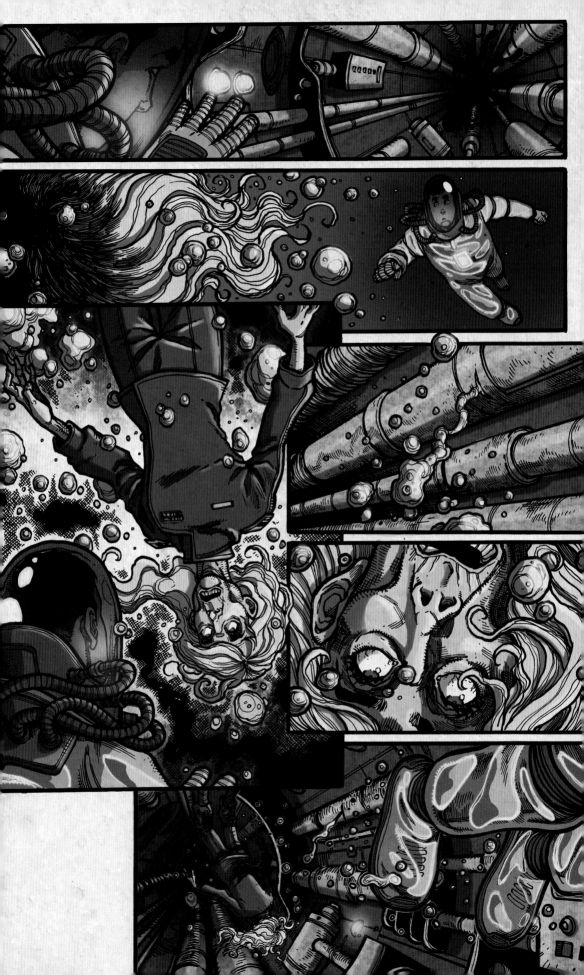

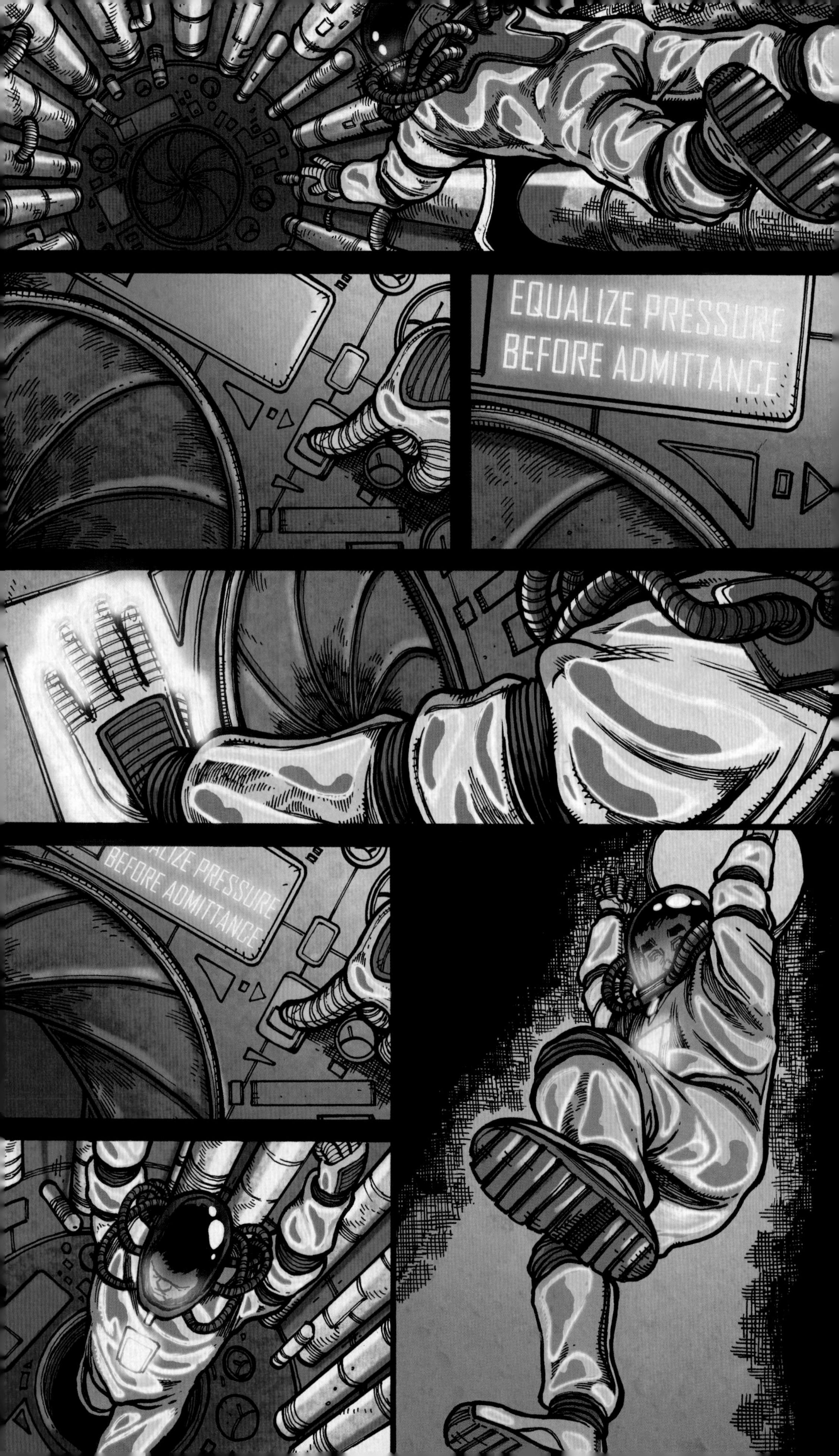
EQUALIZE PRESSURE
BEFORE ADMITTANCE
EQUALIZE PRESSURE
BEFORE ADMITTANCE

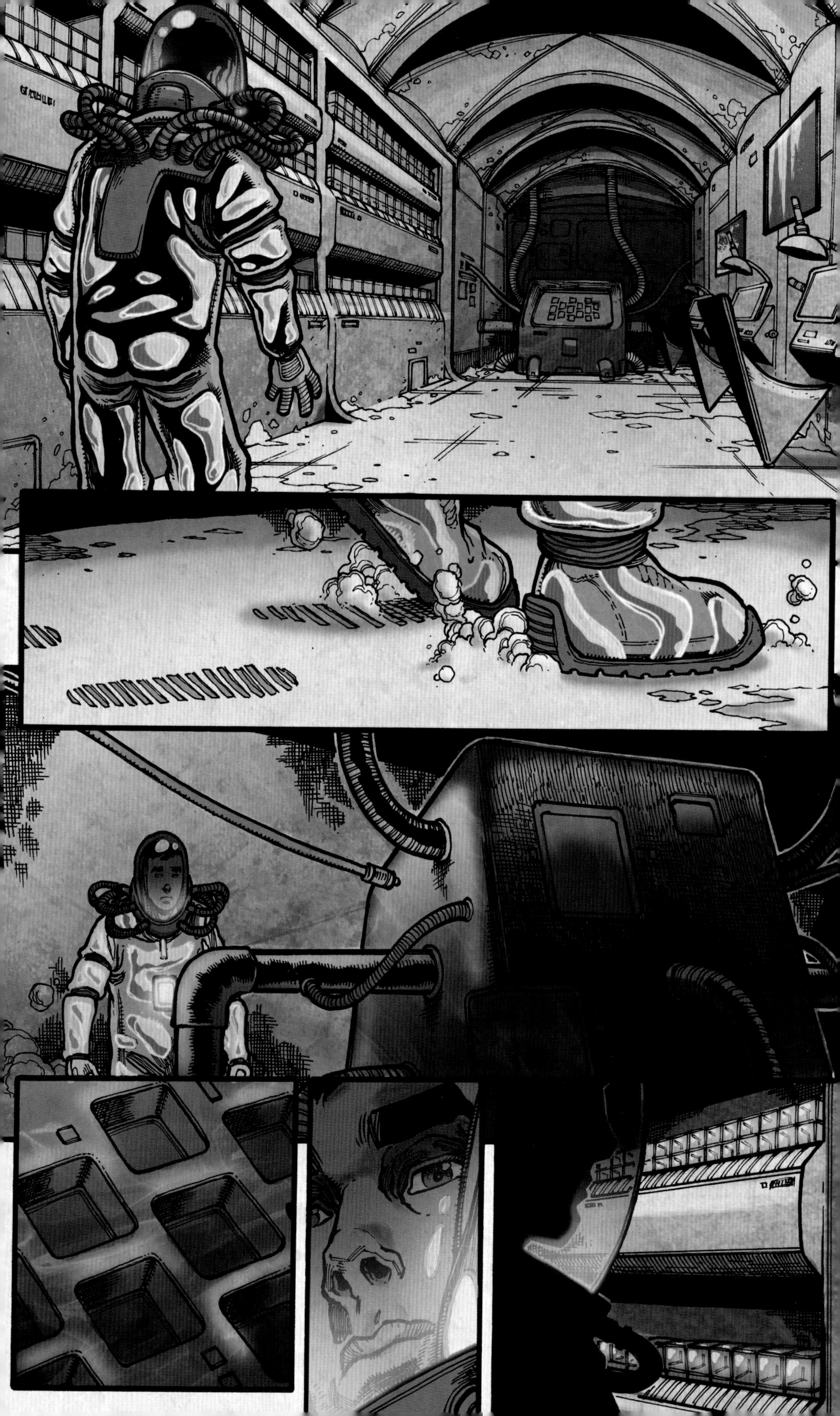

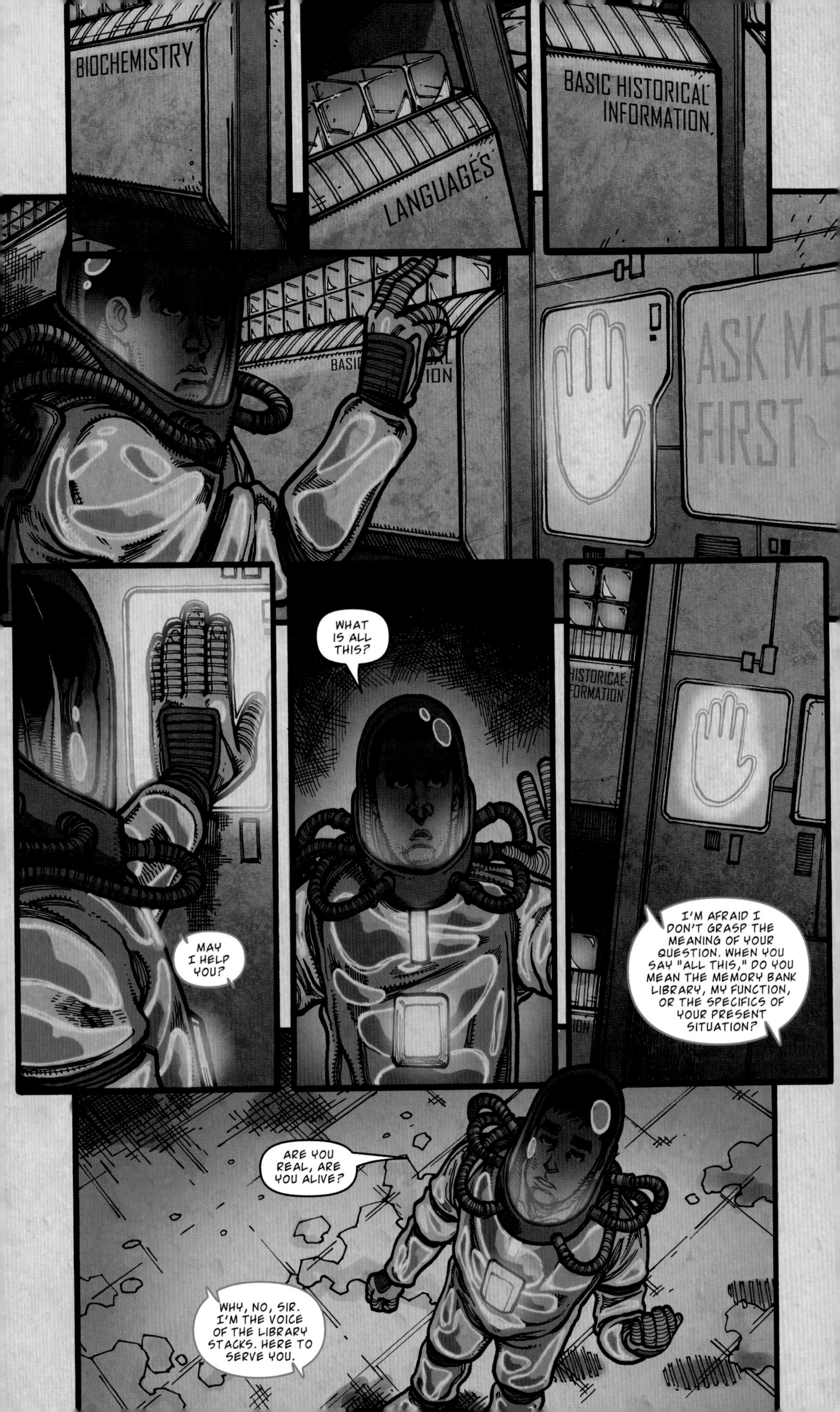
BIOCHEMISTRY
LANGUAGES
BASIC HISTORICAL INFORMATION
ASK ME FIRST
WHAT IS ALL THIS?
MAY I HELP YOU?
I'M AFRAID I DON'T GRASP THE MEANING OF YOUR QUESTION. WHEN YOU SAY "ALL THIS," DO YOU MEAN THE MEMORY BANK LIBRARY, MY FUNCTION, OR THE SPECIFICS OF YOUR PRESENT SITUATION?
ARE YOU REAL, ARE YOU ALIVE?
WHY, NO, SIR. I'M THE VOICE OF THE LIBRARY STACKS. HERE TO SERVE YOU.

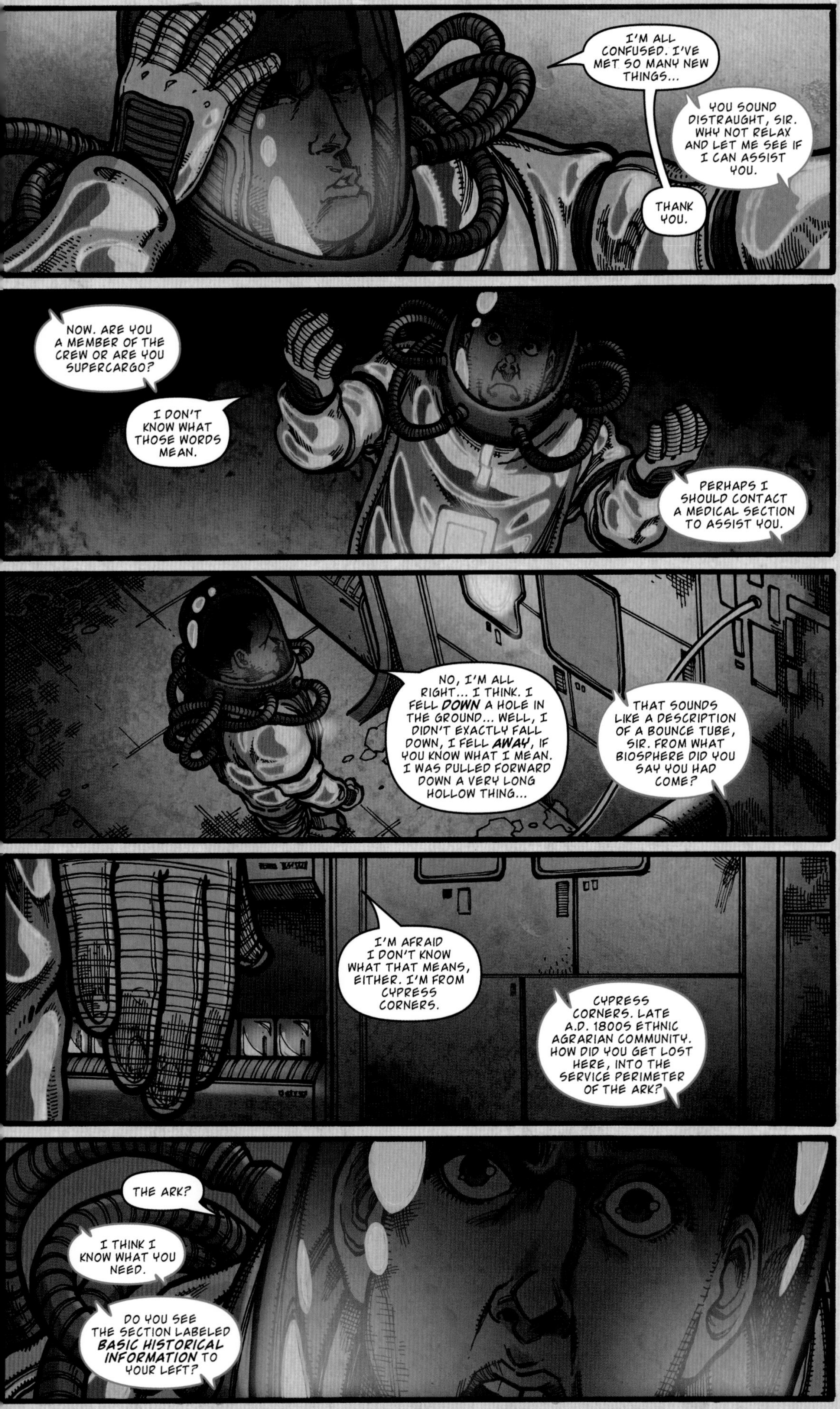
I'M ALL CONFUSED. I'VE MET SO MANY NEW THINGS...
YOU SOUND DISTRAUGHT, SIR. WHY NOT RELAX AND LET ME SEE IF I CAN ASSIST YOU.
THANK YOU.
NOW. ARE YOU A MEMBER OF THE CREW OR ARE YOU SUPERCARGO?
I DON'T KNOW WHAT THOSE WORDS MEAN.
PERHAPS I SHOULD CONTACT A MEDICAL SECTION TO ASSIST YOU.
NO, I'M ALL RIGHT... I THINK. I FELL DOWN A HOLE IN THE GROUND... WELL, I DIDN'T EXACTLY FALL DOWN, I FELL AWAY, IF YOU KNOW WHAT I MEAN. I WAS PULLED FORWARD DOWN A VERY LONG HOLLOW THING...
THAT SOUNDS LIKE A DESCRIPTION OF A BOUNCE TUBE, SIR. FROM WHAT BIOSPHERE DID YOU SAY YOU HAD COME?
I'M AFRAID I DON'T KNOW WHAT THAT MEANS, EITHER. I'M FROM CYPRESS CORNERS.
CYPRESS CORNERS. LATE A.D. 1800S ETHNIC AGRARIAN COMMUNITY. HOW DID YOU GET LOST HERE, INTO THE SERVICE PERIMETER OF THE ARK?
THE ARK?
I THINK I KNOW WHAT YOU NEED.
DO YOU SEE THE SECTION LABELED BASIC HISTORICAL INFORMATION TO YOUR LEFT?

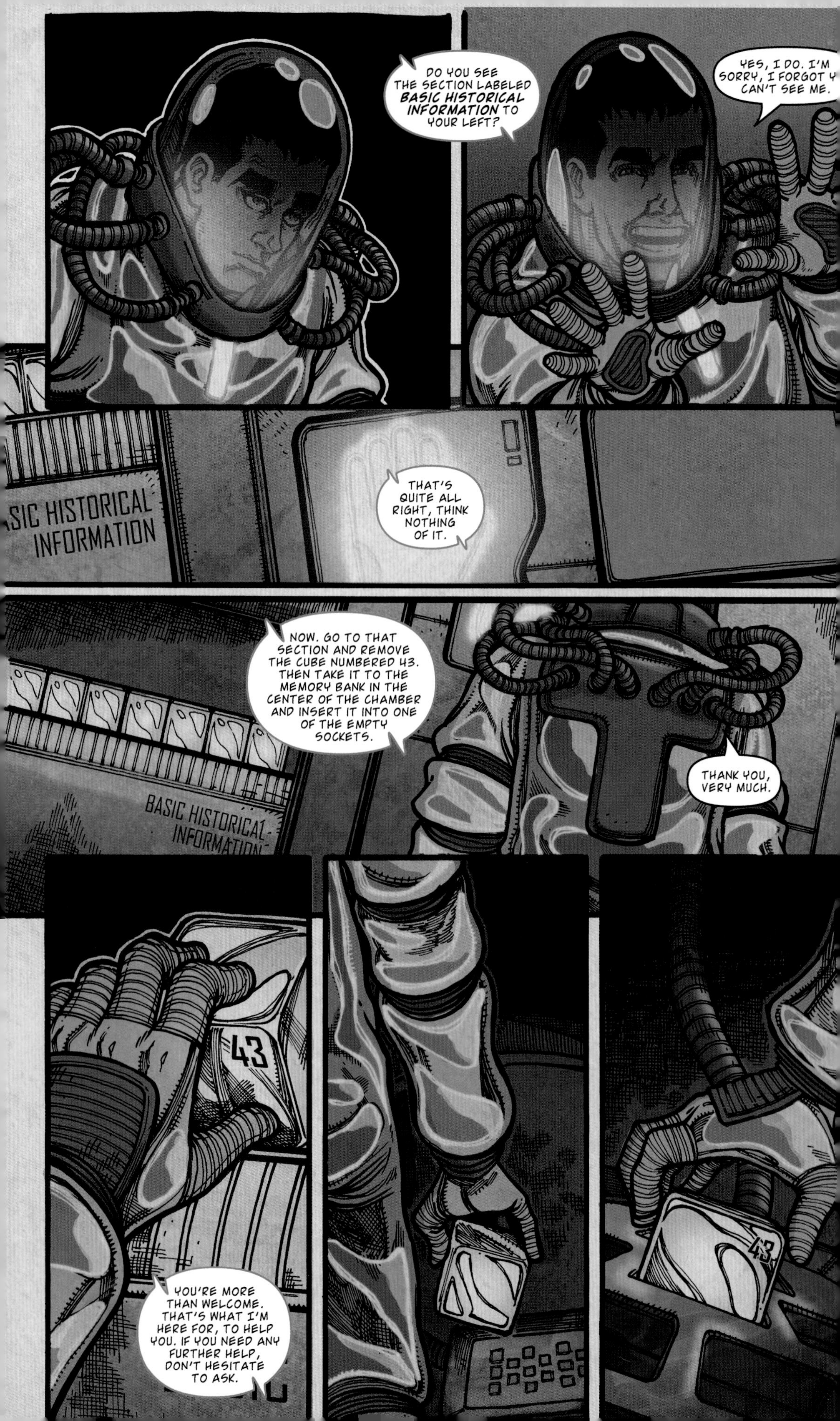
DO YOU SEE THE SECTION LABELED *BASIC HISTORICAL INFORMATION* TO YOUR LEFT?
YES, I DO. I'M SORRY, I FORGOT Y CAN'T SEE ME.
SIC HISTORICAL INFORMATION
THAT'S QUITE ALL RIGHT, THINK NOTHING OF IT.
NOW. GO TO THAT SECTION AND REMOVE THE CUBE NUMBERED 43. THEN TAKE IT TO THE MEMORY BANK IN THE CENTER OF THE CHAMBER AND INSERT IT INTO ONE OF THE EMPTY SOCKETS.
BASIC HISTORICAL INFORMATION
THANK YOU, VERY MUCH.
43
YOU'RE MORE THAN WELCOME. THAT'S WHAT I'M HERE FOR, TO HELP YOU. IF YOU NEED ANY FURTHER HELP, DON'T HESITATE TO ASK.
43

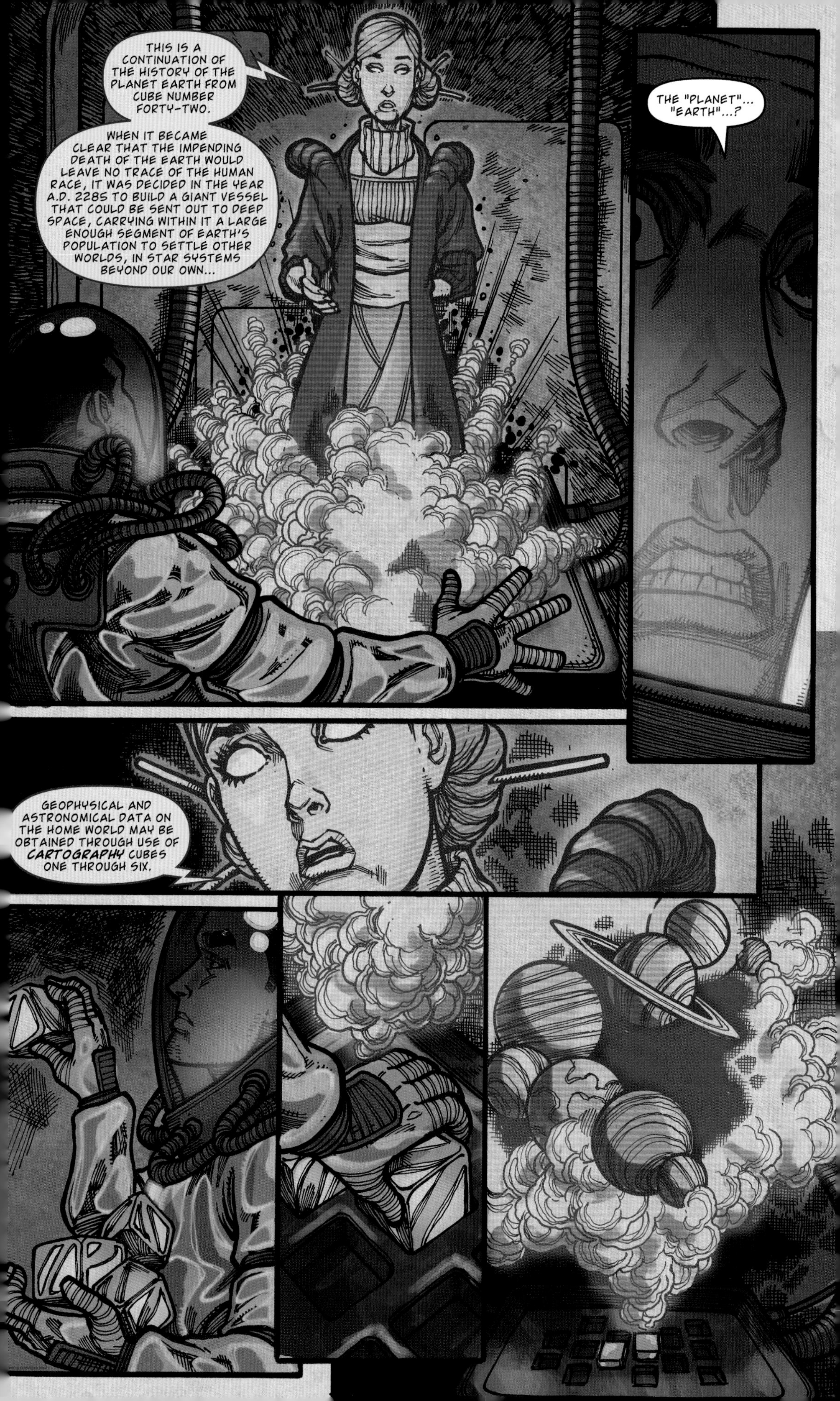
THIS IS A CONTINUATION OF THE HISTORY OF THE PLANET EARTH FROM CUBE NUMBER FORTY-TWO.
WHEN IT BECAME CLEAR THAT THE IMPENDING DEATH OF THE EARTH WOULD LEAVE NO TRACE OF THE HUMAN RACE, IT WAS DECIDED IN THE YEAR A.D. 2285 TO BUILD A GIANT VESSEL THAT COULD BE SENT OUT TO DEEP SPACE, CARRYING WITHIN IT A LARGE ENOUGH SEGMENT OF EARTH'S POPULATION TO SETTLE OTHER WORLDS, IN STAR SYSTEMS BEYOND OUR OWN...
THE "PLANET"... "EARTH"...?
GEOPHYSICAL AND ASTRONOMICAL DATA ON THE HOME WORLD MAY BE OBTAINED THROUGH USE OF *CARTOGRAPHY* CUBES ONE THROUGH SIX.

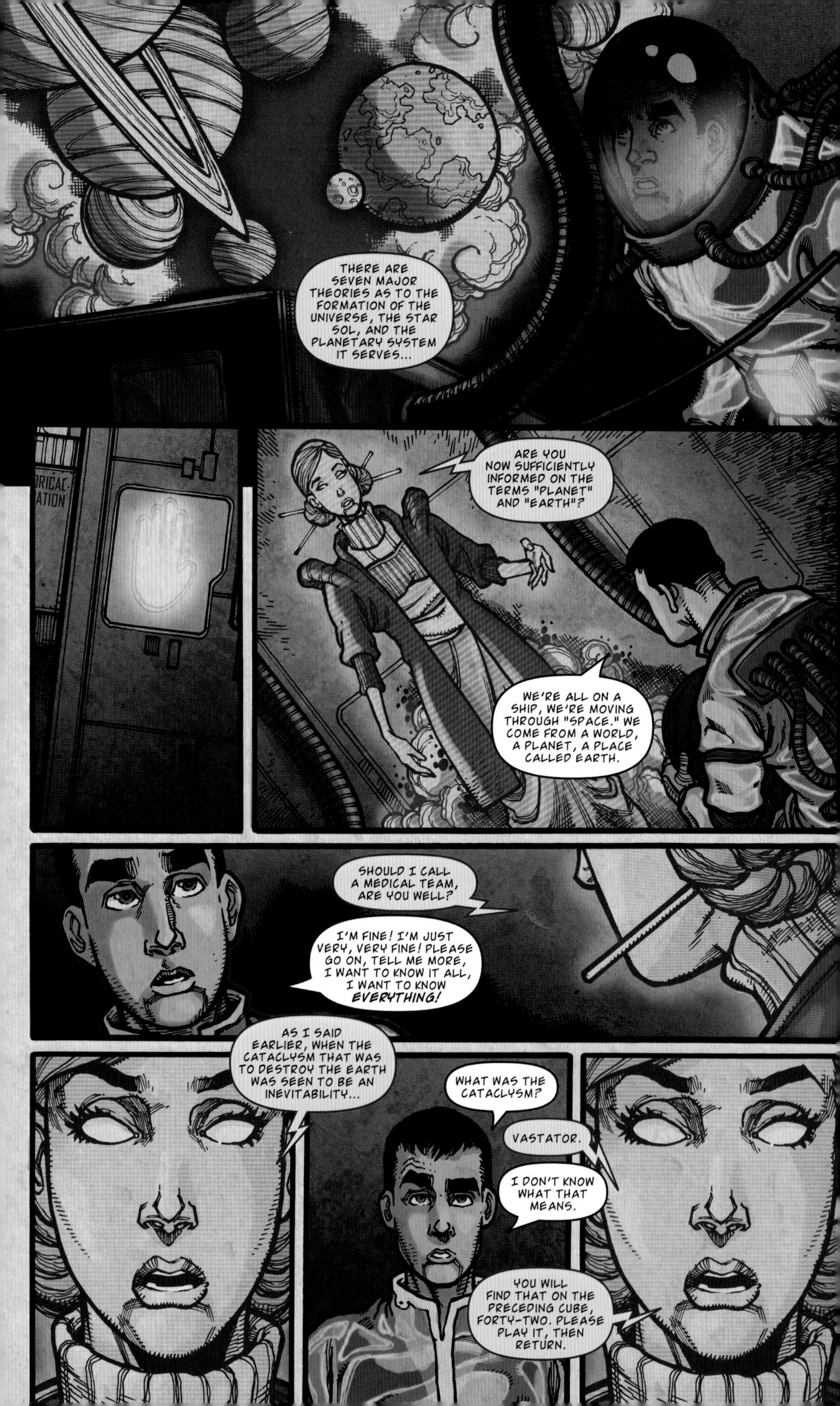
THERE ARE SEVEN MAJOR THEORIES AS TO THE FORMATION OF THE UNIVERSE, THE STAR SOL, AND THE PLANETARY SYSTEM IT SERVES...
ARE YOU NOW SUFFICIENTLY INFORMED ON THE TERMS "PLANET" AND "EARTH"?
WE'RE ALL ON A SHIP, WE'RE MOVING THROUGH "SPACE." WE COME FROM A WORLD, A PLANET, A PLACE CALLED EARTH.
SHOULD I CALL A MEDICAL TEAM, ARE YOU WELL?
I'M FINE! I'M JUST VERY, VERY FINE! PLEASE GO ON, TELL ME MORE, I WANT TO KNOW IT ALL, I WANT TO KNOW EVERYTHING!
AS I SAID EARLIER, WHEN THE CATACLYSM THAT WAS TO DESTROY THE EARTH WAS SEEN TO BE AN INEVITABILITY...
WHAT WAS THE CATACLYSM?
VASTATOR.
I DON'T KNOW WHAT THAT MEANS.
YOU WILL FIND THAT ON THE PRECEDING CUBE, FORTY-TWO. PLEASE PLAY IT, THEN RETURN.

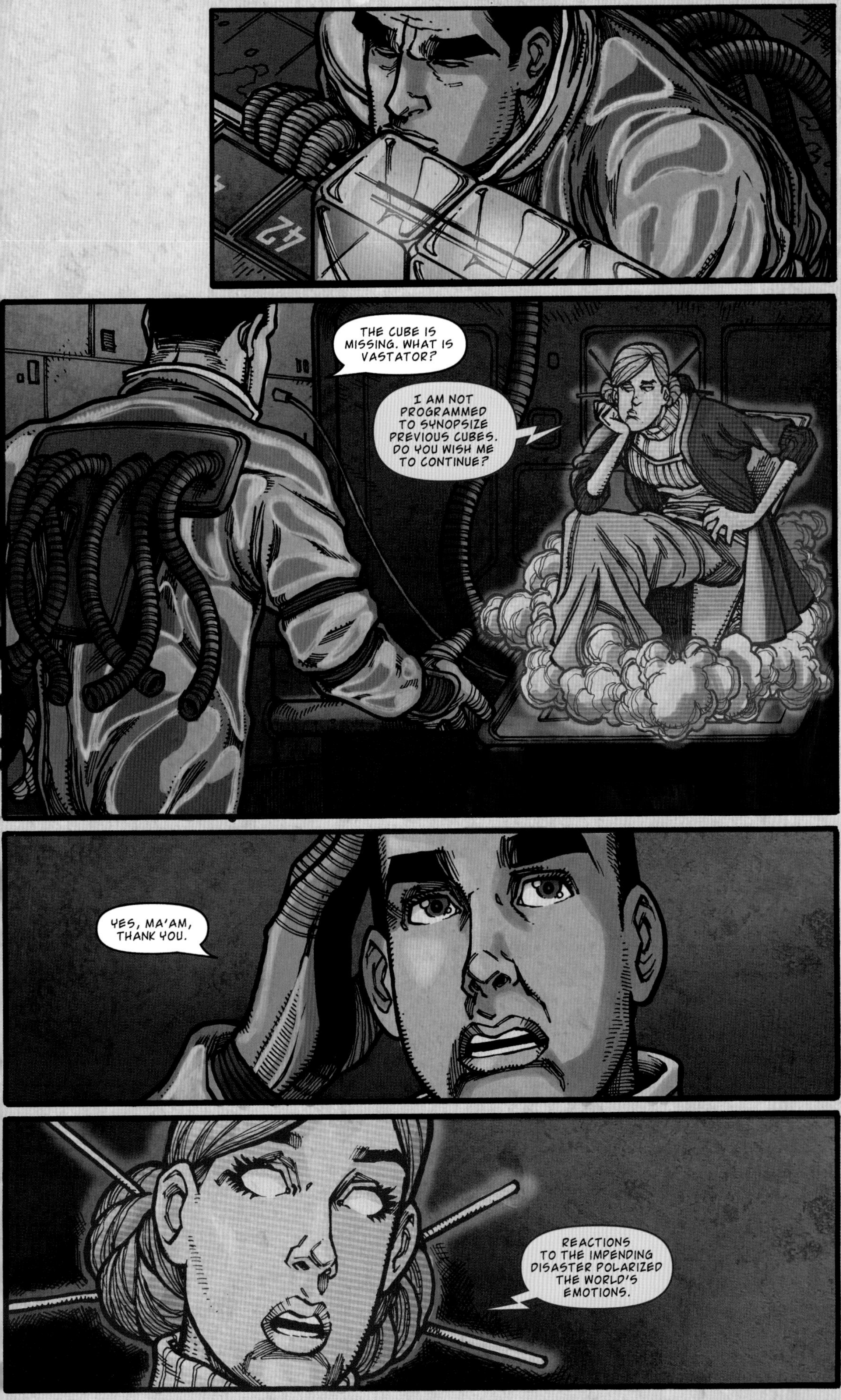
42
THE CUBE IS MISSING. WHAT IS VASTATOR?
I AM NOT PROGRAMMED TO SYNOPSIZE PREVIOUS CUBES. DO YOU WISH ME TO CONTINUE?
YES, MA'AM, THANK YOU.
REACTIONS TO THE IMPENDING DISASTER POLARIZED THE WORLD'S EMOTIONS.

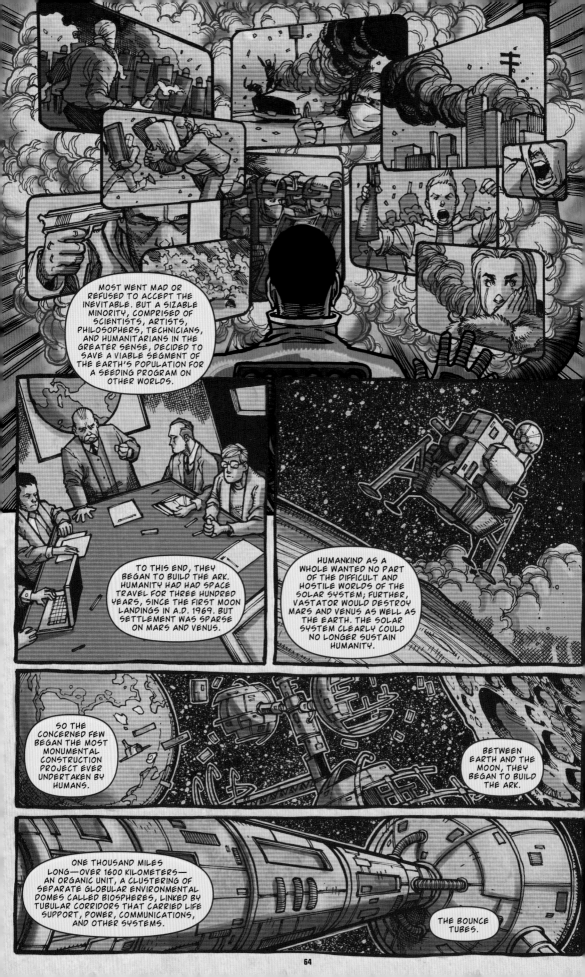

MOST WENT MAD OR REFUSED TO ACCEPT THE INEVITABLE. BUT A SIZABLE MINORITY, COMPRISED OF SCIENTISTS, ARTISTS, PHILOSOPHERS, TECHNICIANS, AND HUMANITARIANS IN THE GREATER SENSE, DECIDED TO SAVE A VIABLE SEGMENT OF THE EARTH'S POPULATION FOR A SEEDING PROGRAM ON OTHER WORLDS.

TO THIS END, THEY BEGAN TO BUILD THE ARK. HUMANITY HAD HAD SPACE TRAVEL FOR THREE HUNDRED YEARS, SINCE THE FIRST MOON LANDINGS IN A.D. 1969. BUT SETTLEMENT WAS SPARSE ON MARS AND VENUS.

HUMANKIND AS A WHOLE WANTED NO PART OF THE DIFFICULT AND HOSTILE WORLDS OF THE SOLAR SYSTEM; FURTHER, VASTATOR WOULD DESTROY MARS AND VENUS AS WELL AS THE EARTH. THE SOLAR SYSTEM CLEARLY COULD NO LONGER SUSTAIN HUMANITY.

SO THE CONCERNED FEW BEGAN THE MOST MONUMENTAL CONSTRUCTION PROJECT EVER UNDERTAKEN BY HUMANS.

BETWEEN EARTH AND THE MOON, THEY BEGAN TO BUILD THE ARK.

ONE THOUSAND MILES LONG—OVER 1600 KILOMETERS—AN ORGANIC UNIT, A CLUSTERING OF SEPARATE GLOBULAR ENVIRONMENTAL DOMES CALLED BIOSPHERES, LINKED BY TUBULAR CORRIDORS THAT CARRIED LIFE SUPPORT, POWER, COMMUNICATIONS, AND OTHER SYSTEMS.

THE BOUNCE TUBES.

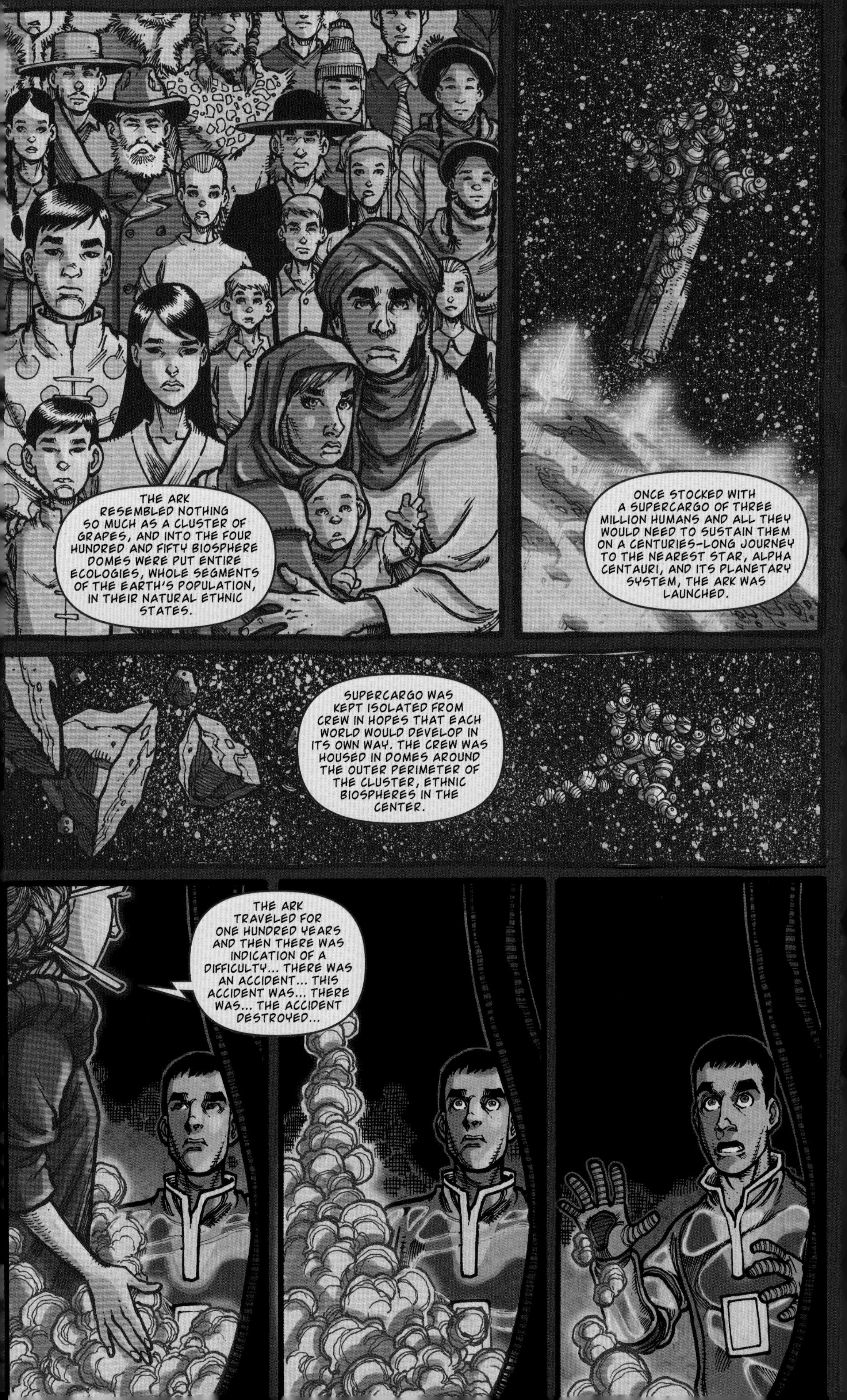
THE ARK RESEMBLED NOTHING SO MUCH AS A CLUSTER OF GRAPES, AND INTO THE FOUR HUNDRED AND FIFTY BIOSPHERE DOMES WERE PUT ENTIRE ECOLOGIES, WHOLE SEGMENTS OF THE EARTH'S POPULATION, IN THEIR NATURAL ETHNIC STATES.
ONCE STOCKED WITH A SUPERCARGO OF THREE MILLION HUMANS AND ALL THEY WOULD NEED TO SUSTAIN THEM ON A CENTURIES-LONG JOURNEY TO THE NEAREST STAR, ALPHA CENTAURI, AND ITS PLANETARY SYSTEM, THE ARK WAS LAUNCHED.
SUPERCARGO WAS KEPT ISOLATED FROM CREW IN HOPES THAT EACH WORLD WOULD DEVELOP IN ITS OWN WAY. THE CREW WAS HOUSED IN DOMES AROUND THE OUTER PERIMETER OF THE CLUSTER, ETHNIC BIOSPHERES IN THE CENTER.
THE ARK TRAVELED FOR ONE HUNDRED YEARS AND THEN THERE WAS INDICATION OF A DIFFICULTY... THERE WAS AN ACCIDENT... THIS ACCIDENT WAS... THERE WAS... THE ACCIDENT DESTROYED...

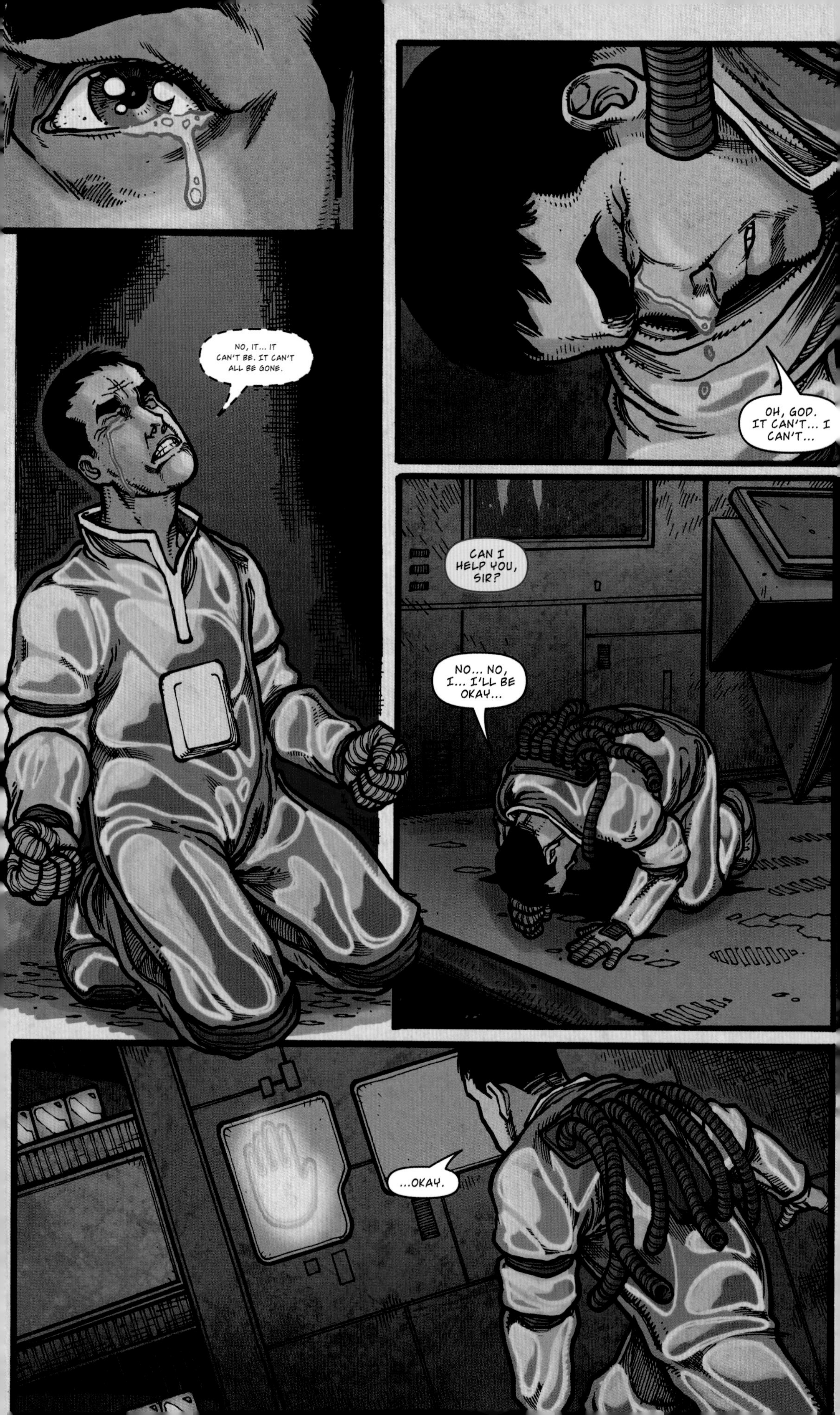

NO, IT... IT CAN'T BE. IT CAN'T ALL BE GONE.
OH, GOD. IT CAN'T... I CAN'T...
CAN I HELP YOU, SIR?
NO... NO, I... I'LL BE OKAY...
...OKAY.

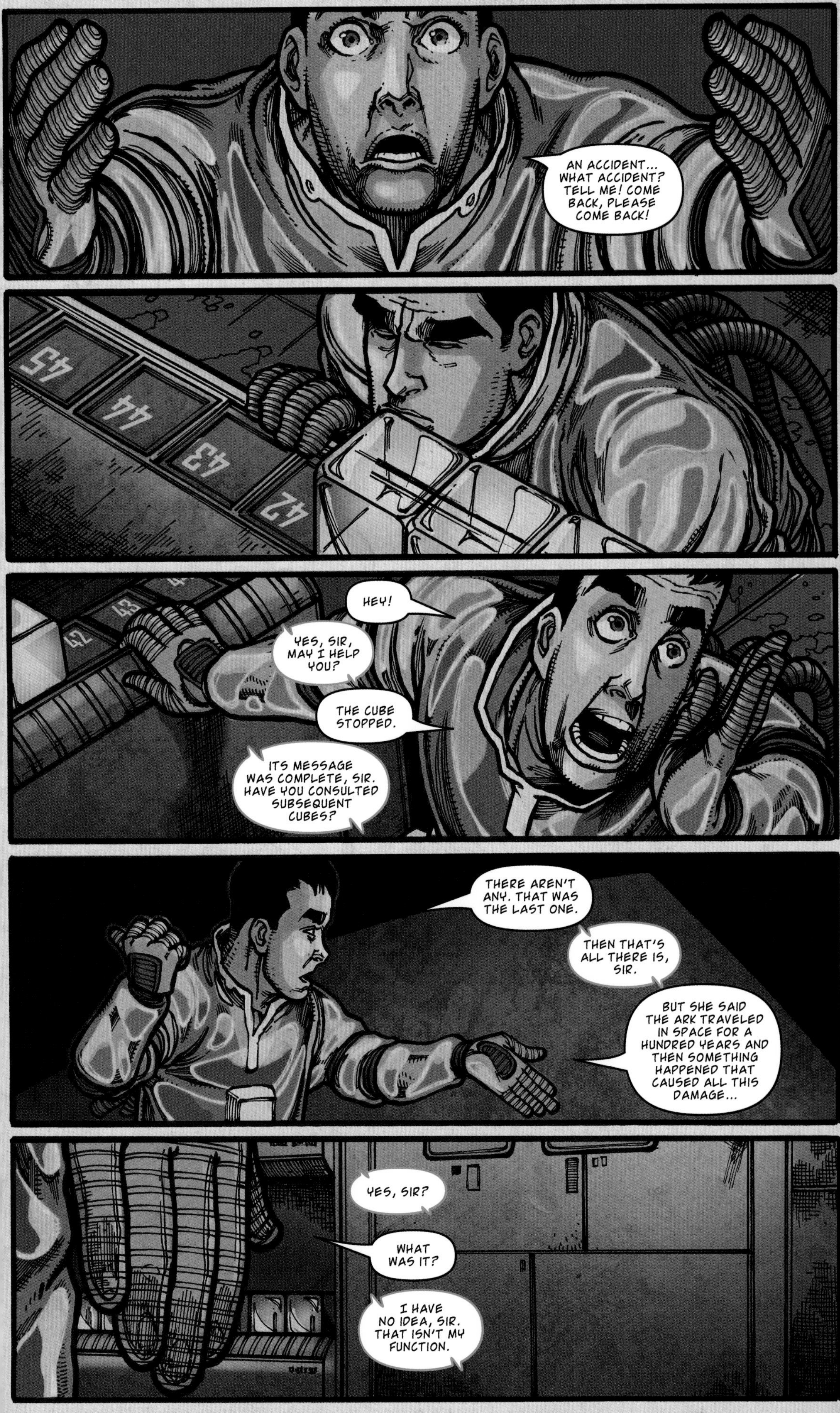
AN ACCIDENT... WHAT ACCIDENT? TELL ME! COME BACK, PLEASE COME BACK!
45
44
43
42
HEY!
YES, SIR, MAY I HELP YOU?
THE CUBE STOPPED.
ITS MESSAGE WAS COMPLETE, SIR. HAVE YOU CONSULTED SUBSEQUENT CUBES?
THERE AREN'T ANY. THAT WAS THE LAST ONE.
THEN THAT'S ALL THERE IS, SIR.
BUT SHE SAID THE ARK TRAVELED IN SPACE FOR A HUNDRED YEARS AND THEN SOMETHING HAPPENED THAT CAUSED ALL THIS DAMAGE...
YES, SIR?
WHAT WAS IT?
I HAVE NO IDEA, SIR. THAT ISN'T MY FUNCTION.

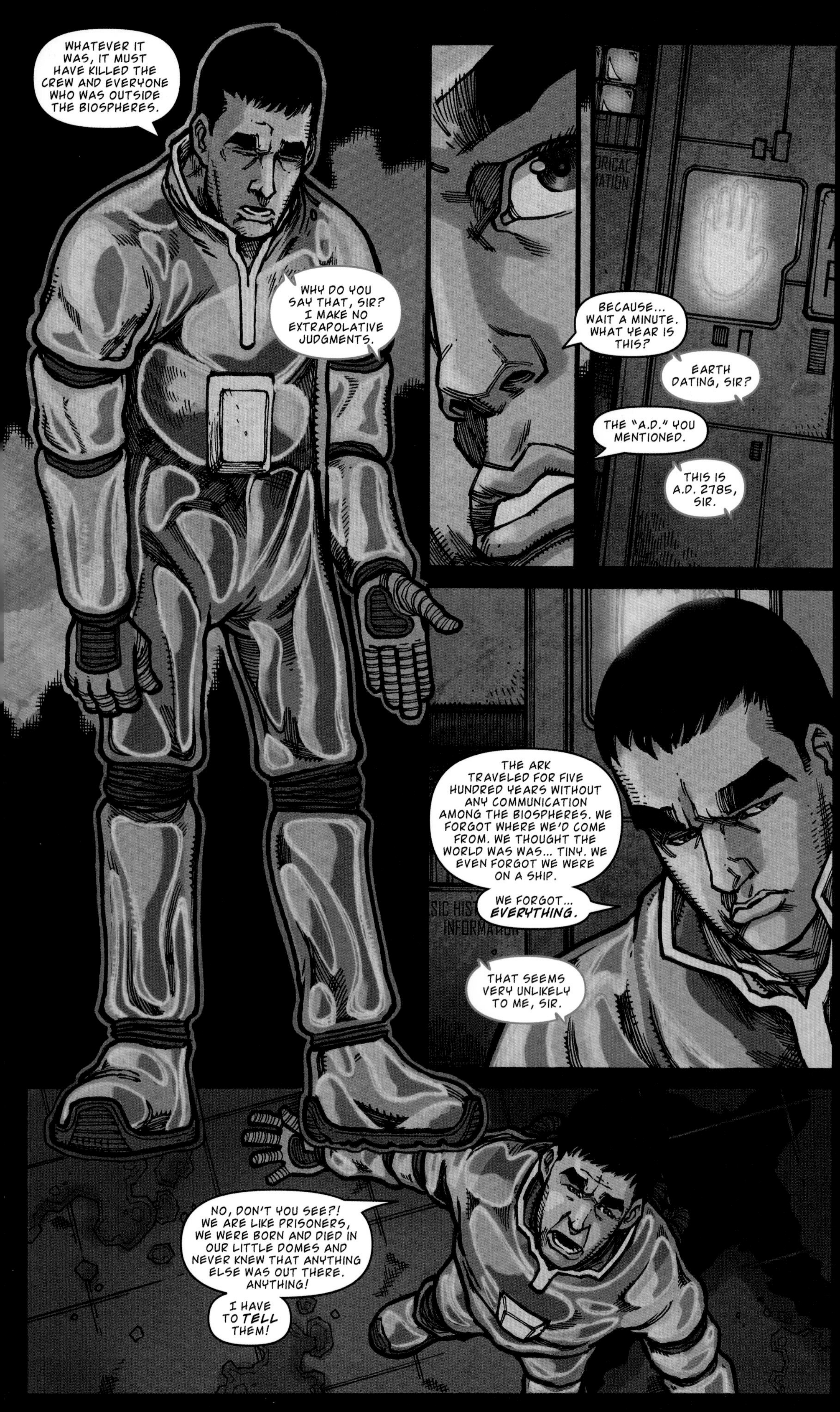
WHATEVER IT WAS, IT MUST HAVE KILLED THE CREW AND EVERYONE WHO WAS OUTSIDE THE BIOSPHERES.
WHY DO YOU SAY THAT, SIR? I MAKE NO EXTRAPOLATIVE JUDGMENTS.
BECAUSE... WAIT A MINUTE. WHAT YEAR IS THIS?
EARTH DATING, SIR?
THE "A.D." YOU MENTIONED.
THIS IS A.D. 2785, SIR.
THE ARK TRAVELED FOR FIVE HUNDRED YEARS WITHOUT ANY COMMUNICATION AMONG THE BIOSPHERES. WE FORGOT WHERE WE'D COME FROM. WE THOUGHT THE WORLD WAS WAS... TINY. WE EVEN FORGOT WE WERE ON A SHIP.
WE FORGOT... *EVERYTHING.*
THAT SEEMS VERY UNLIKELY TO ME, SIR.
NO, DON'T YOU SEE?! WE ARE LIKE PRISONERS, WE WERE BORN AND DIED IN OUR LITTLE DOMES AND NEVER KNEW THAT ANYTHING ELSE WAS OUT THERE. ANYTHING!
I HAVE TO *TELL* THEM!

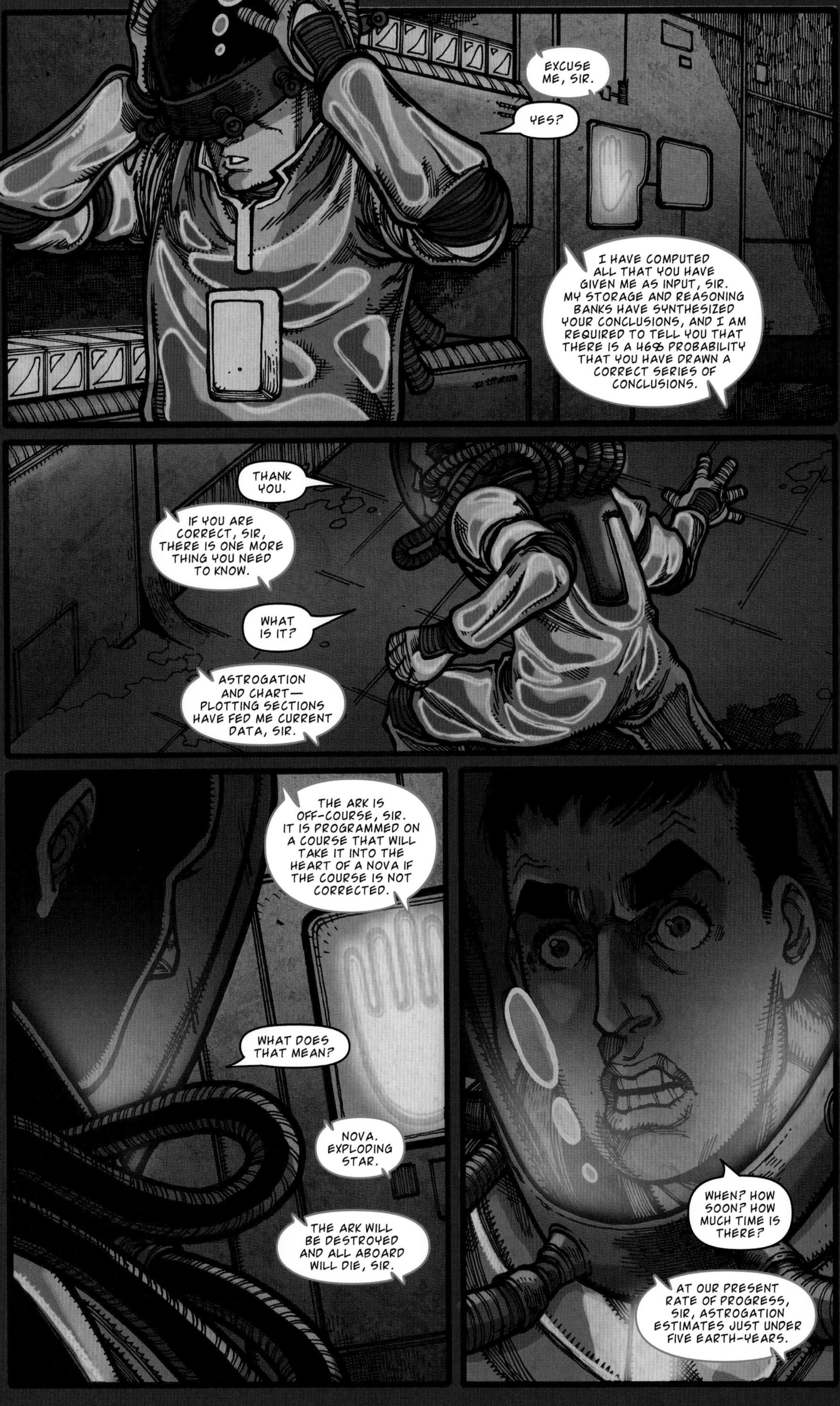
EXCUSE ME, SIR.
YES?
I HAVE COMPUTED ALL THAT YOU HAVE GIVEN ME AS INPUT, SIR. MY STORAGE AND REASONING BANKS HAVE SYNTHESIZED YOUR CONCLUSIONS, AND I AM REQUIRED TO TELL YOU THAT THERE IS A 46% PROBABILITY THAT YOU HAVE DRAWN A CORRECT SERIES OF CONCLUSIONS.
THANK YOU.
IF YOU ARE CORRECT, SIR, THERE IS ONE MORE THING YOU NEED TO KNOW.
WHAT IS IT?
ASTROGATION AND CHART—PLOTTING SECTIONS HAVE FED ME CURRENT DATA, SIR.
THE ARK IS OFF-COURSE, SIR. IT IS PROGRAMMED ON A COURSE THAT WILL TAKE IT INTO THE HEART OF A NOVA IF THE COURSE IS NOT CORRECTED.
WHAT DOES THAT MEAN?
NOVA. EXPLODING STAR.
THE ARK WILL BE DESTROYED AND ALL ABOARD WILL DIE, SIR.
WHEN? HOW SOON? HOW MUCH TIME IS THERE?
AT OUR PRESENT RATE OF PROGRESS, SIR, ASTROGATION ESTIMATES JUST UNDER FIVE EARTH-YEARS.

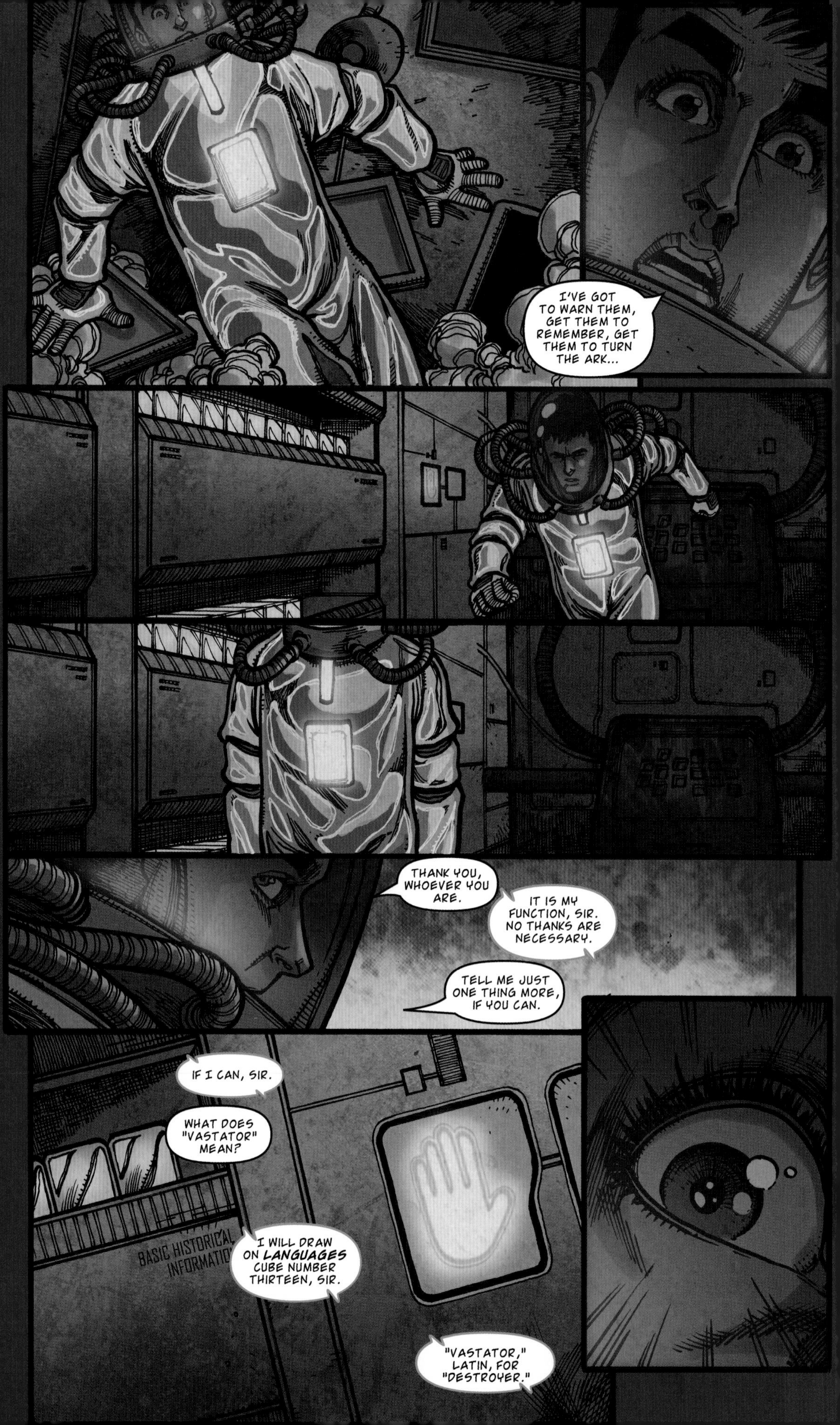

I'VE GOT TO WARN THEM, GET THEM TO REMEMBER, GET THEM TO TURN THE ARK...
THANK YOU, WHOEVER YOU ARE.
IT IS MY FUNCTION, SIR. NO THANKS ARE NECESSARY.
TELL ME JUST ONE THING MORE, IF YOU CAN.
IF I CAN, SIR.
WHAT DOES "VASTATOR" MEAN?
BASIC HISTORICAL INFORMATIO
I WILL DRAW ON LANGUAGES CUBE NUMBER THIRTEEN, SIR.
"VASTATOR," LATIN, FOR "DESTROYER."

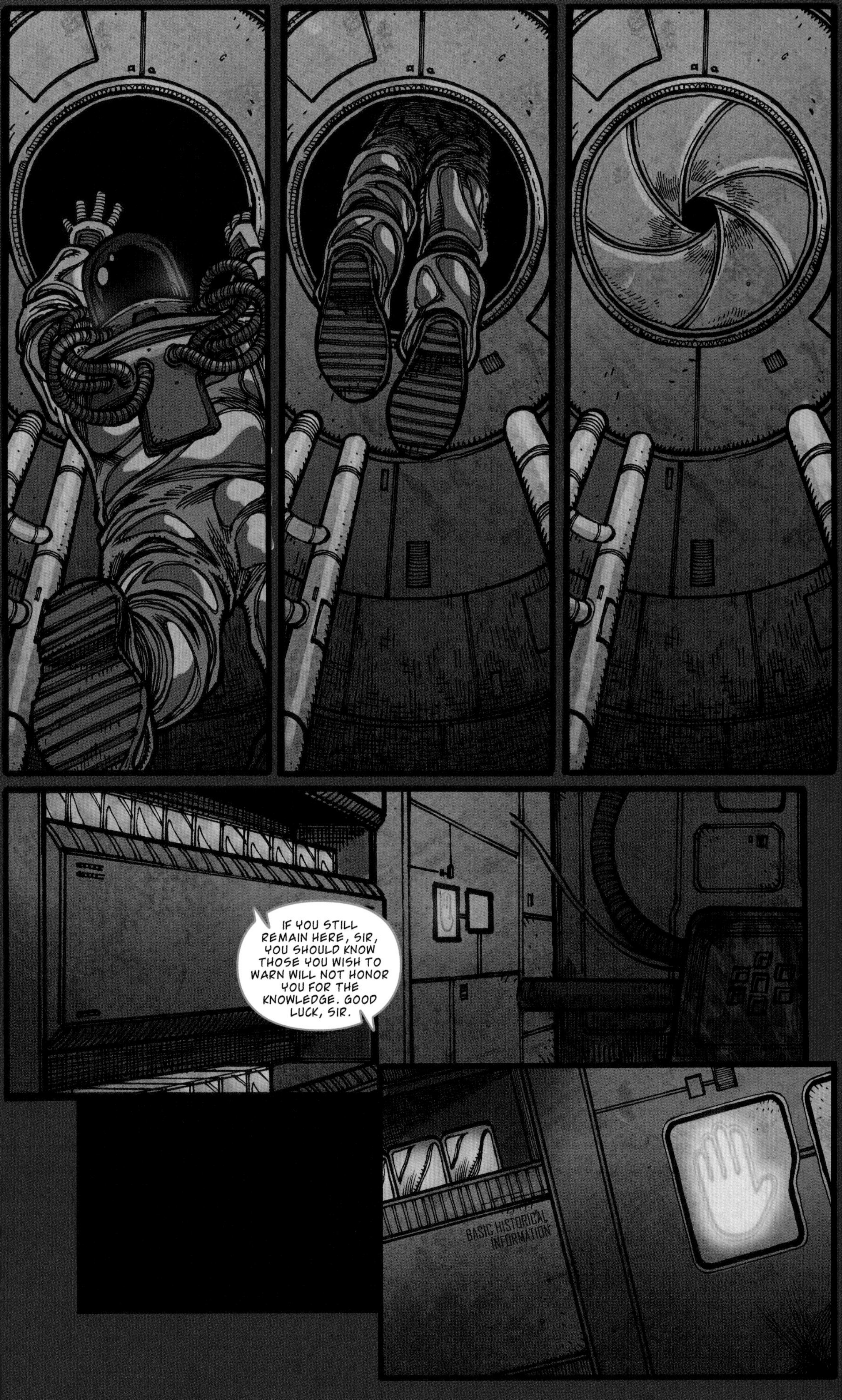
IF YOU STILL REMAIN HERE, SIR, YOU SHOULD KNOW THOSE YOU WISH TO WARN WILL NOT HONOR YOU FOR THE KNOWLEDGE. GOOD LUCK, SIR.
BASIC HISTORICAL INFORMATION

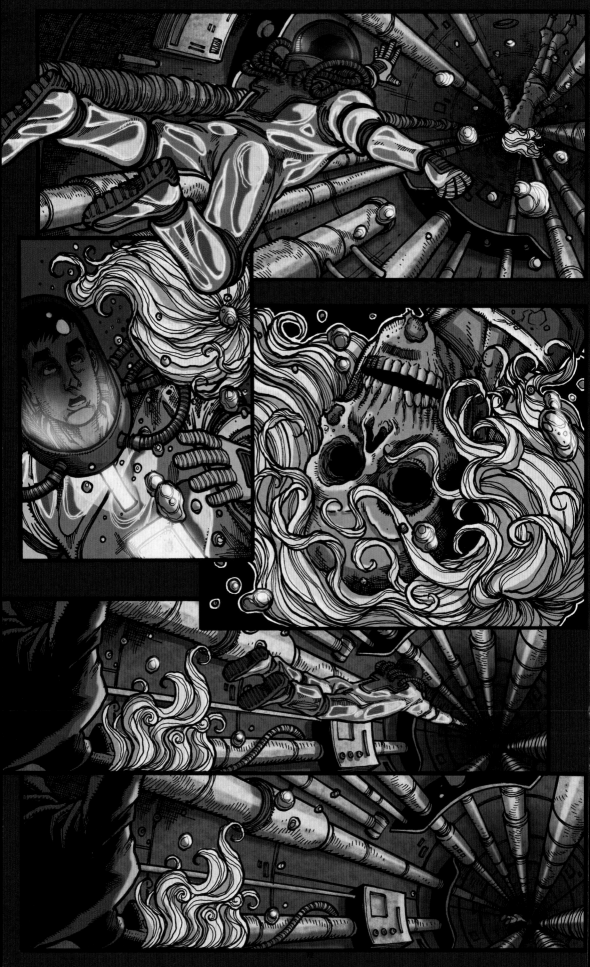

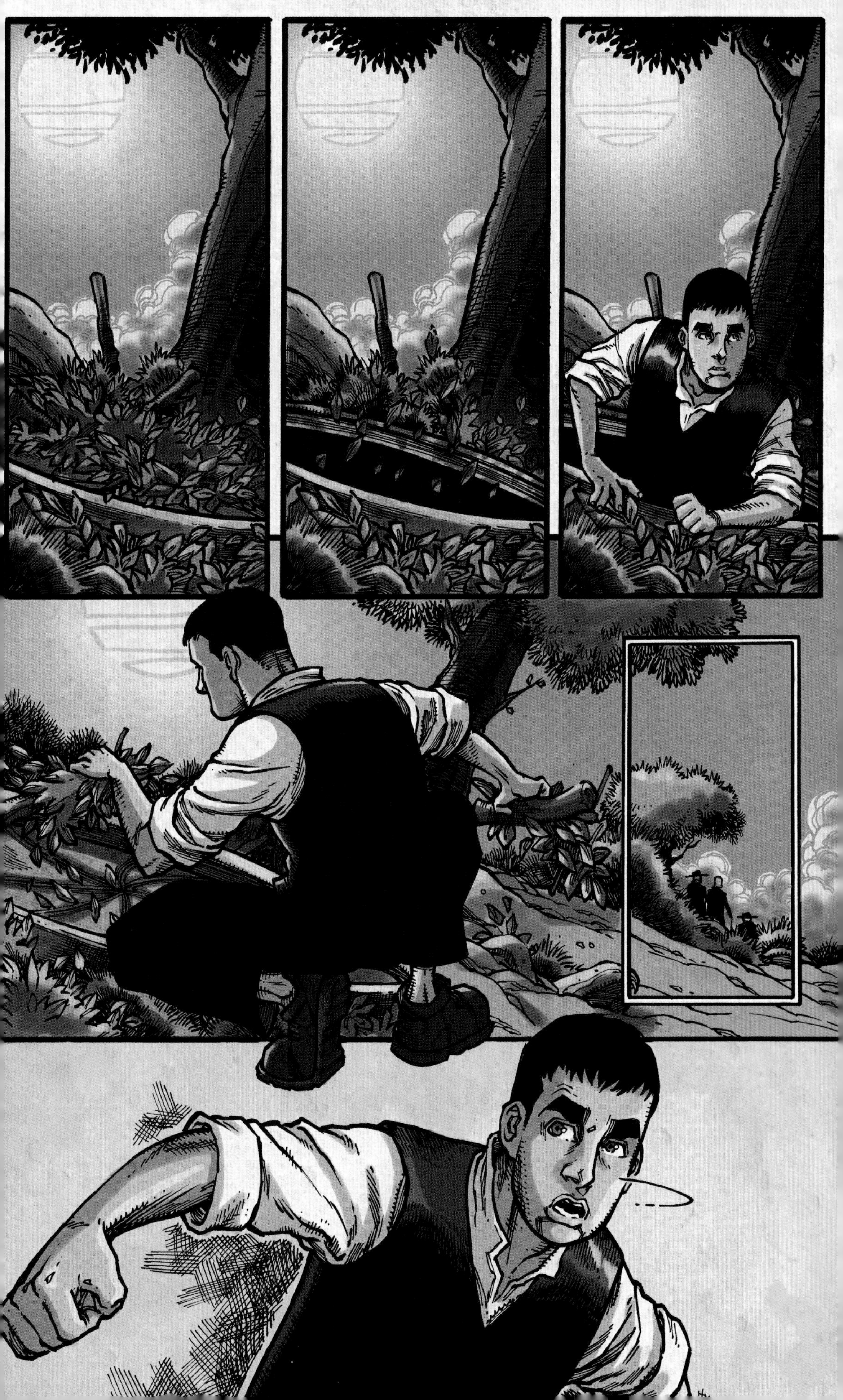

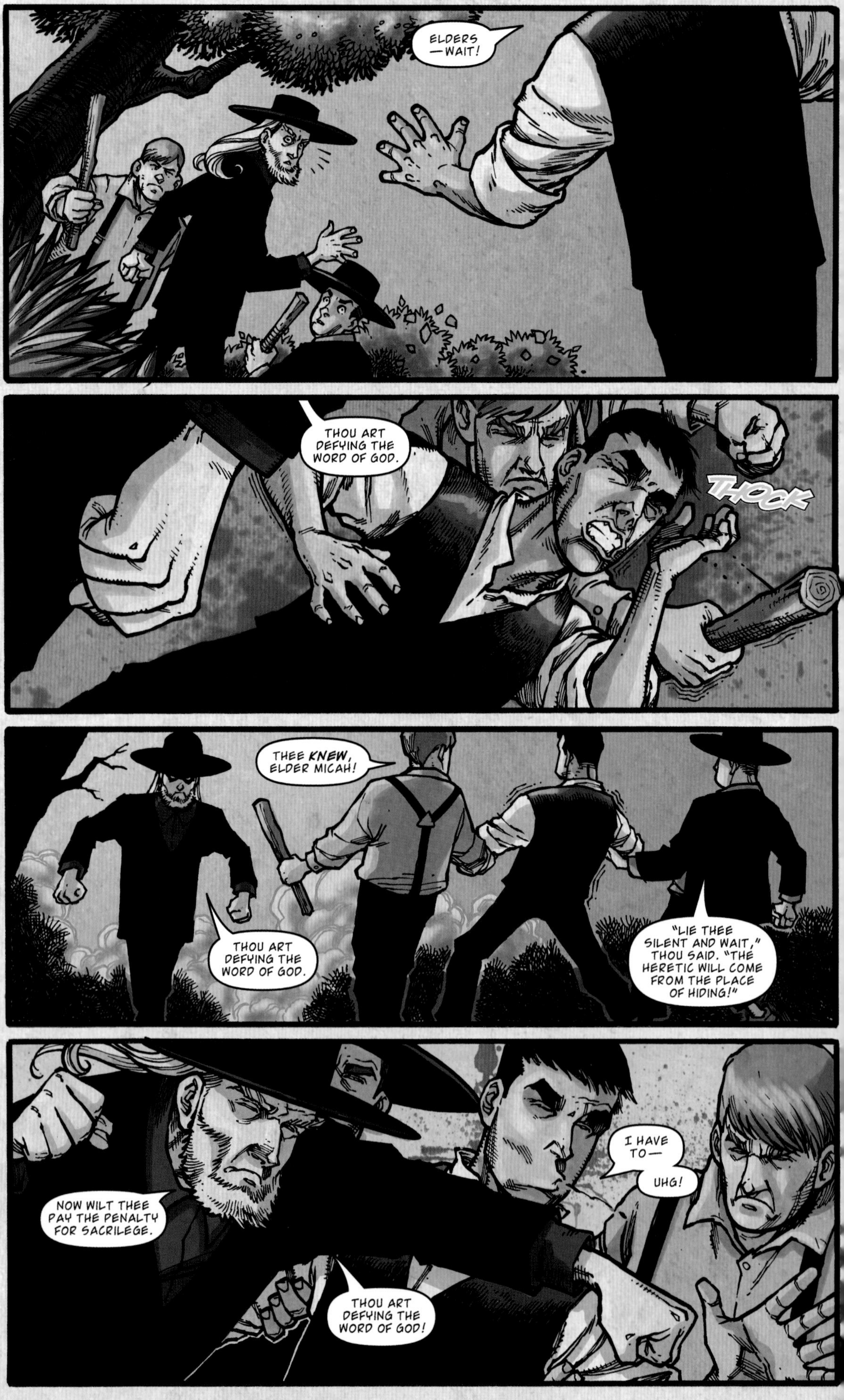
ELDERS —WAIT!
THOU ART DEFYING THE WORD OF GOD.
THOCK
THEE KNEW, ELDER MICAH!
THOU ART DEFYING THE WORD OF GOD.
"LIE THEE SILENT AND WAIT," THOU SAID. "THE HERETIC WILL COME FROM THE PLACE OF HIDING!"
I HAVE TO—
UHG!
NOW WILT THEE PAY THE PENALTY FOR SACRILEGE.
THOU ART DEFYING THE WORD OF GOD!

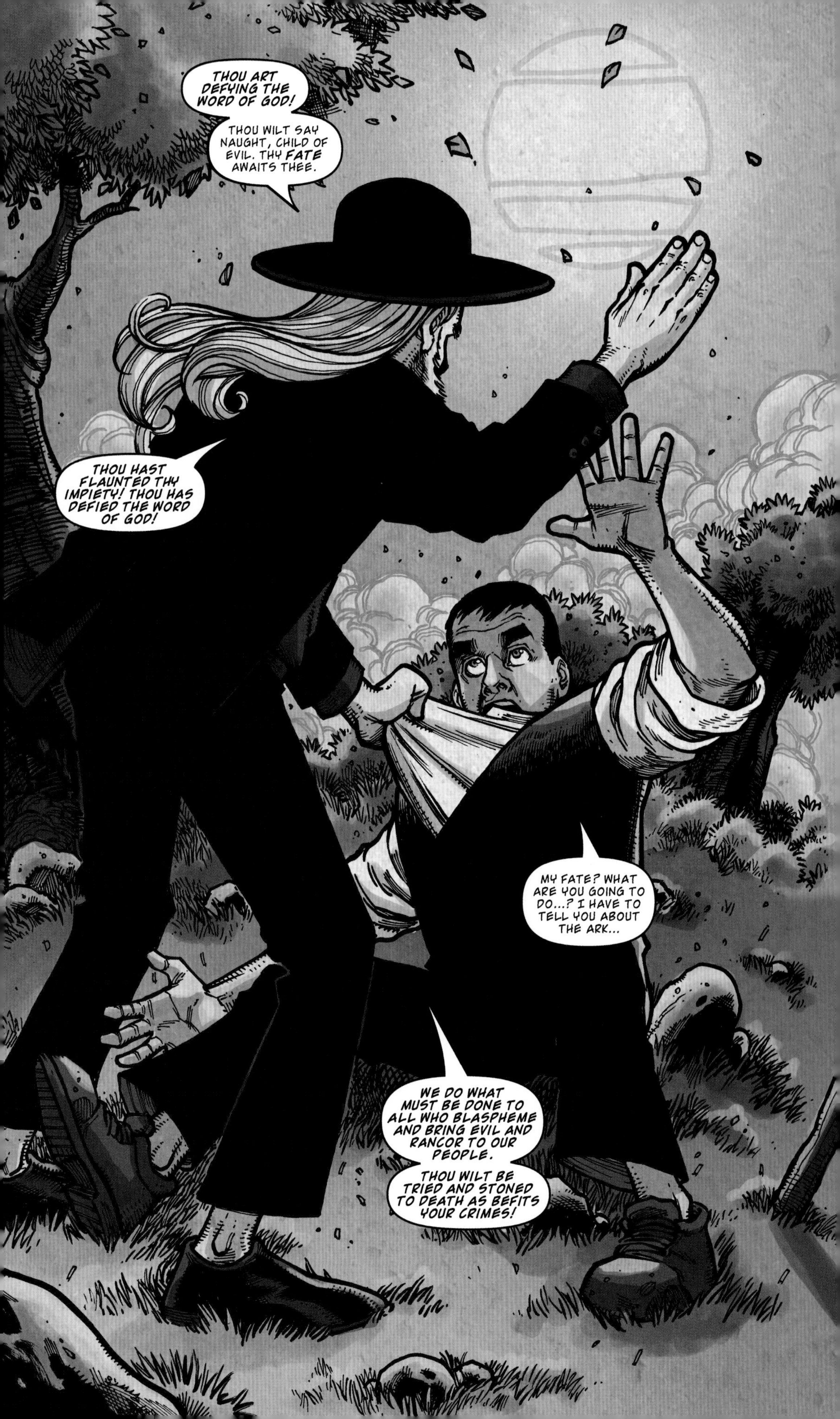
THOU ART DEFYING THE WORD OF GOD!
THOU WILT SAY NAUGHT, CHILD OF EVIL. THY FATE AWAITS THEE.
THOU HAST FLAUNTED THY IMPIETY! THOU HAS DEFIED THE WORD OF GOD!
MY FATE? WHAT ARE YOU GOING TO DO...? I HAVE TO TELL YOU ABOUT THE ARK...
WE DO WHAT MUST BE DONE TO ALL WHO BLASPHEME AND BRING EVIL AND RANCOR TO OUR PEOPLE.
THOU WILT BE TRIED AND STONED TO DEATH AS BEFITS YOUR CRIMES!

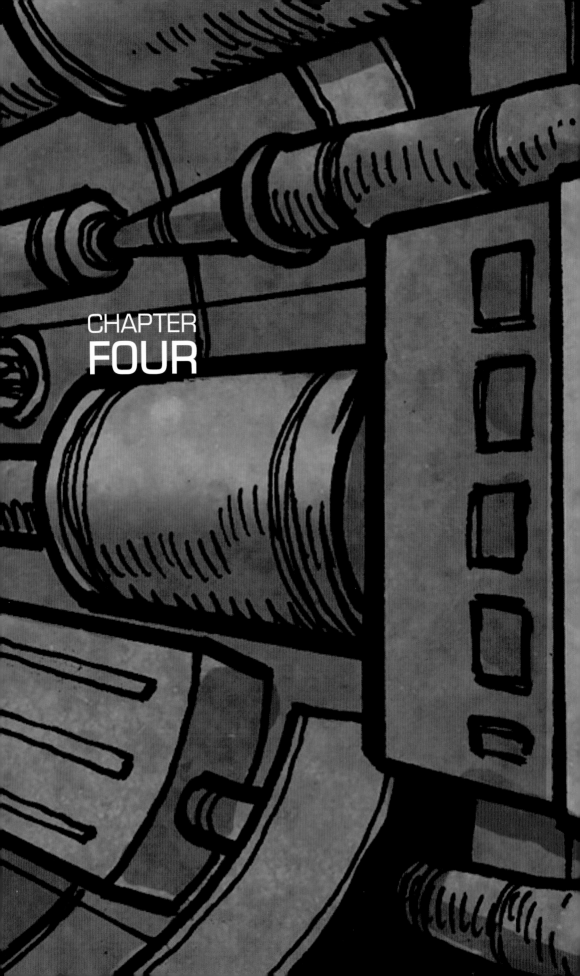

CHAPTER
FOUR

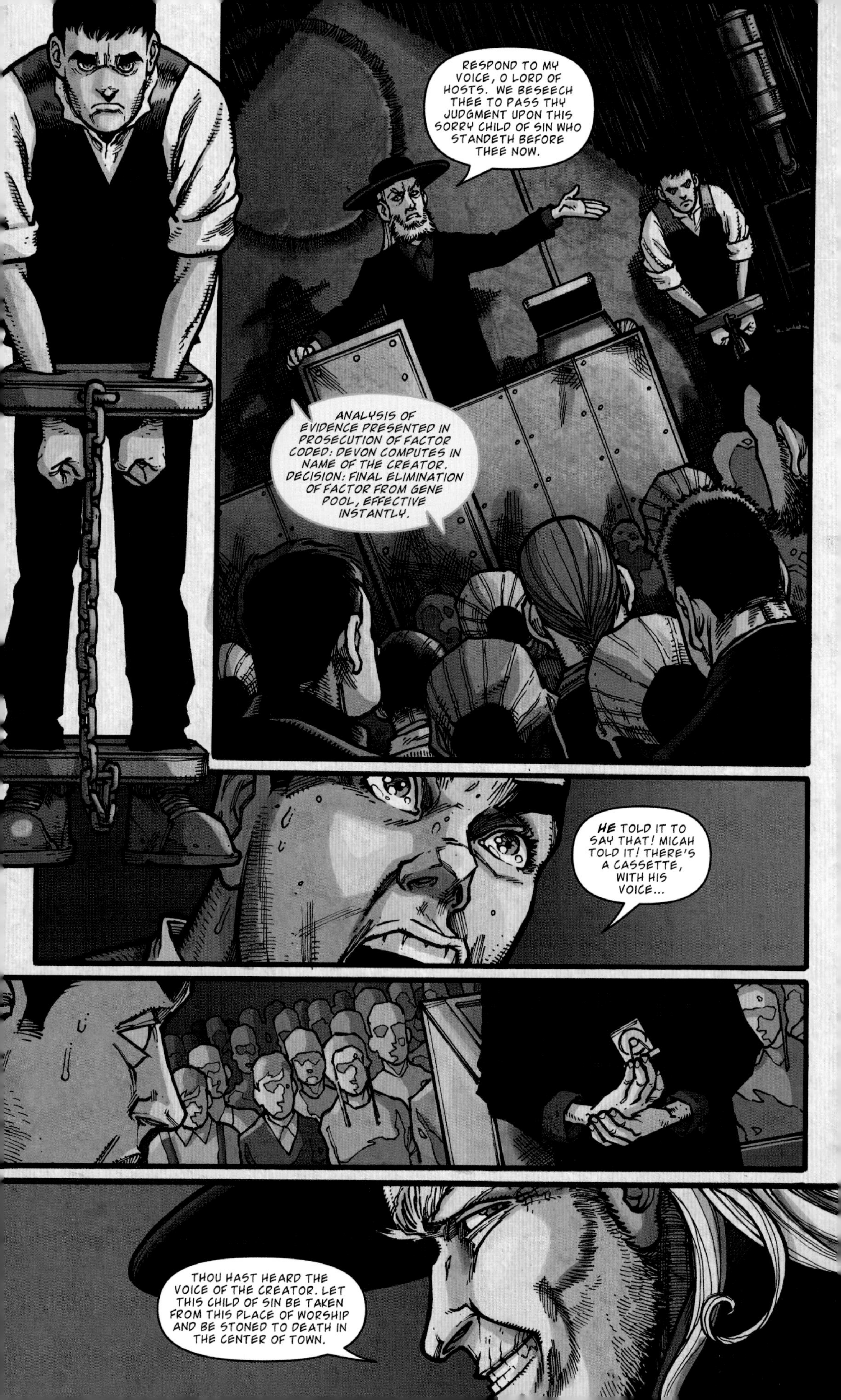

RESPOND TO MY VOICE, O LORD OF HOSTS. WE BESEECH THEE TO PASS THY JUDGMENT UPON THIS SORRY CHILD OF SIN WHO STANDETH BEFORE THEE NOW.
ANALYSIS OF EVIDENCE PRESENTED IN PROSECUTION OF FACTOR CODED: DEVON COMPUTES IN NAME OF THE CREATOR. DECISION: FINAL ELIMINATION OF FACTOR FROM GENE POOL, EFFECTIVE INSTANTLY.
HE TOLD IT TO SAY THAT! MICAH TOLD IT! THERE'S A CASSETTE, WITH HIS VOICE...
THOU HAST HEARD THE VOICE OF THE CREATOR. LET THIS CHILD OF SIN BE TAKEN FROM THIS PLACE OF WORSHIP AND BE STONED TO DEATH IN THE CENTER OF TOWN.

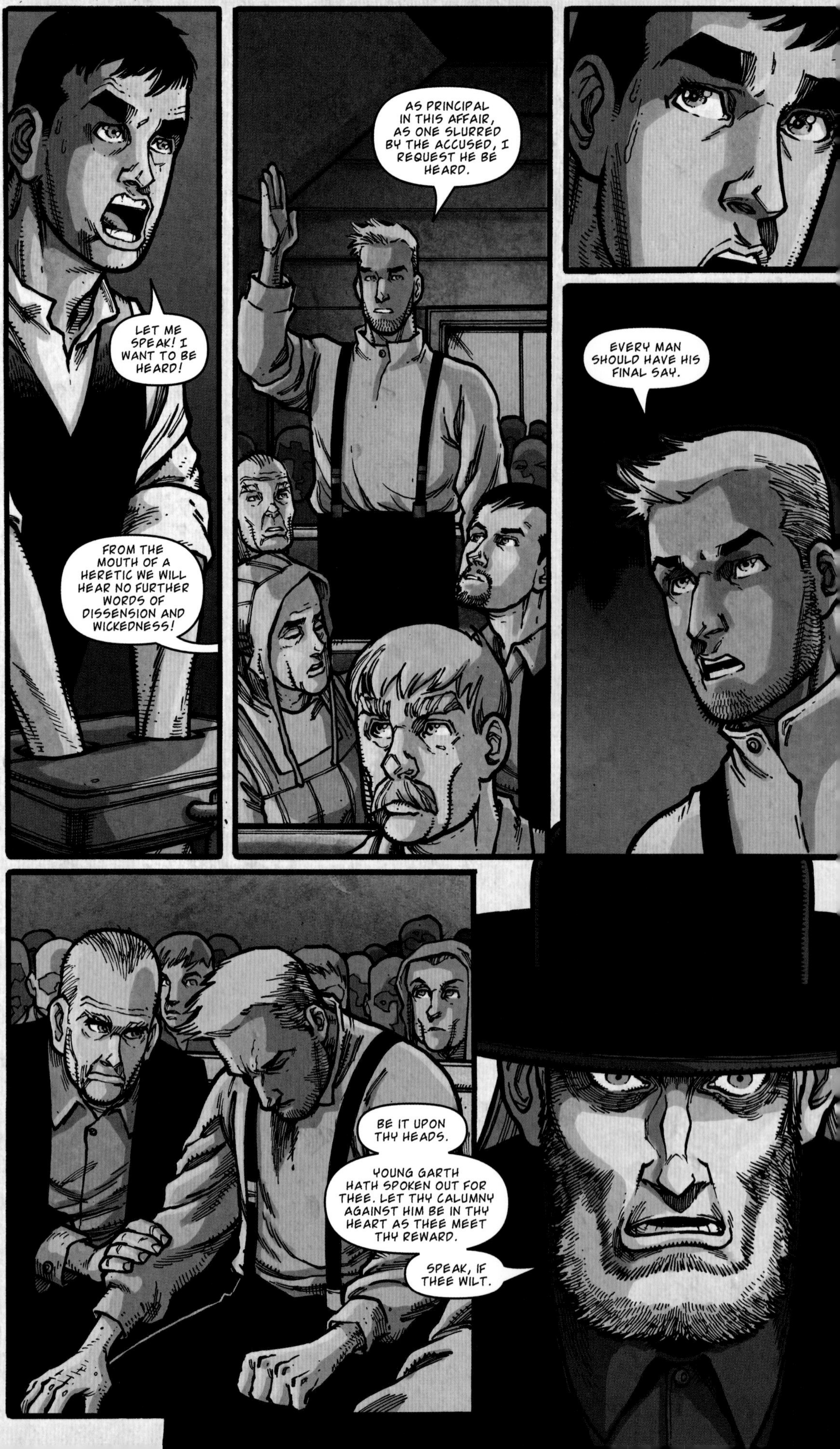
LET ME SPEAK! I WANT TO BE HEARD!
FROM THE MOUTH OF A HERETIC WE WILL HEAR NO FURTHER WORDS OF DISSENSION AND WICKEDNESS!
AS PRINCIPAL IN THIS AFFAIR, AS ONE SLURRED BY THE ACCUSED, I REQUEST HE BE HEARD.
EVERY MAN SHOULD HAVE HIS FINAL SAY.
BE IT UPON THY HEADS.
YOUNG GARTH HATH SPOKEN OUT FOR THEE. LET THY CALUMNY AGAINST HIM BE IN THY HEART AS THEE MEET THY REWARD.
SPEAK, IF THEE WILT.

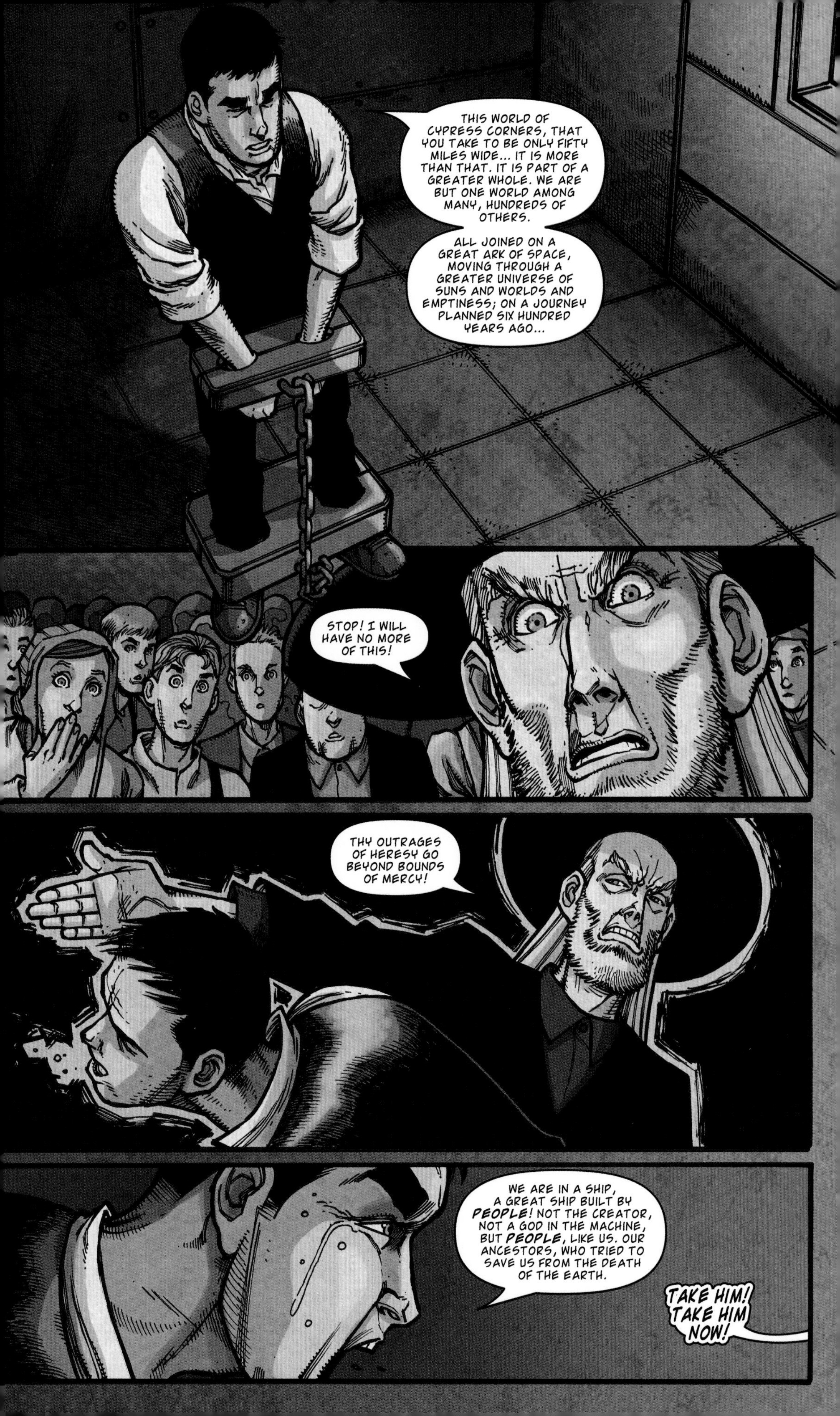
THIS WORLD OF CYPRESS CORNERS, THAT YOU TAKE TO BE ONLY FIFTY MILES WIDE... IT IS MORE THAN THAT. IT IS PART OF A GREATER WHOLE. WE ARE BUT ONE WORLD AMONG MANY, HUNDREDS OF OTHERS.
ALL JOINED ON A GREAT ARK OF SPACE, MOVING THROUGH A GREATER UNIVERSE OF SUNS AND WORLDS AND EMPTINESS; ON A JOURNEY PLANNED SIX HUNDRED YEARS AGO...
STOP! I WILL HAVE NO MORE OF THIS!
THY OUTRAGES OF HERESY GO BEYOND BOUNDS OF MERCY!
WE ARE IN A SHIP, A GREAT SHIP BUILT BY *PEOPLE!* NOT THE CREATOR, NOT A GOD IN THE MACHINE, BUT *PEOPLE*, LIKE US. OUR ANCESTORS, WHO TRIED TO SAVE US FROM THE DEATH OF THE EARTH.
TAKE HIM! TAKE HIM NOW!

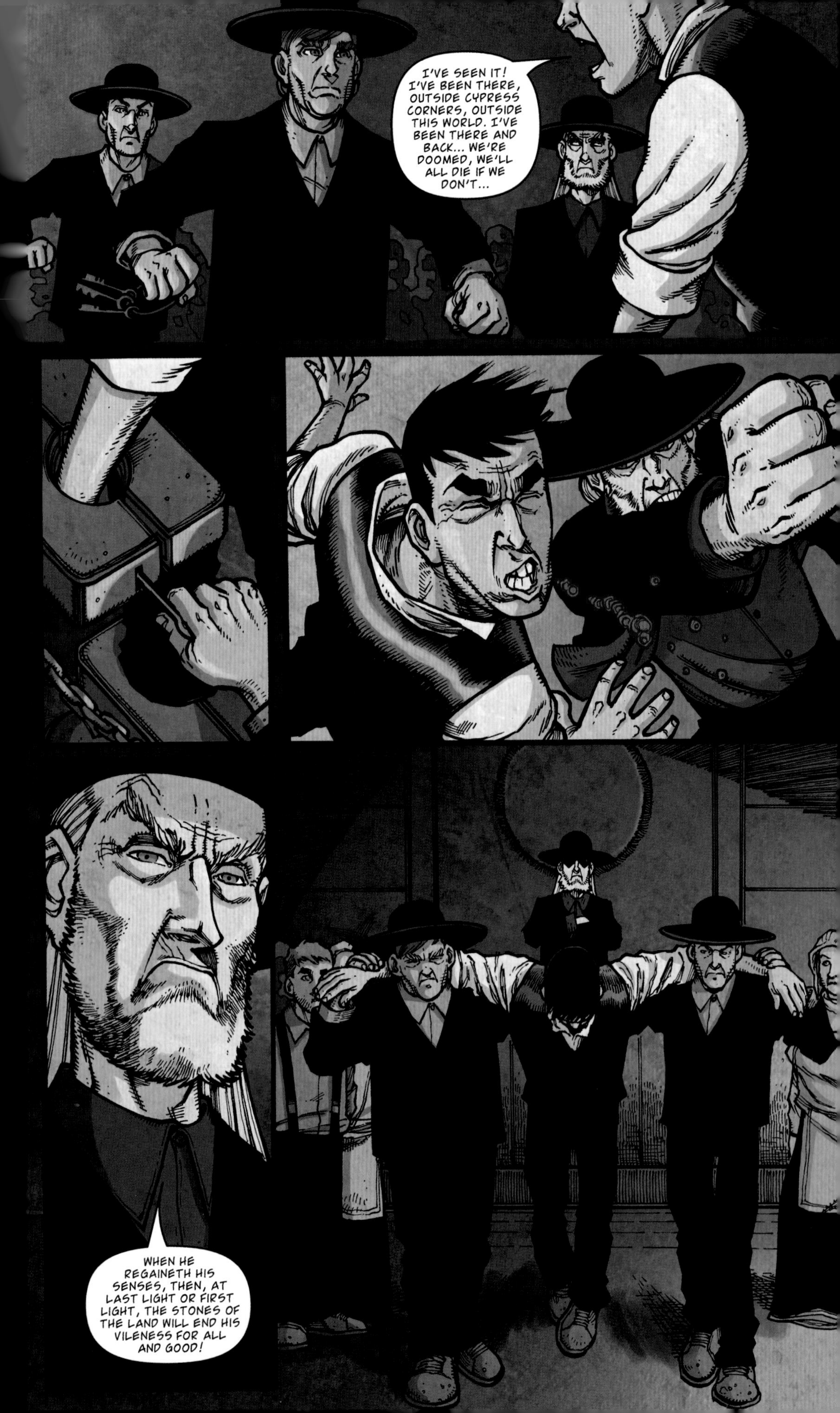
I'VE SEEN IT! I'VE BEEN THERE, OUTSIDE CYPRESS CORNERS, OUTSIDE THIS WORLD. I'VE BEEN THERE AND BACK... WE'RE DOOMED, WE'LL ALL DIE IF WE DON'T...
WHEN HE REGAINETH HIS SENSES, THEN, AT LAST LIGHT OR FIRST LIGHT, THE STONES OF THE LAND WILL END HIS VILENESS FOR ALL AND GOOD!

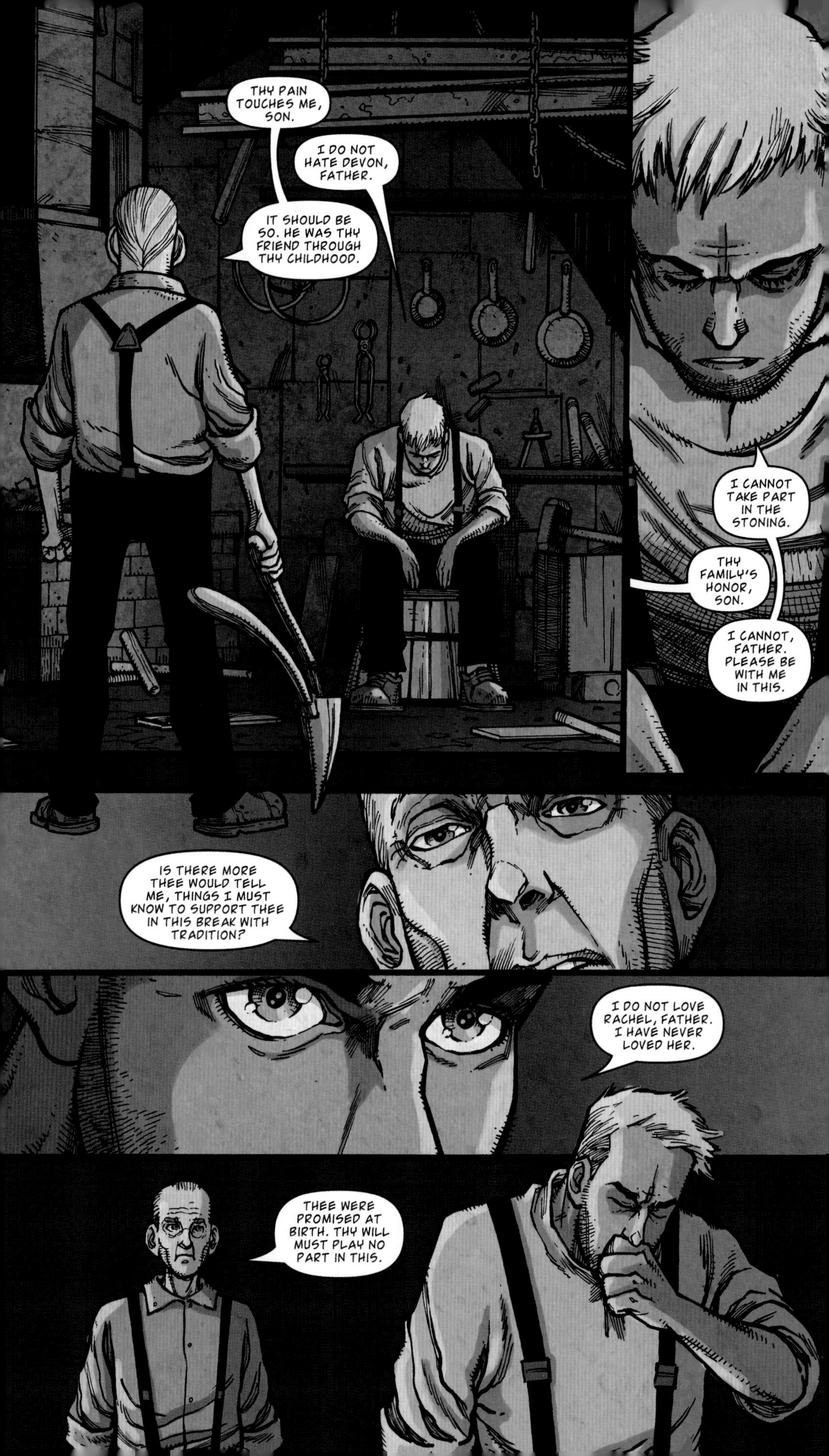
THY PAIN TOUCHES ME, SON.
I DO NOT HATE DEVON, FATHER.
IT SHOULD BE SO. HE WAS THY FRIEND THROUGH THY CHILDHOOD.
I CANNOT TAKE PART IN THE STONING.
THY FAMILY'S HONOR, SON.
I CANNOT, FATHER. PLEASE BE WITH ME IN THIS.
IS THERE MORE THEE WOULD TELL ME, THINGS I MUST KNOW TO SUPPORT THEE IN THIS BREAK WITH TRADITION?
I DO NOT LOVE RACHEL, FATHER. I HAVE NEVER LOVED HER.
THEE WERE PROMISED AT BIRTH. THY WILL MUST PLAY NO PART IN THIS.

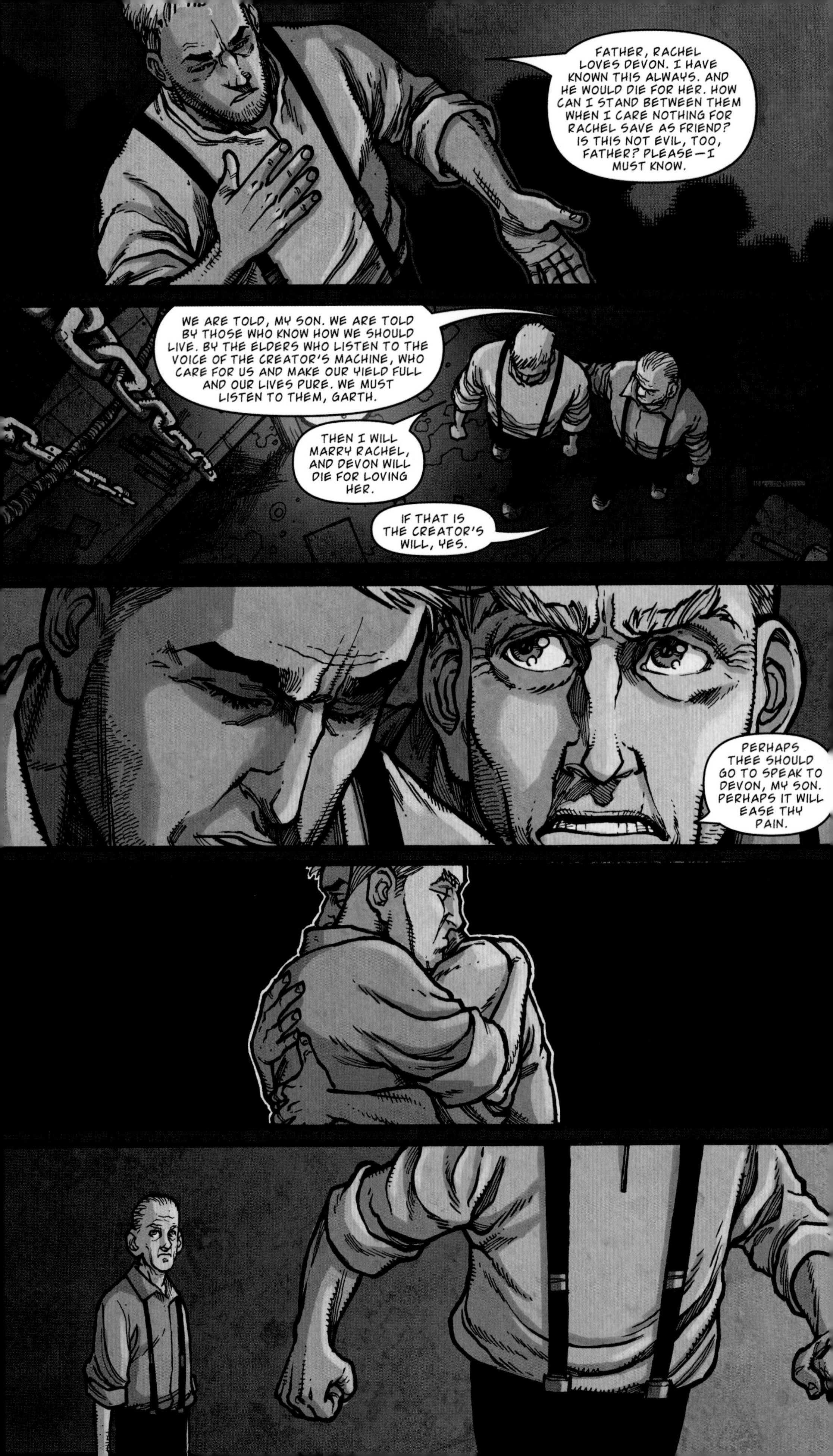
FATHER, RACHEL LOVES DEVON. I HAVE KNOWN THIS ALWAYS. AND HE WOULD DIE FOR HER. HOW CAN I STAND BETWEEN THEM WHEN I CARE NOTHING FOR RACHEL SAVE AS FRIEND? IS THIS NOT EVIL, TOO, FATHER? PLEASE—I MUST KNOW.
WE ARE TOLD, MY SON. WE ARE TOLD BY THOSE WHO KNOW HOW WE SHOULD LIVE. BY THE ELDERS WHO LISTEN TO THE VOICE OF THE CREATOR'S MACHINE, WHO CARE FOR US AND MAKE OUR YIELD FULL AND OUR LIVES PURE. WE MUST LISTEN TO THEM, GARTH.
THEN I WILL MARRY RACHEL, AND DEVON WILL DIE FOR LOVING HER.
IF THAT IS THE CREATOR'S WILL, YES.
PERHAPS THEE SHOULD GO TO SPEAK TO DEVON, MY SON. PERHAPS IT WILL EASE THY PAIN.

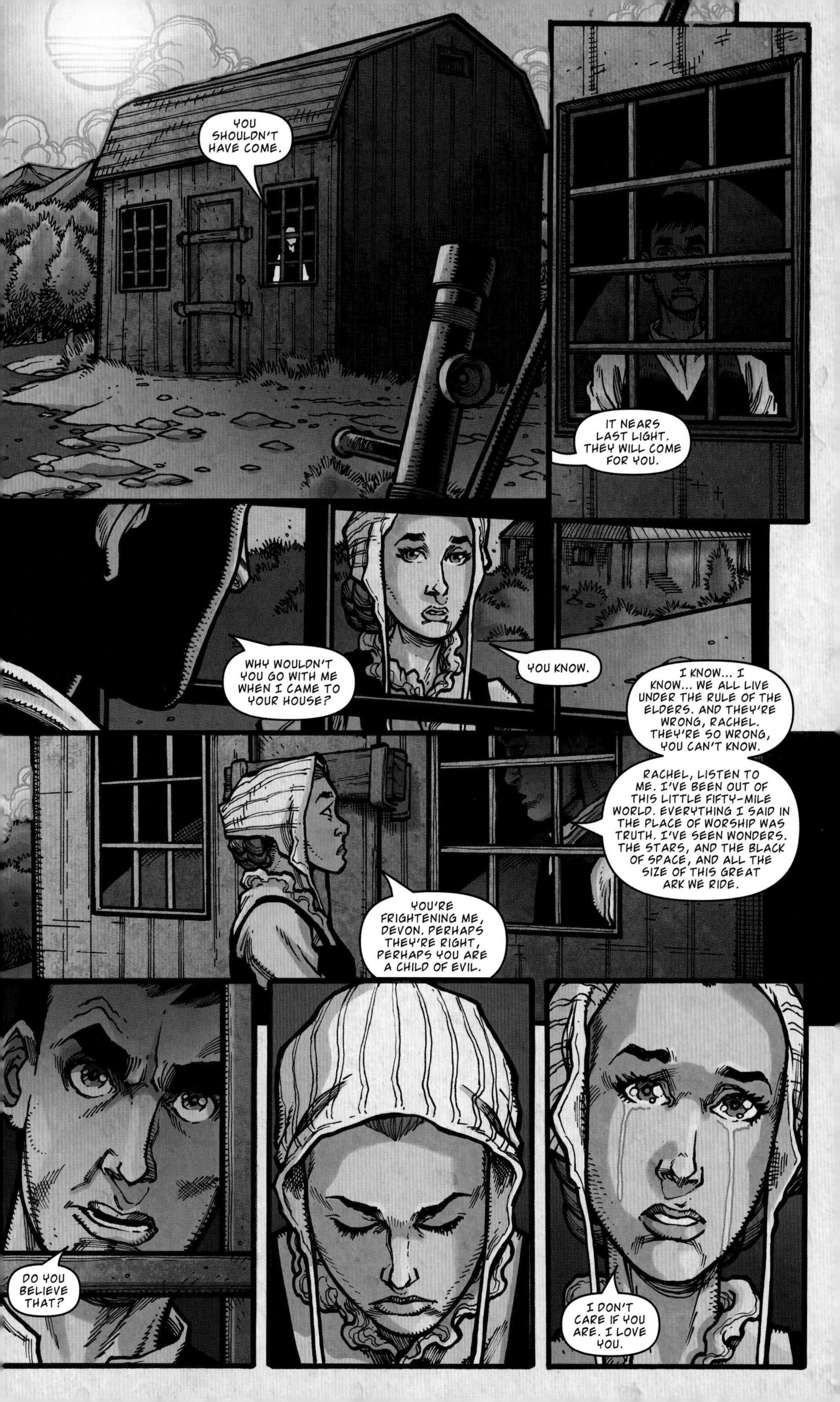
YOU SHOULDN'T HAVE COME.
IT NEARS LAST LIGHT. THEY WILL COME FOR YOU.
WHY WOULDN'T YOU GO WITH ME WHEN I CAME TO YOUR HOUSE?
YOU KNOW.
I KNOW... I KNOW... WE ALL LIVE UNDER THE RULE OF THE ELDERS. AND THEY'RE WRONG, RACHEL. THEY'RE SO WRONG, YOU CAN'T KNOW.
RACHEL, LISTEN TO ME. I'VE BEEN OUT OF THIS LITTLE FIFTY-MILE WORLD. EVERYTHING I SAID IN THE PLACE OF WORSHIP WAS TRUTH. I'VE SEEN WONDERS. THE STARS, AND THE BLACK OF SPACE, AND ALL THE SIZE OF THIS GREAT ARK WE RIDE.
YOU'RE FRIGHTENING ME, DEVON. PERHAPS THEY'RE RIGHT, PERHAPS YOU ARE A CHILD OF EVIL.
DO YOU BELIEVE THAT?
I DON'T CARE IF YOU ARE. I LOVE YOU.

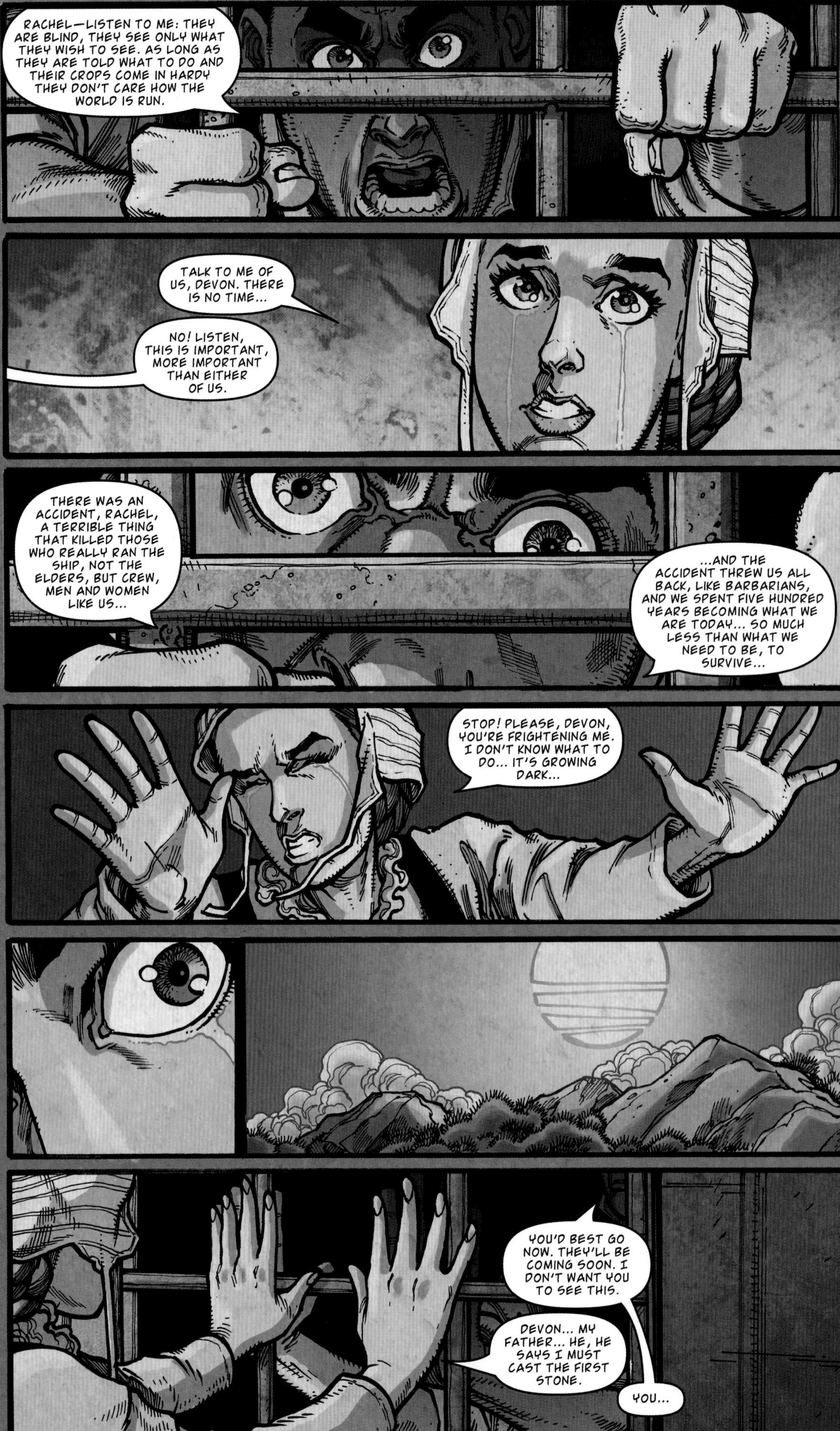
RACHEL—LISTEN TO ME: THEY ARE BLIND, THEY SEE ONLY WHAT THEY WISH TO SEE. AS LONG AS THEY ARE TOLD WHAT TO DO AND THEIR CROPS COME IN HARDY THEY DON'T CARE HOW THE WORLD IS RUN.
TALK TO ME OF US, DEVON. THERE IS NO TIME...
NO! LISTEN, THIS IS IMPORTANT, MORE IMPORTANT THAN EITHER OF US.
THERE WAS AN ACCIDENT, RACHEL, A TERRIBLE THING THAT KILLED THOSE WHO REALLY RAN THE SHIP, NOT THE ELDERS, BUT CREW, MEN AND WOMEN LIKE US...
...AND THE ACCIDENT THREW US ALL BACK, LIKE BARBARIANS, AND WE SPENT FIVE HUNDRED YEARS BECOMING WHAT WE ARE TODAY... SO MUCH LESS THAN WHAT WE NEED TO BE, TO SURVIVE...
STOP! PLEASE, DEVON, YOU'RE FRIGHTENING ME. I DON'T KNOW WHAT TO DO... IT'S GROWING DARK...
YOU'D BEST GO NOW. THEY'LL BE COMING SOON. I DON'T WANT YOU TO SEE THIS.
DEVON... MY FATHER... HE, HE SAYS I MUST CAST THE FIRST STONE.
YOU...

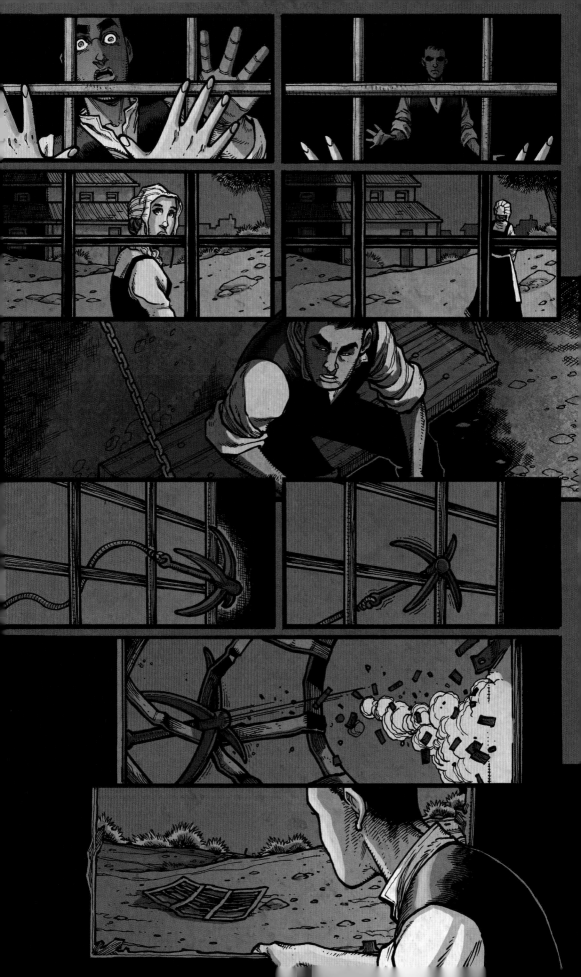

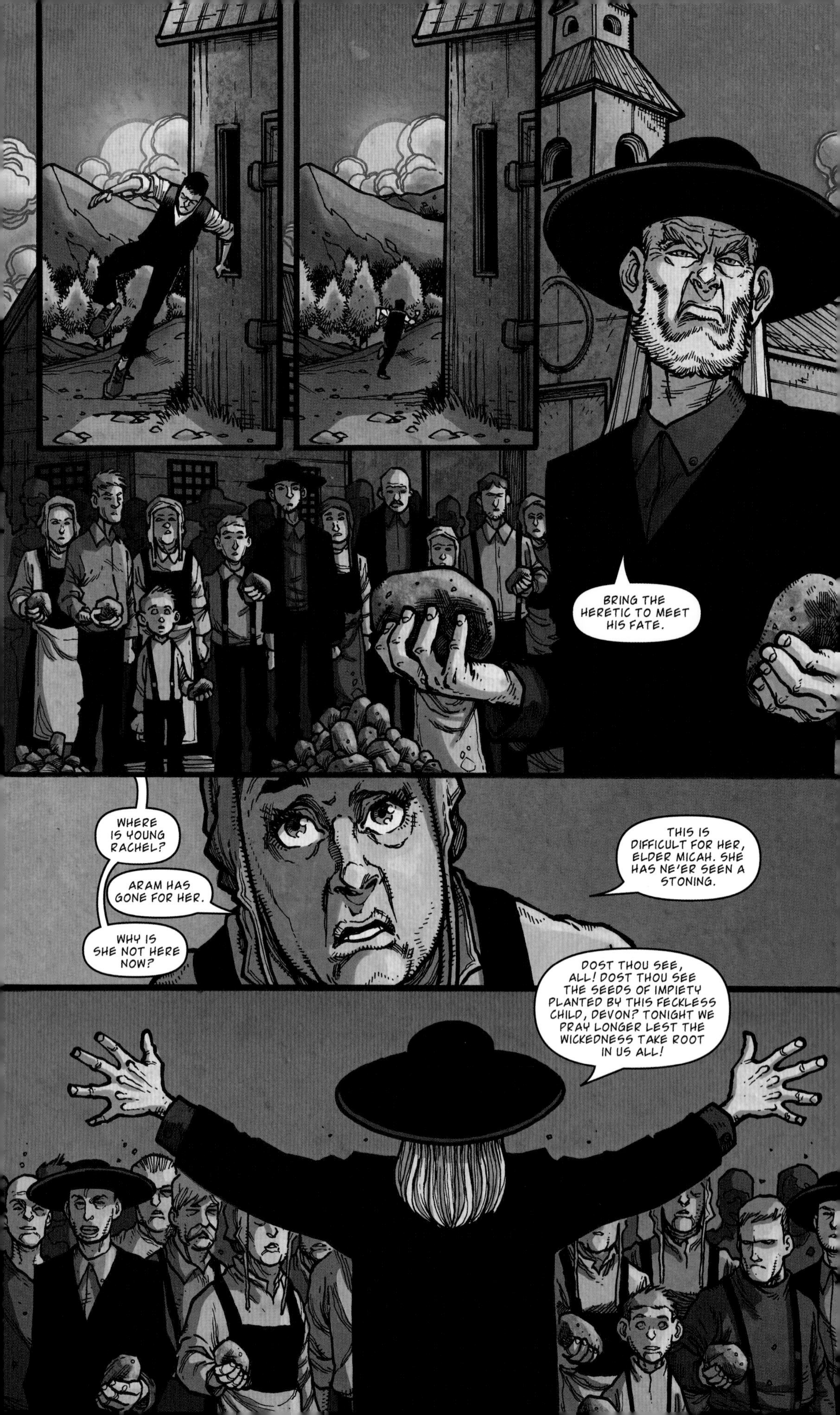
BRING THE HERETIC TO MEET HIS FATE.
WHERE IS YOUNG RACHEL?
ARAM HAS GONE FOR HER.
WHY IS SHE NOT HERE NOW?
THIS IS DIFFICULT FOR HER, ELDER MICAH. SHE HAS NE'ER SEEN A STONING.
DOST THOU SEE, ALL! DOST THOU SEE THE SEEDS OF IMPIETY PLANTED BY THIS FECKLESS CHILD, DEVON? TONIGHT WE PRAY LONGER LEST THE WICKEDNESS TAKE ROOT IN US ALL!

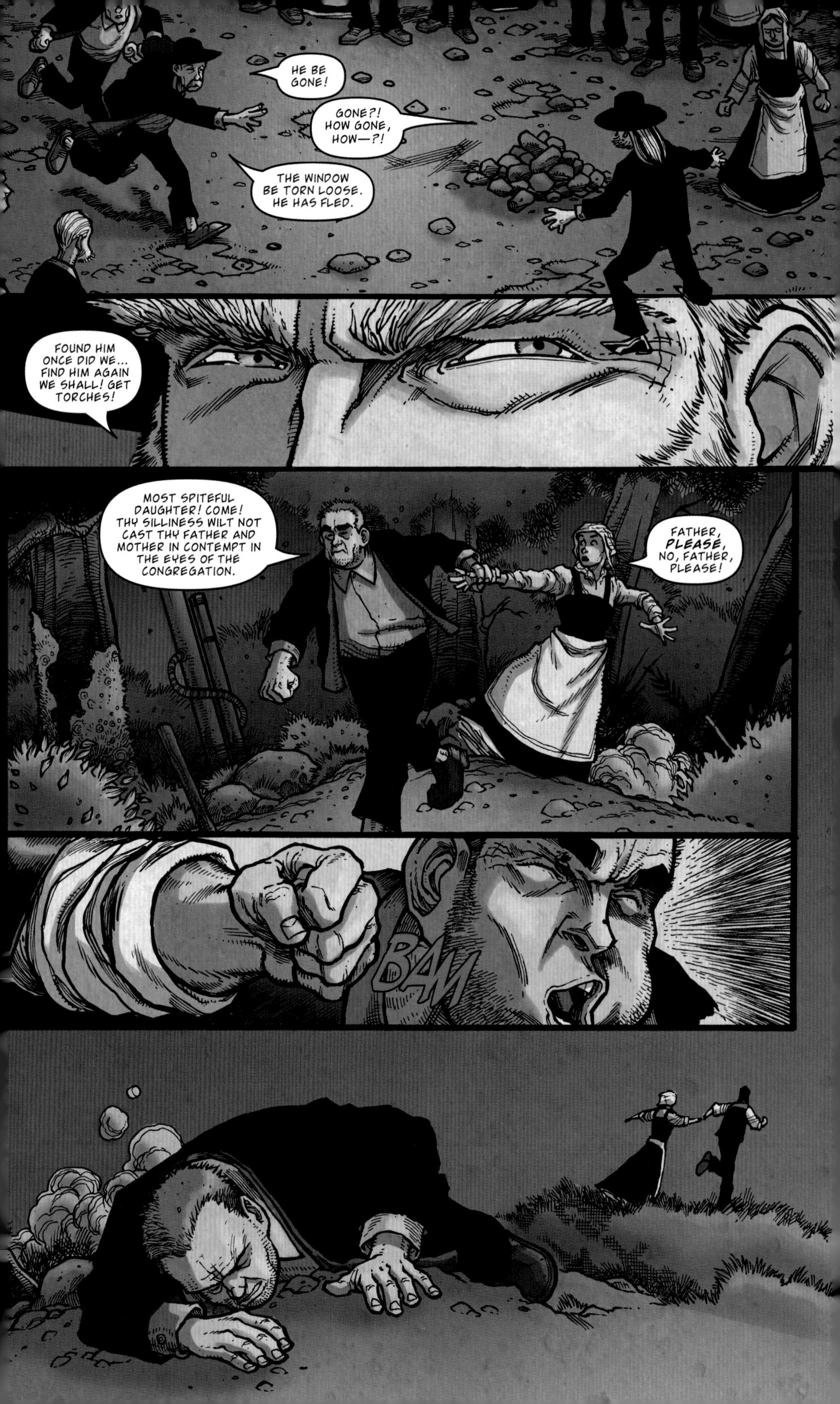

HE BE GONE!
GONE?! HOW GONE, HOW—?!
THE WINDOW BE TORN LOOSE. HE HAS FLED.
FOUND HIM ONCE DID WE... FIND HIM AGAIN WE SHALL! GET TORCHES!
MOST SPITEFUL DAUGHTER! COME! THY SILLINESS WILT NOT CAST THY FATHER AND MOTHER IN CONTEMPT IN THE EYES OF THE CONGREGATION.
FATHER, PLEASE, NO, FATHER, PLEASE!
BAM

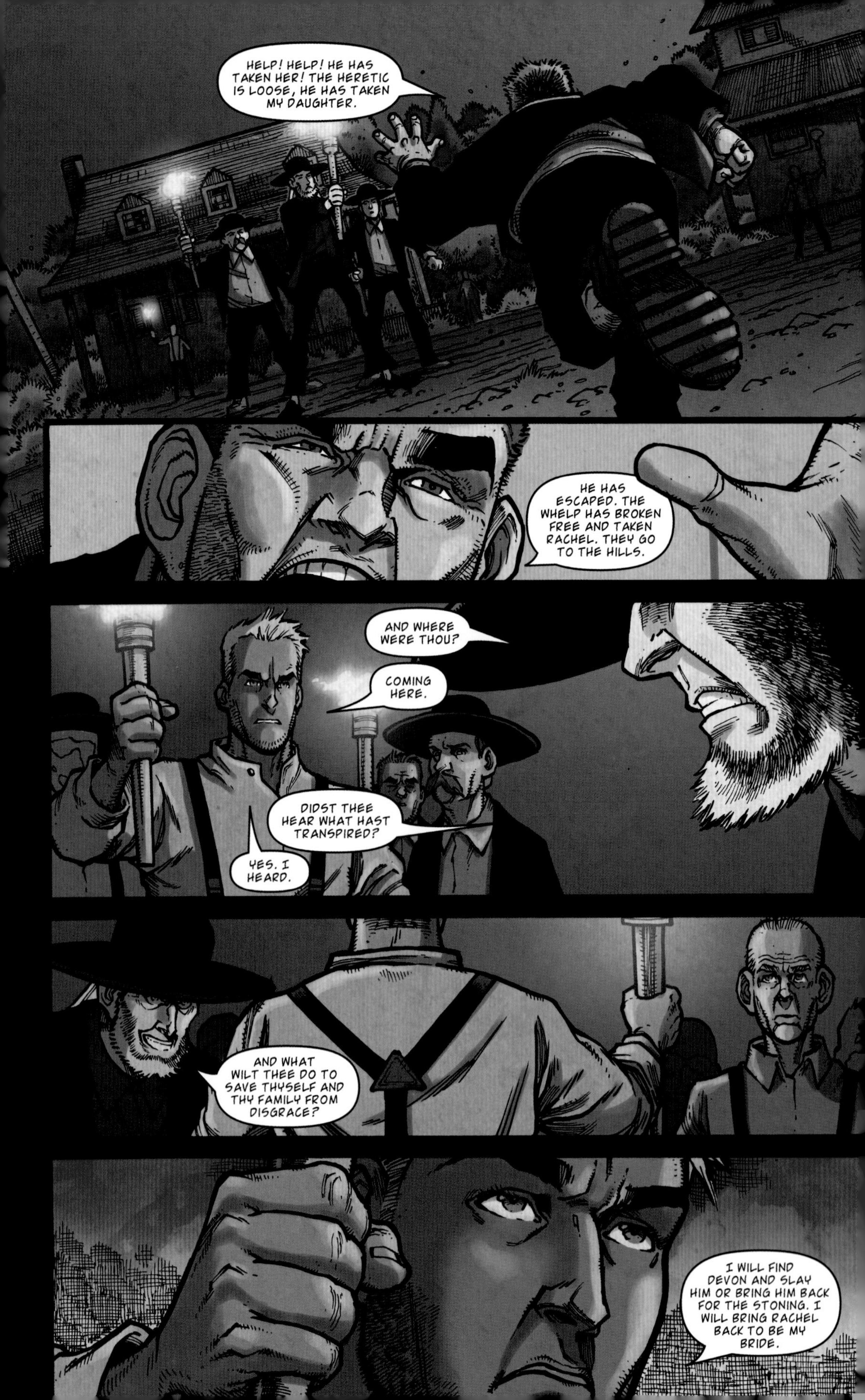
HELP! HELP! HE HAS TAKEN HER! THE HERETIC IS LOOSE, HE HAS TAKEN MY DAUGHTER.
HE HAS ESCAPED. THE WHELP HAS BROKEN FREE AND TAKEN RACHEL. THEY GO TO THE HILLS.
AND WHERE WERE THOU?
COMING HERE.
DIDST THEE HEAR WHAT HAST TRANSPIRED?
YES. I HEARD.
AND WHAT WILT THEE DO TO SAVE THYSELF AND THY FAMILY FROM DISGRACE?
I WILL FIND DEVON AND SLAY HIM OR BRING HIM BACK FOR THE STONING. I WILL BRING RACHEL BACK TO BE MY BRIDE.

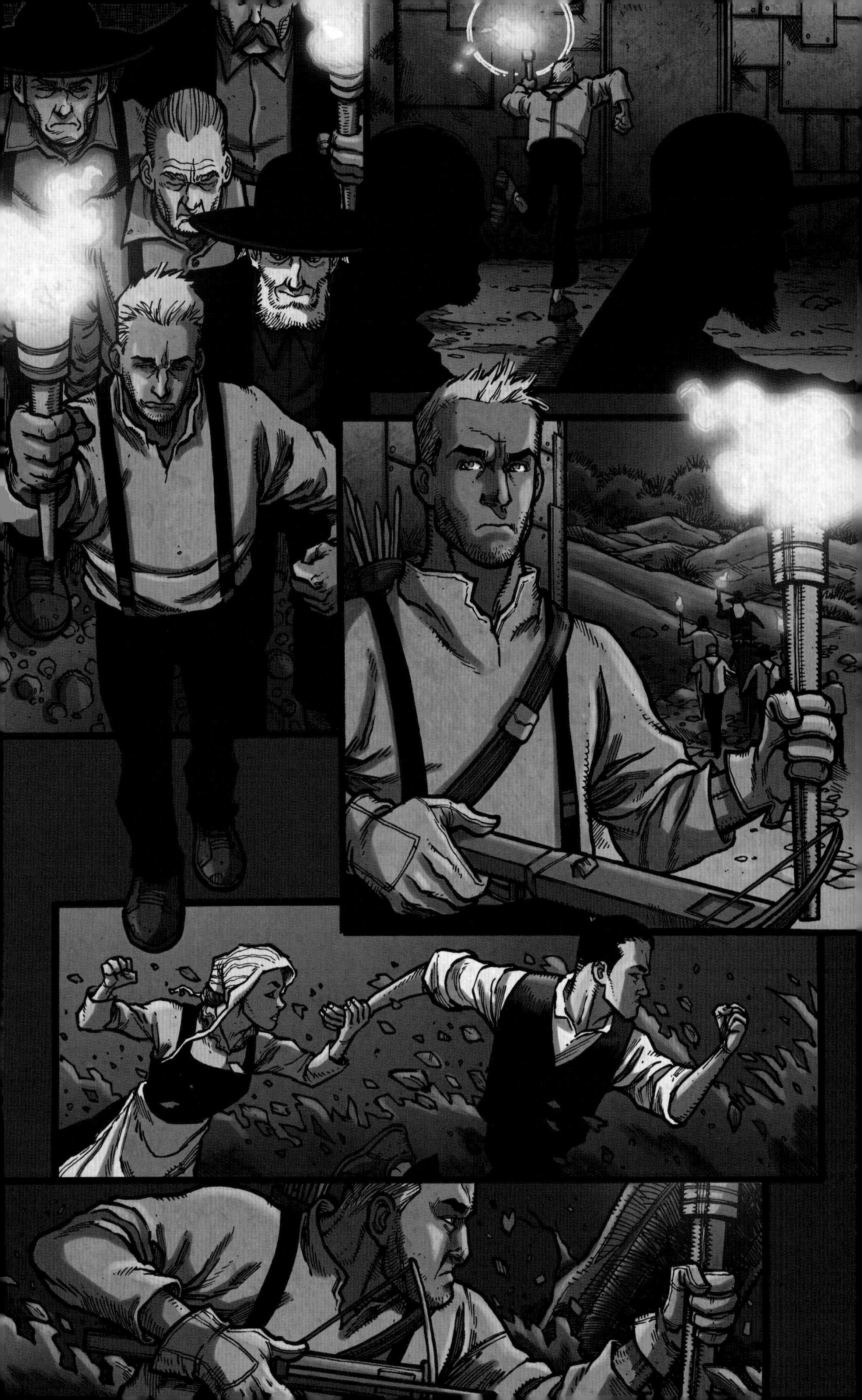

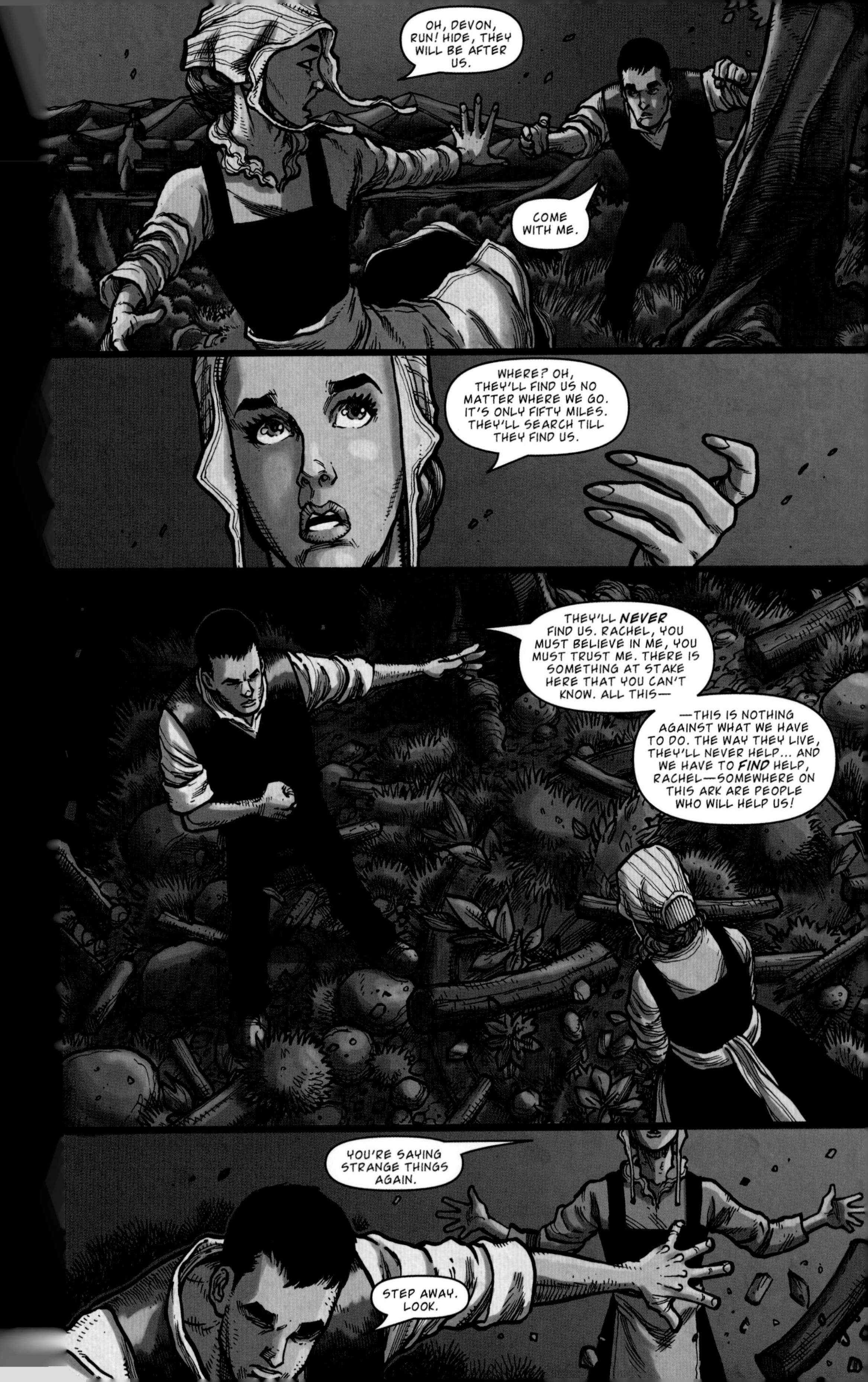
OH, DEVON, RUN! HIDE, THEY WILL BE AFTER US.
COME WITH ME.
WHERE? OH, THEY'LL FIND US NO MATTER WHERE WE GO. IT'S ONLY FIFTY MILES. THEY'LL SEARCH TILL THEY FIND US.
THEY'LL NEVER FIND US. RACHEL, YOU MUST BELIEVE IN ME, YOU MUST TRUST ME. THERE IS SOMETHING AT STAKE HERE THAT YOU CAN'T KNOW. ALL THIS—
—THIS IS NOTHING AGAINST WHAT WE HAVE TO DO. THE WAY THEY LIVE, THEY'LL NEVER HELP... AND WE HAVE TO FIND HELP, RACHEL—SOMEWHERE ON THIS ARK ARE PEOPLE WHO WILL HELP US!
YOU'RE SAYING STRANGE THINGS AGAIN.
STEP AWAY. LOOK.

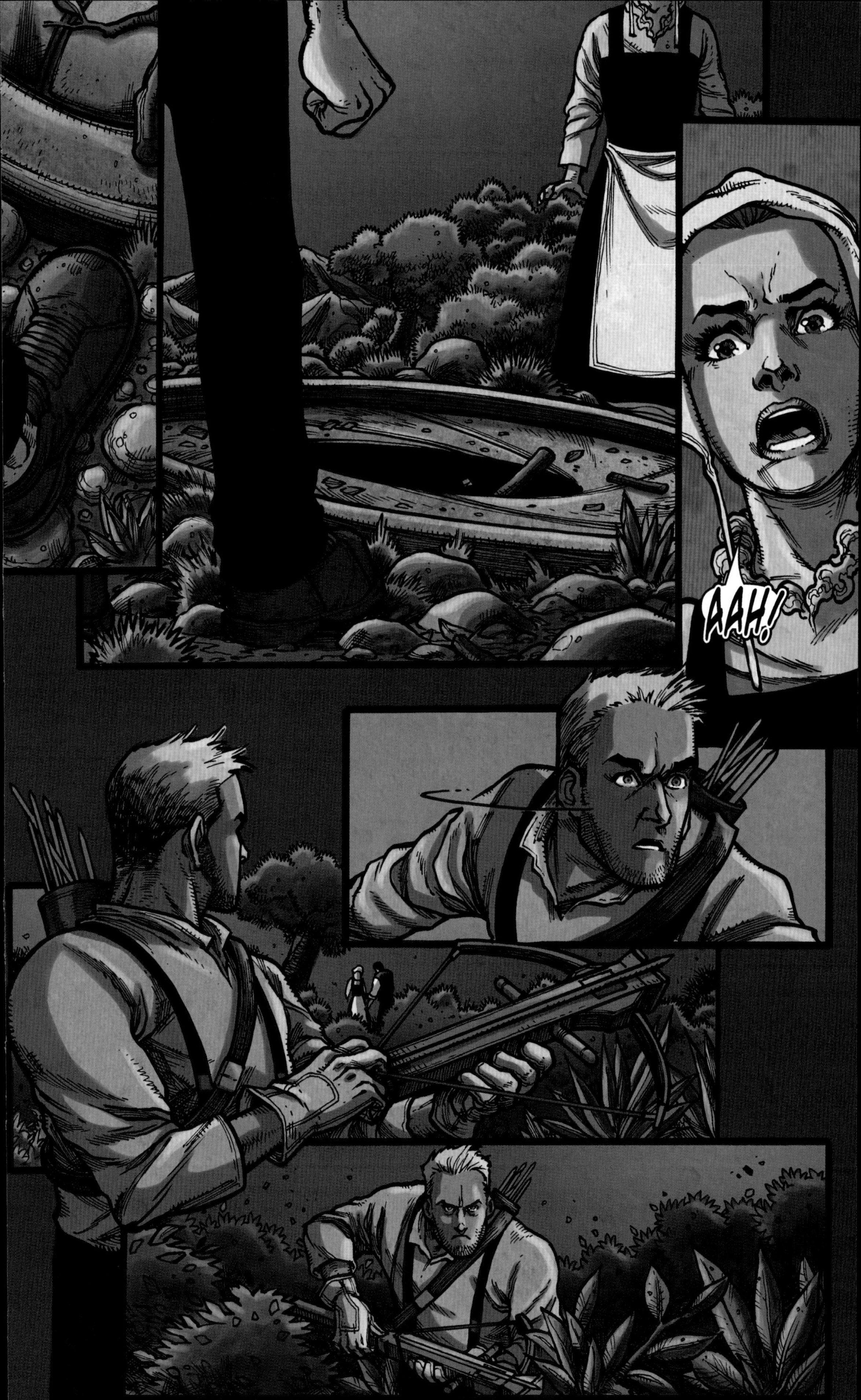
AAH!

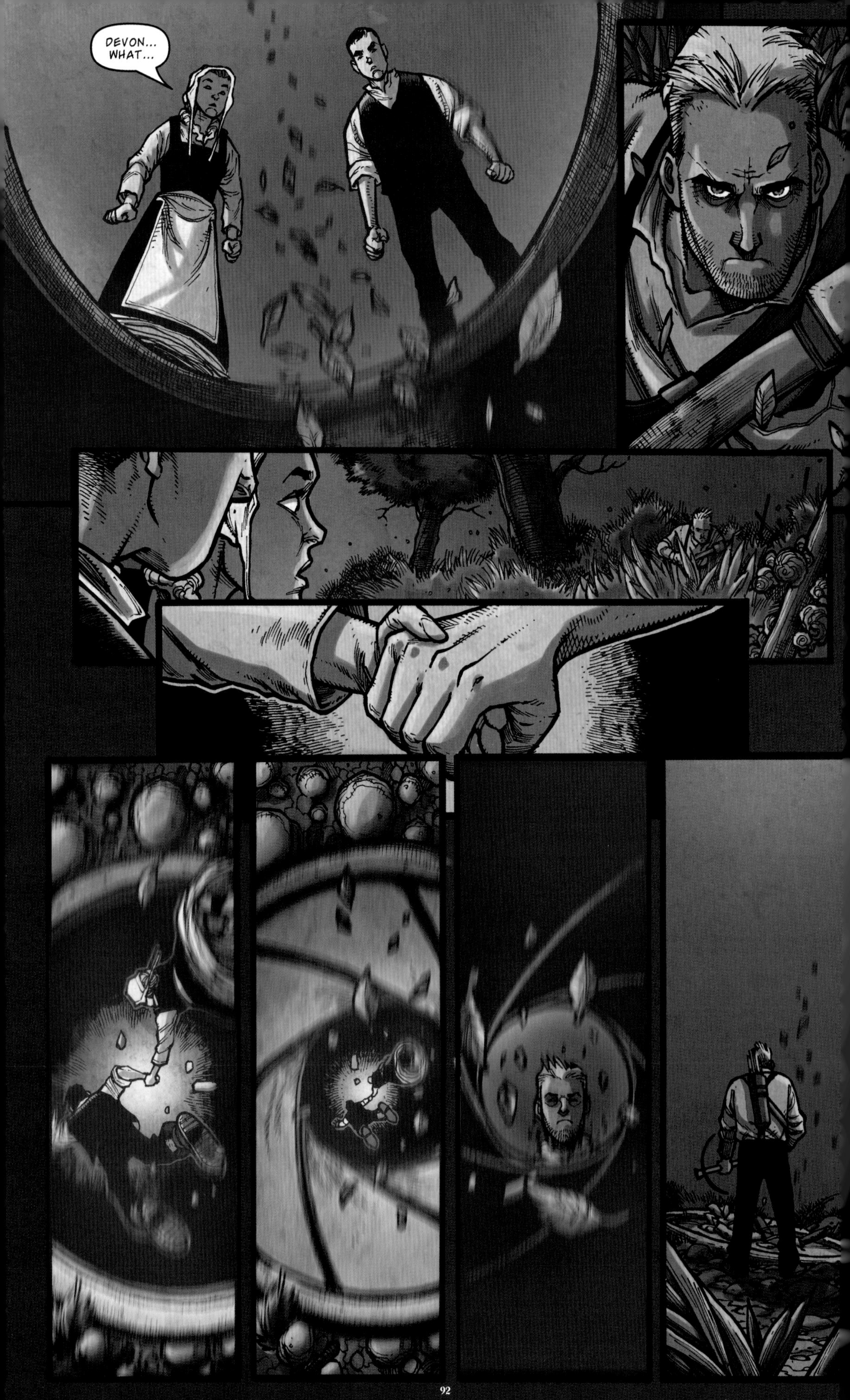
DEVON...
WHAT...

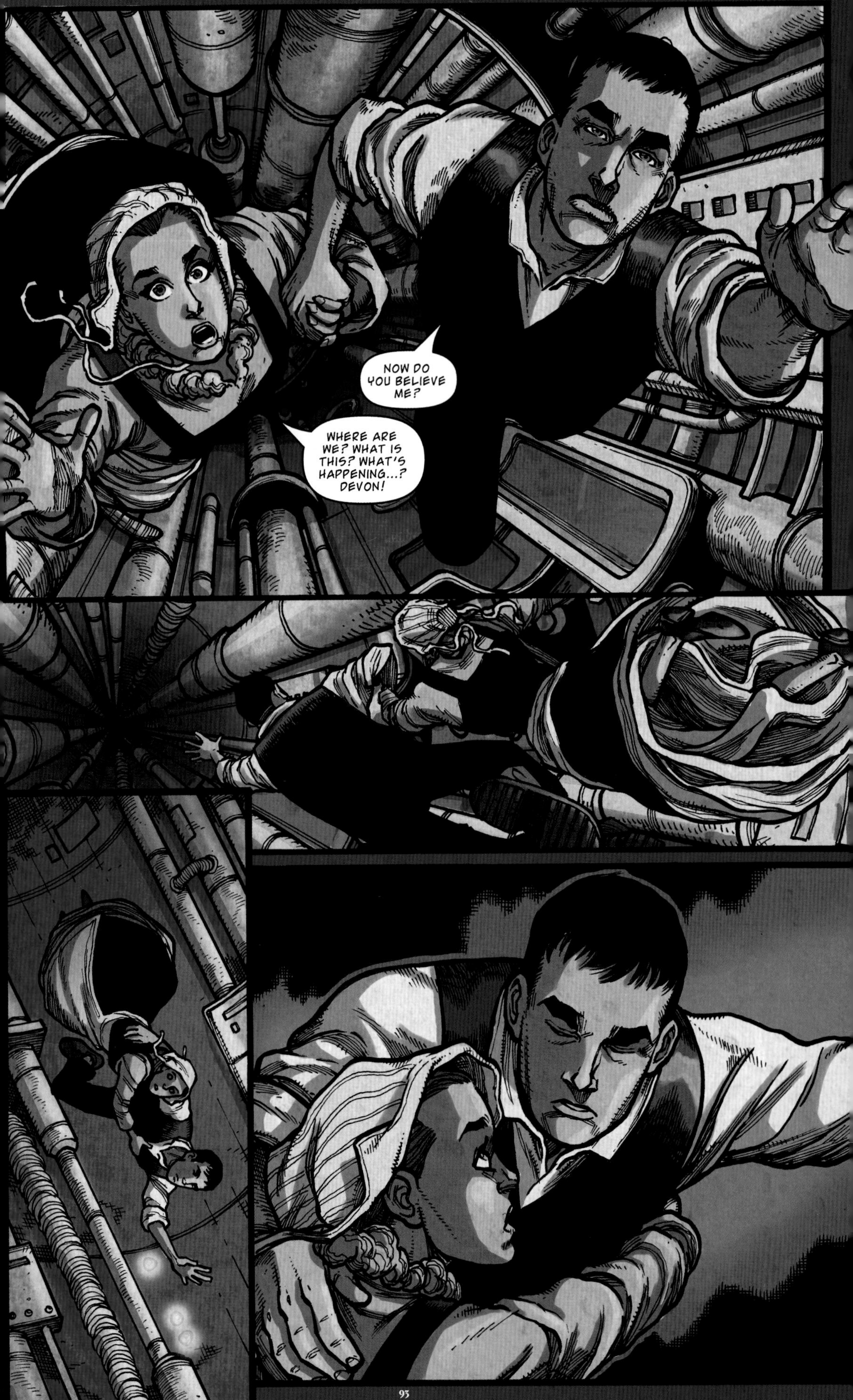
NOW DO YOU BELIEVE ME?
WHERE ARE WE? WHAT IS THIS? WHAT'S HAPPENING...? DEVON!

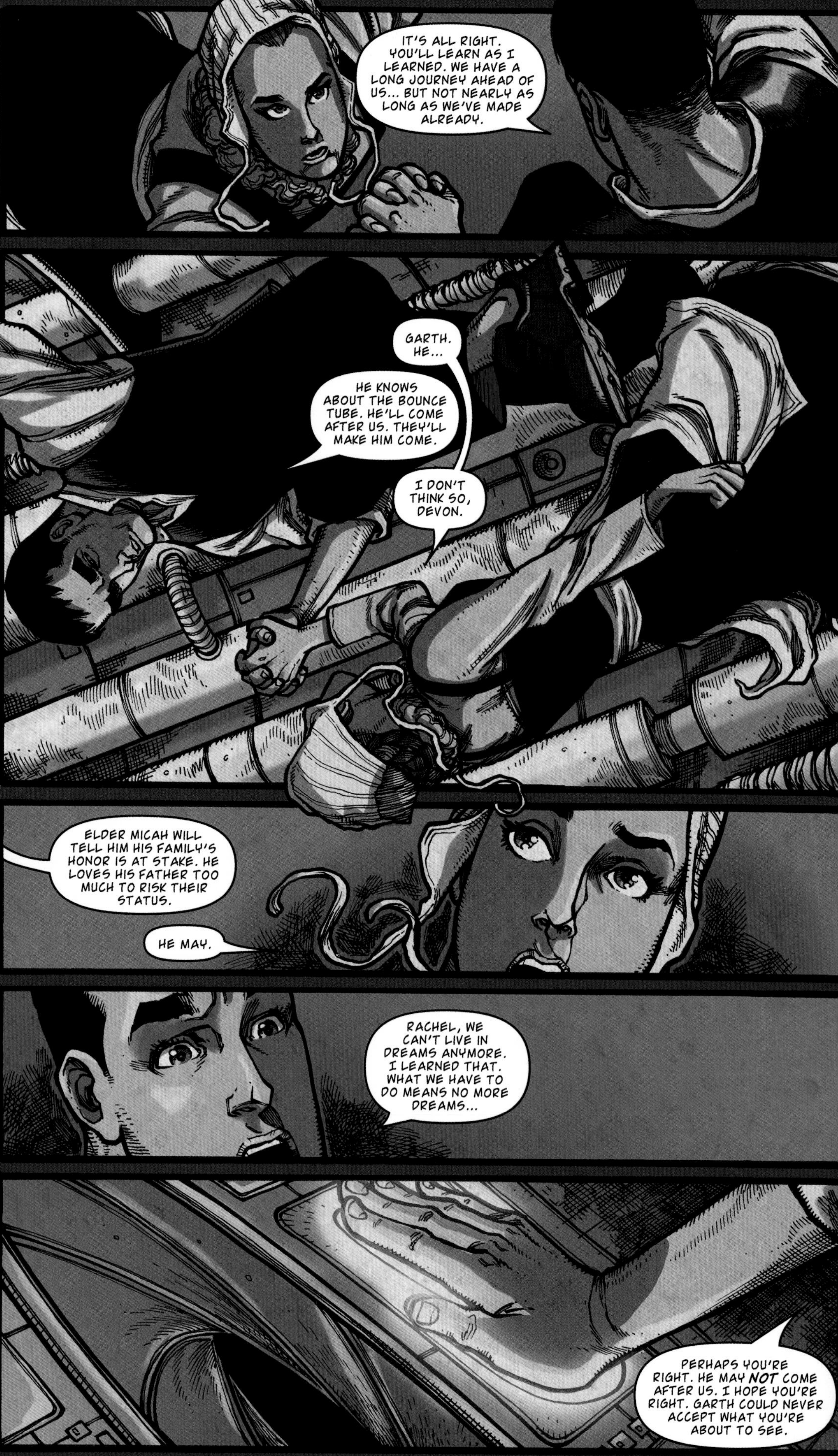
IT'S ALL RIGHT. YOU'LL LEARN AS I LEARNED. WE HAVE A LONG JOURNEY AHEAD OF US... BUT NOT NEARLY AS LONG AS WE'VE MADE ALREADY.
GARTH. HE...
HE KNOWS ABOUT THE BOUNCE TUBE. HE'LL COME AFTER US. THEY'LL MAKE HIM COME.
I DON'T THINK SO, DEVON.
ELDER MICAH WILL TELL HIM HIS FAMILY'S HONOR IS AT STAKE. HE LOVES HIS FATHER TOO MUCH TO RISK THEIR STATUS.
HE MAY.
RACHEL, WE CAN'T LIVE IN DREAMS ANYMORE. I LEARNED THAT. WHAT WE HAVE TO DO MEANS NO MORE DREAMS...
PERHAPS YOU'RE RIGHT. HE MAY *NOT* COME AFTER US. I HOPE YOU'RE RIGHT. GARTH COULD NEVER ACCEPT WHAT YOU'RE ABOUT TO SEE.

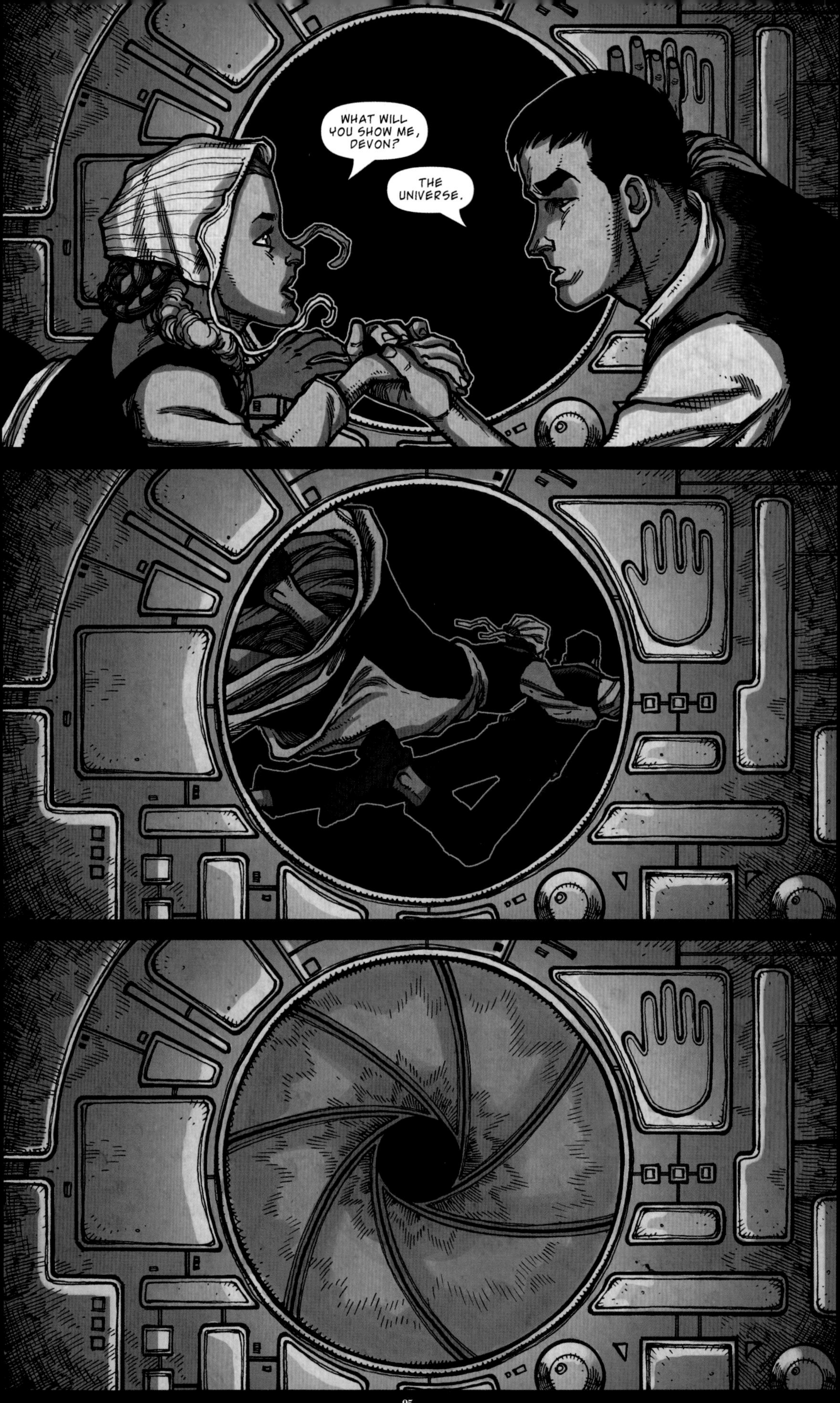
WHAT WILL YOU SHOW ME, DEVON?
THE UNIVERSE.

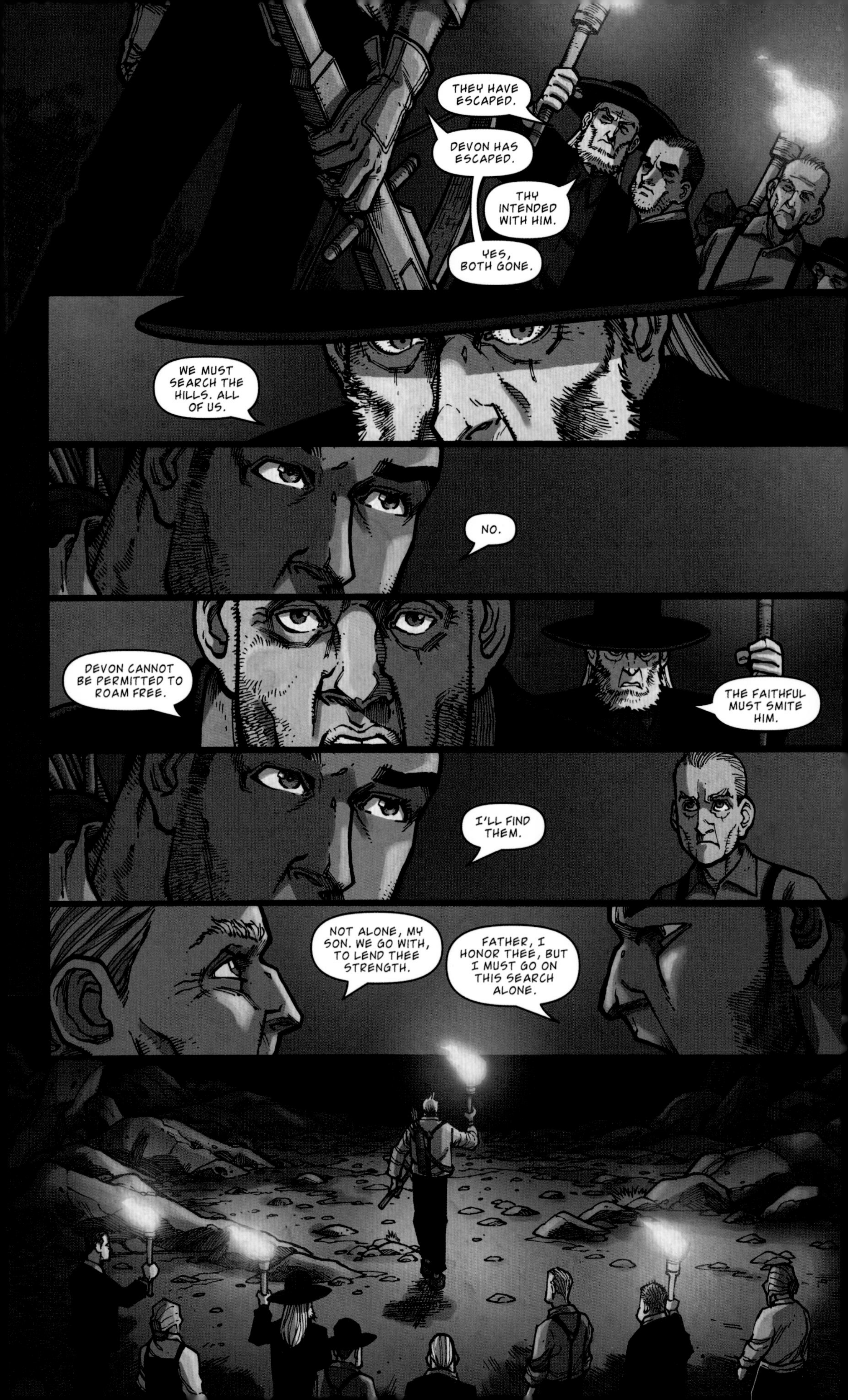

THEY HAVE ESCAPED.
DEVON HAS ESCAPED.
THY INTENDED WITH HIM.
YES, BOTH GONE.
WE MUST SEARCH THE HILLS. ALL OF US.
NO.
DEVON CANNOT BE PERMITTED TO ROAM FREE.
THE FAITHFUL MUST SMITE HIM.
I'LL FIND THEM.
NOT ALONE, MY SON. WE GO WITH, TO LEND THEE STRENGTH.
FATHER, I HONOR THEE, BUT I MUST GO ON THIS SEARCH ALONE.

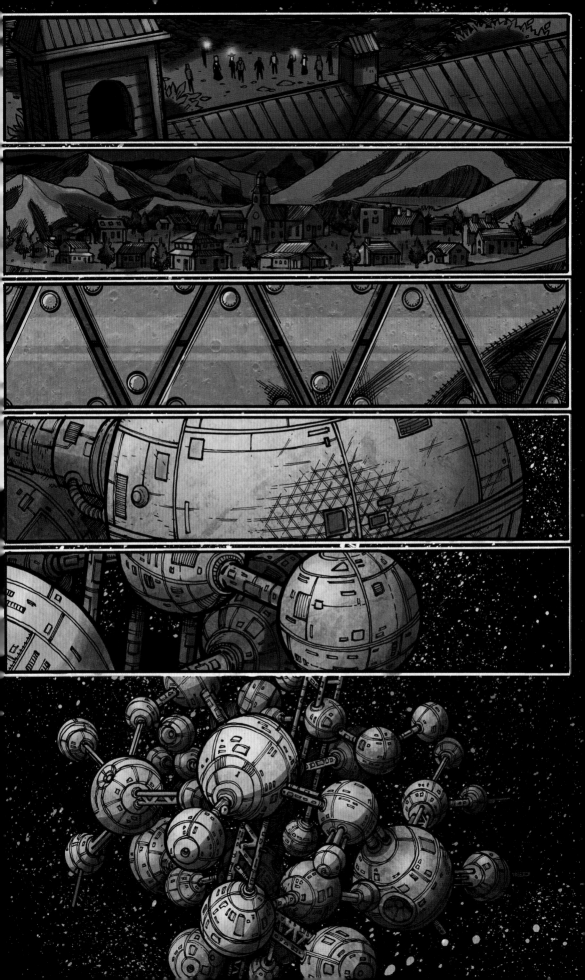

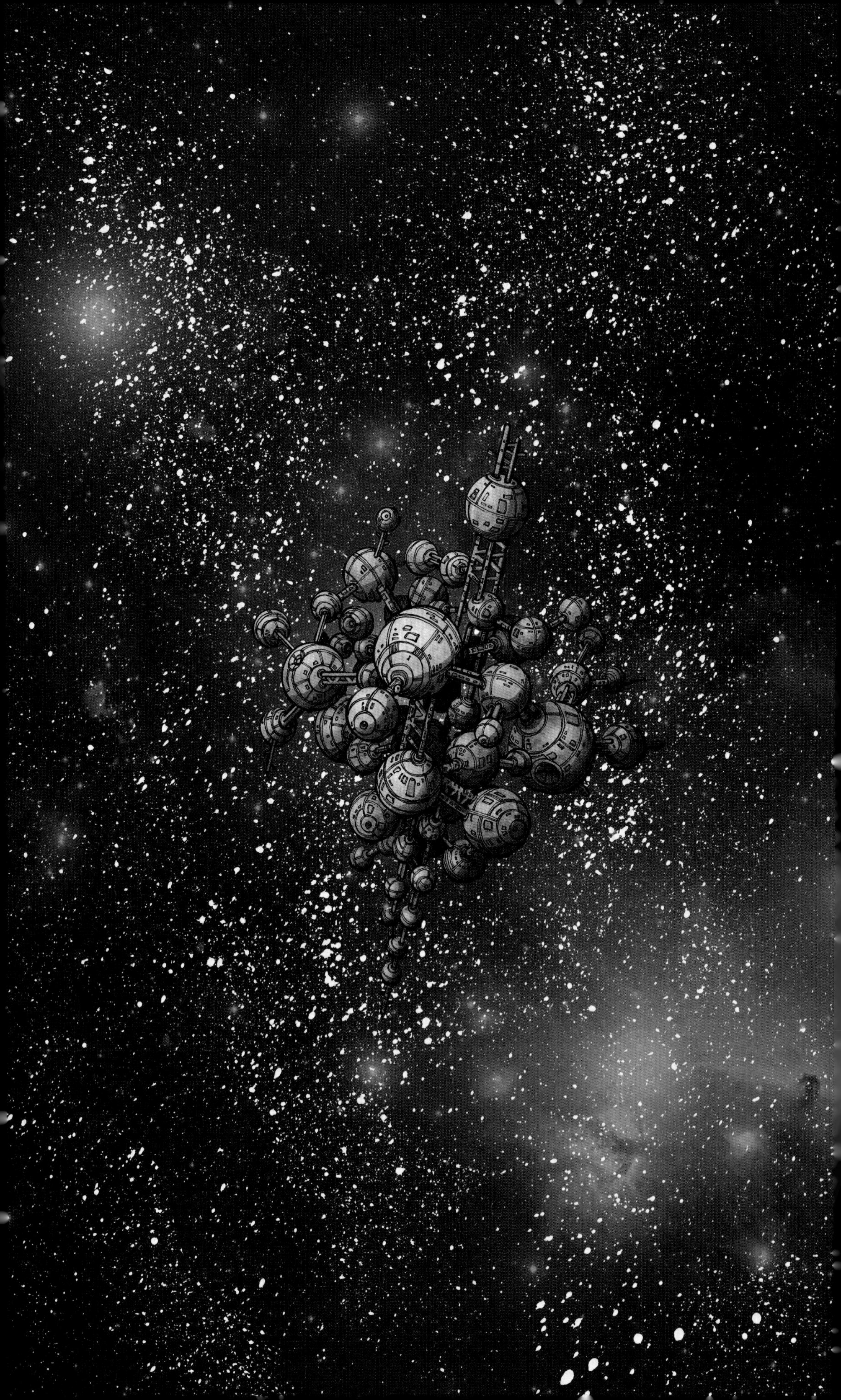

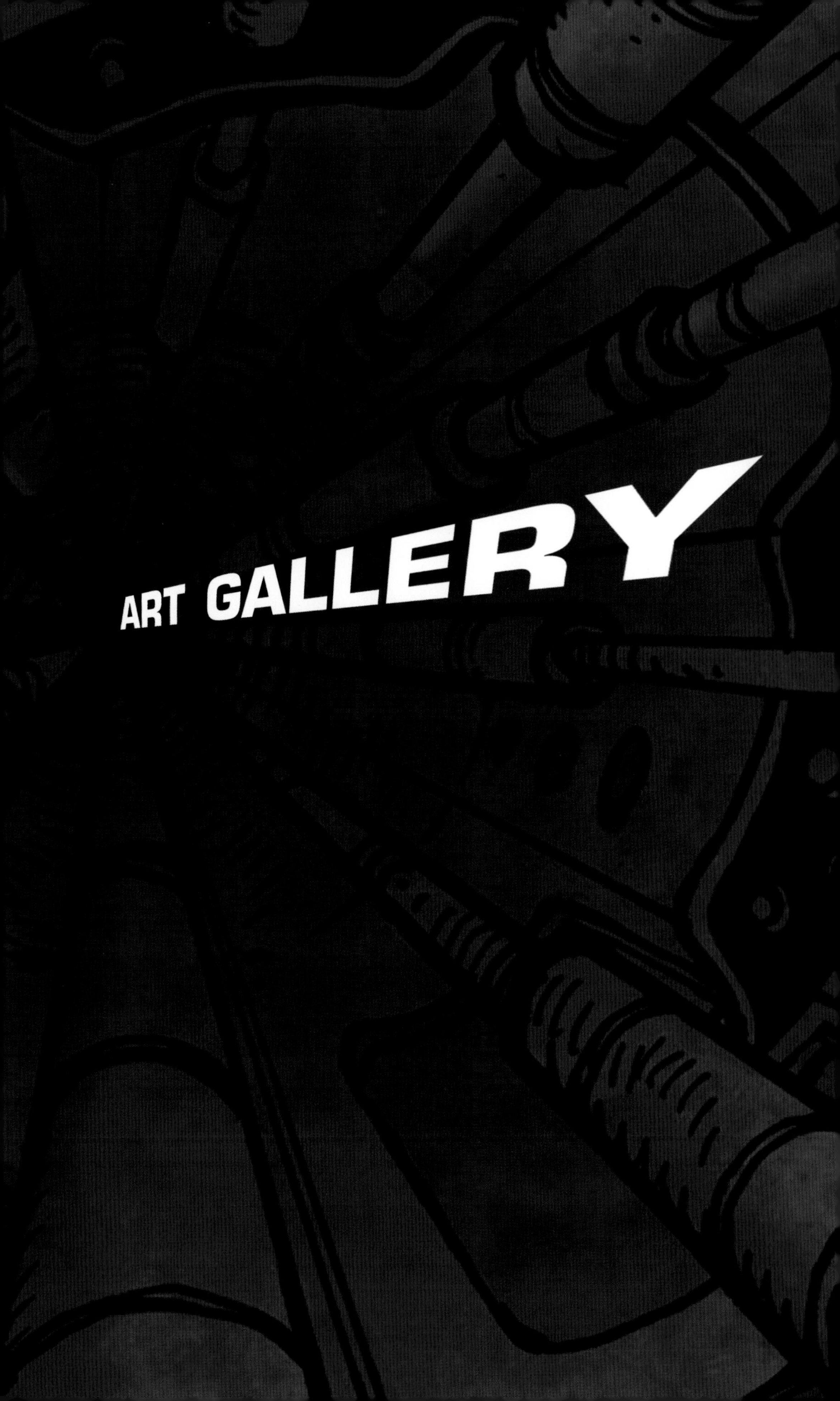
ART GALLERY

ART BY **JOHN K. SNYDER III**
COLORS BY **JASON WRIGHT**

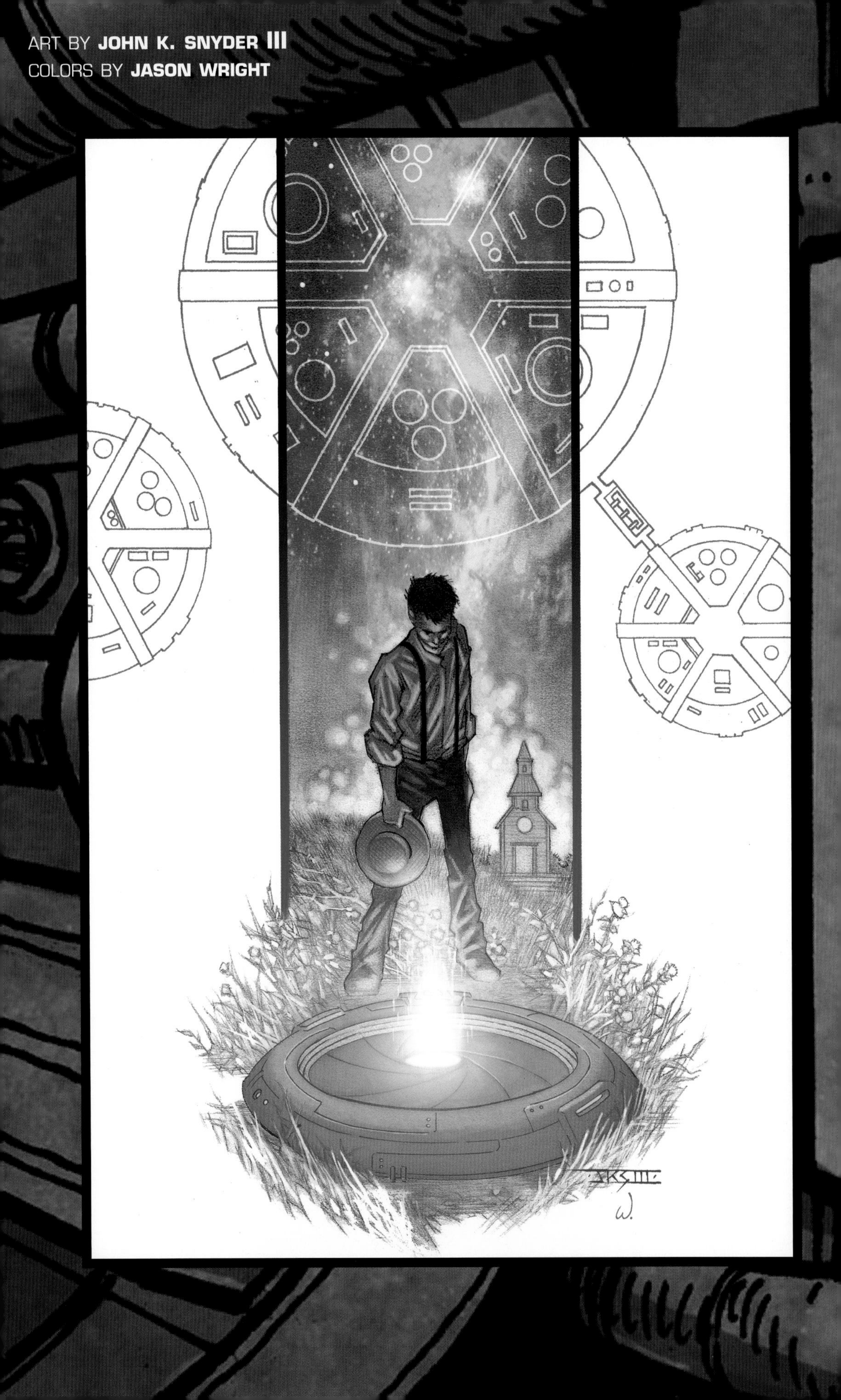

ART BY **JOHN K. SNYDER III**
COLORS BY **JASON WRIGHT**

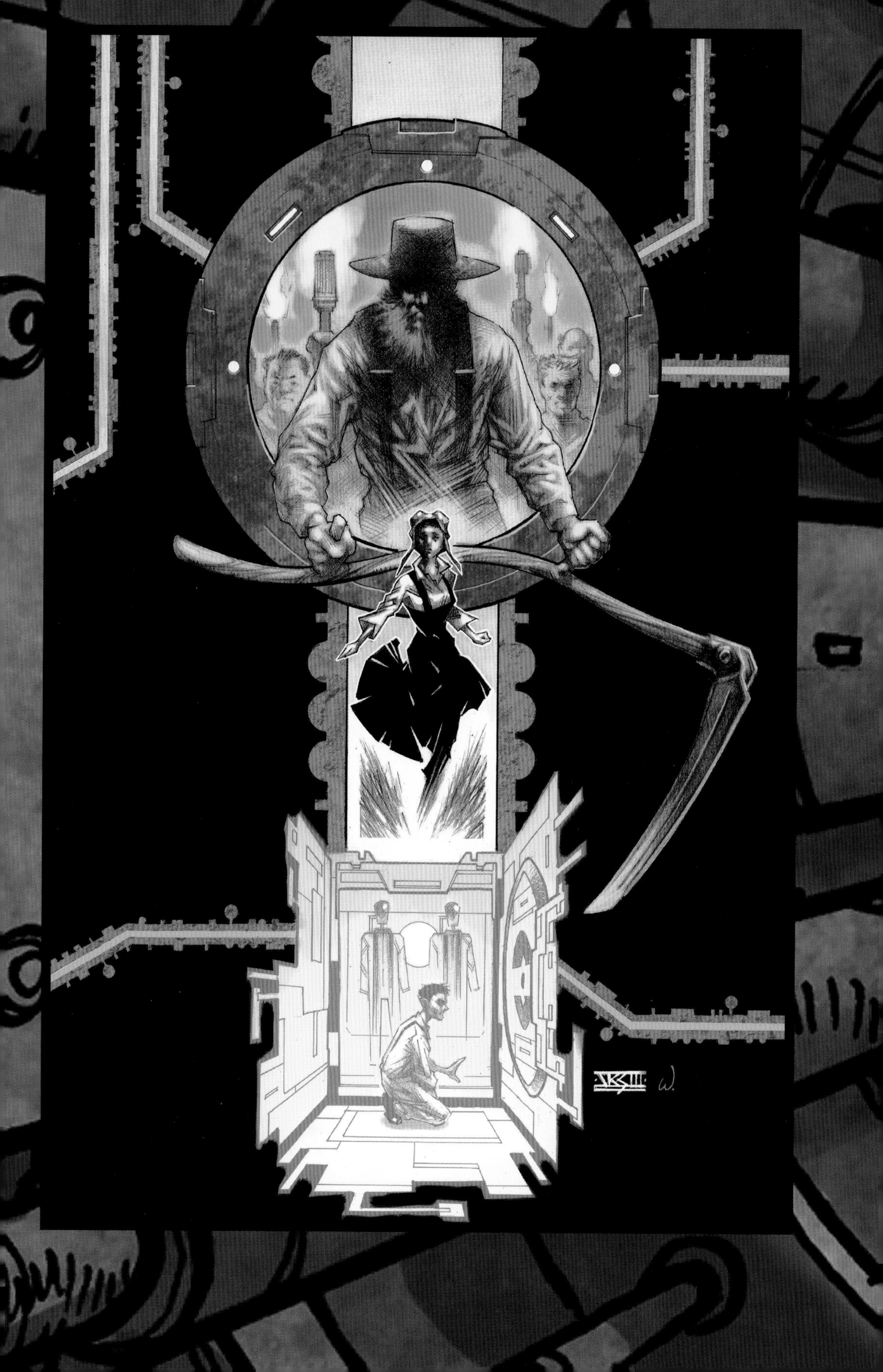

ART BY **JOHN K. SNYDER III**
COLORS BY **JASON WRIGHT**

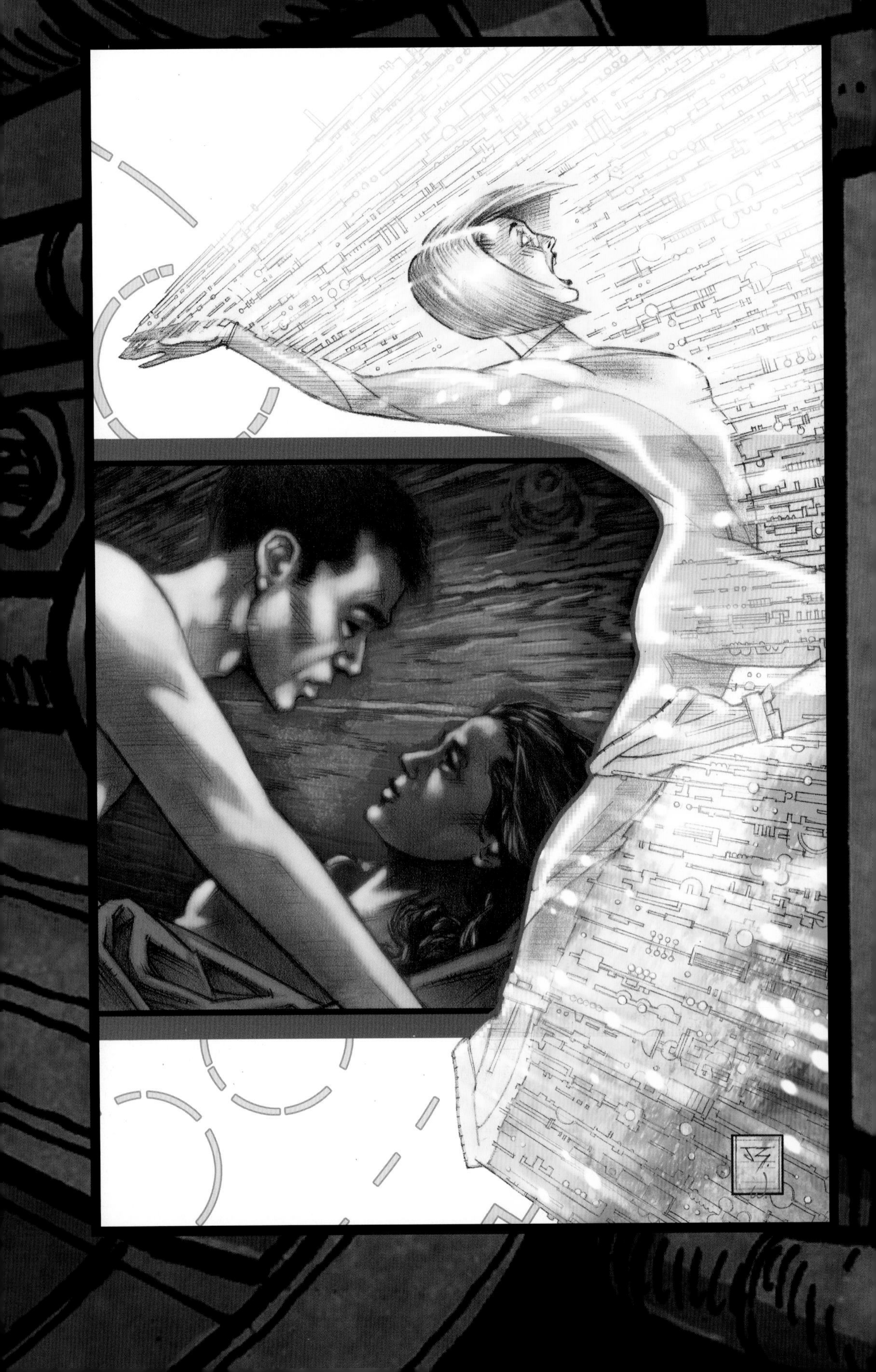

ART BY **JOHN K. SNYDER III**
COLORS BY **JASON WRIGHT**

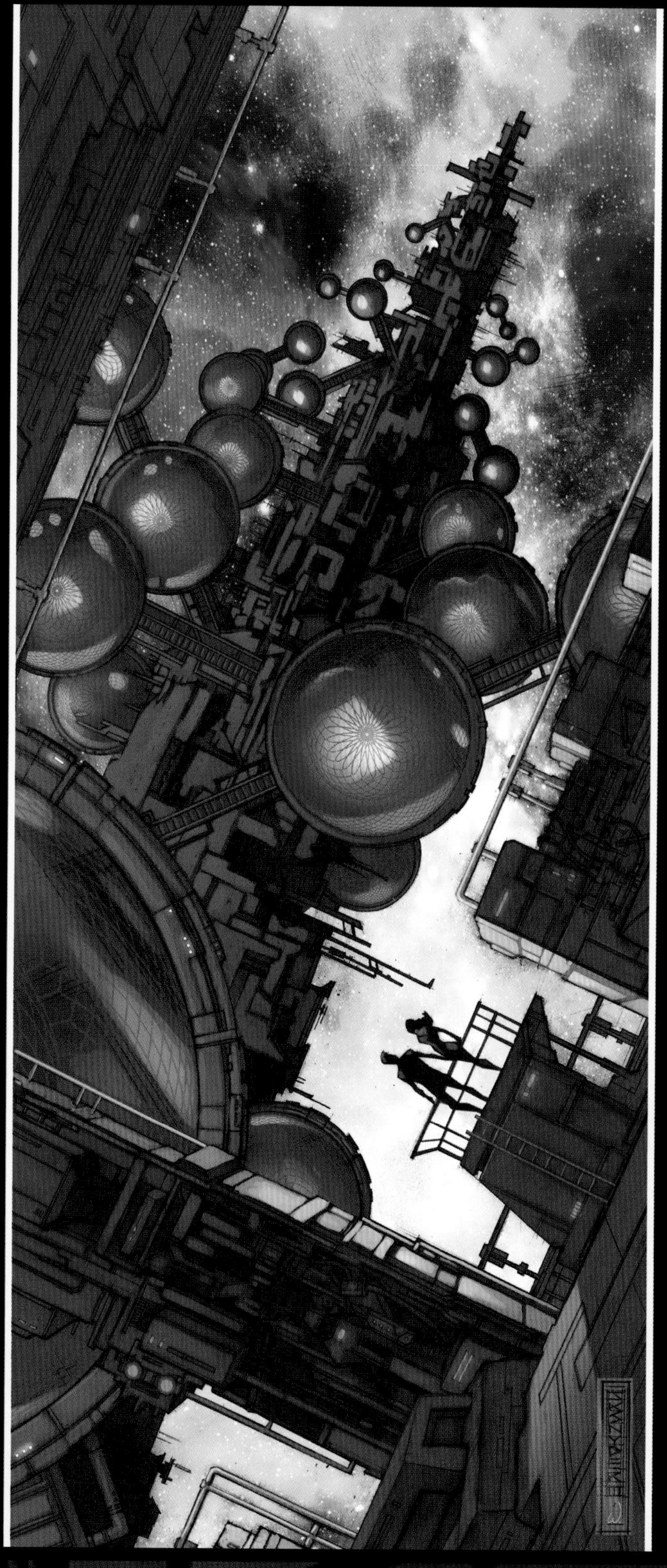

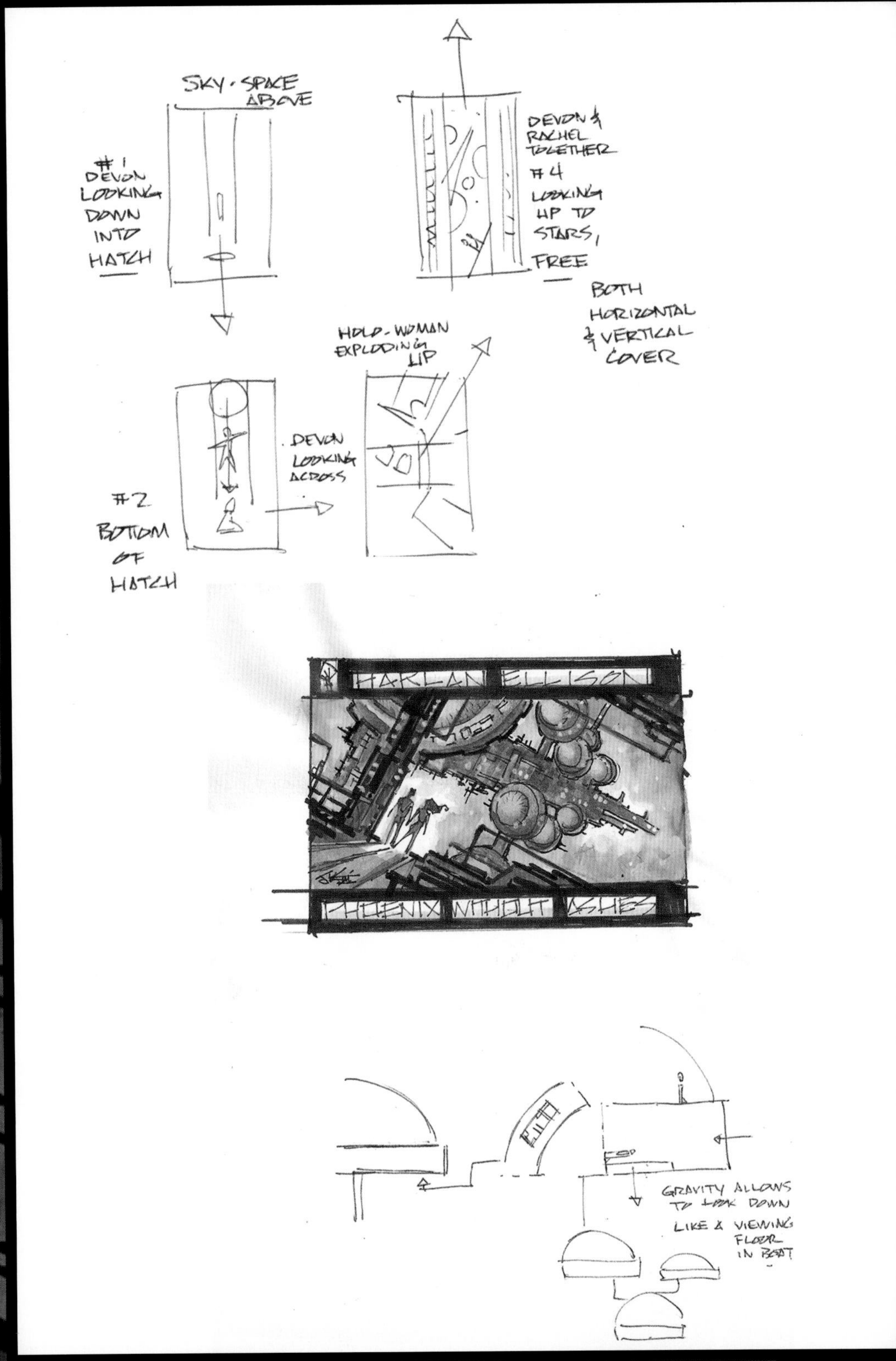
SKY · SPACE ABOVE
#1 DEVON LOOKING DOWN INTO HATCH
DEVON & RACHEL TOGETHER #4 LOOKING UP TO STARS, FREE
BOTH HORIZONTAL & VERTICAL COVER
HOLD-WOMAN EXPLODING UP
· DEVON LOOKING ACROSS
#2 BOTTOM OF HATCH
HARLAN ELLISON
PHOENIX WITHOUT ASHES
GRAVITY ALLOWS TO LOOK DOWN LIKE A VIEWING FLOOR IN BOAT

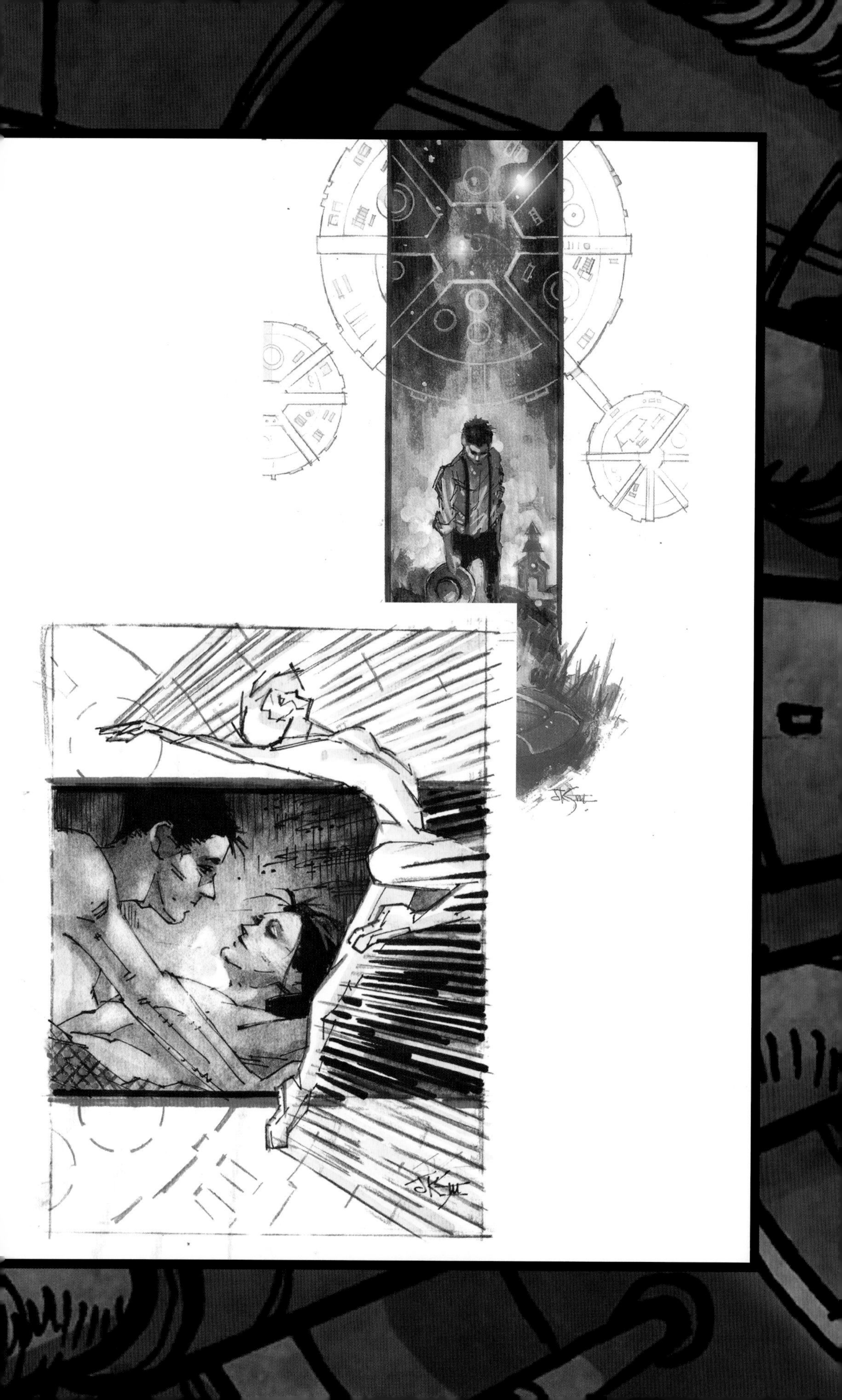

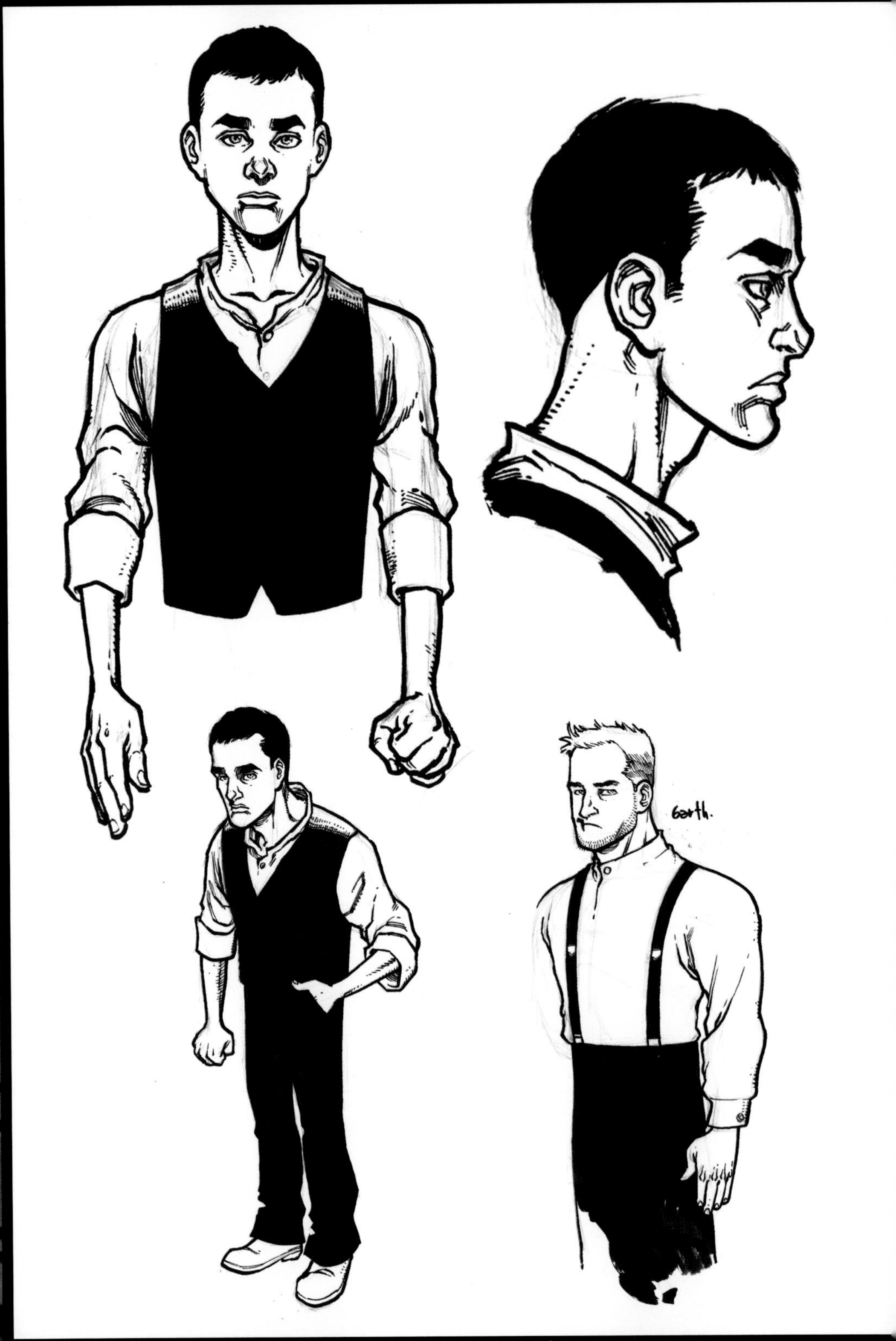
Garth.

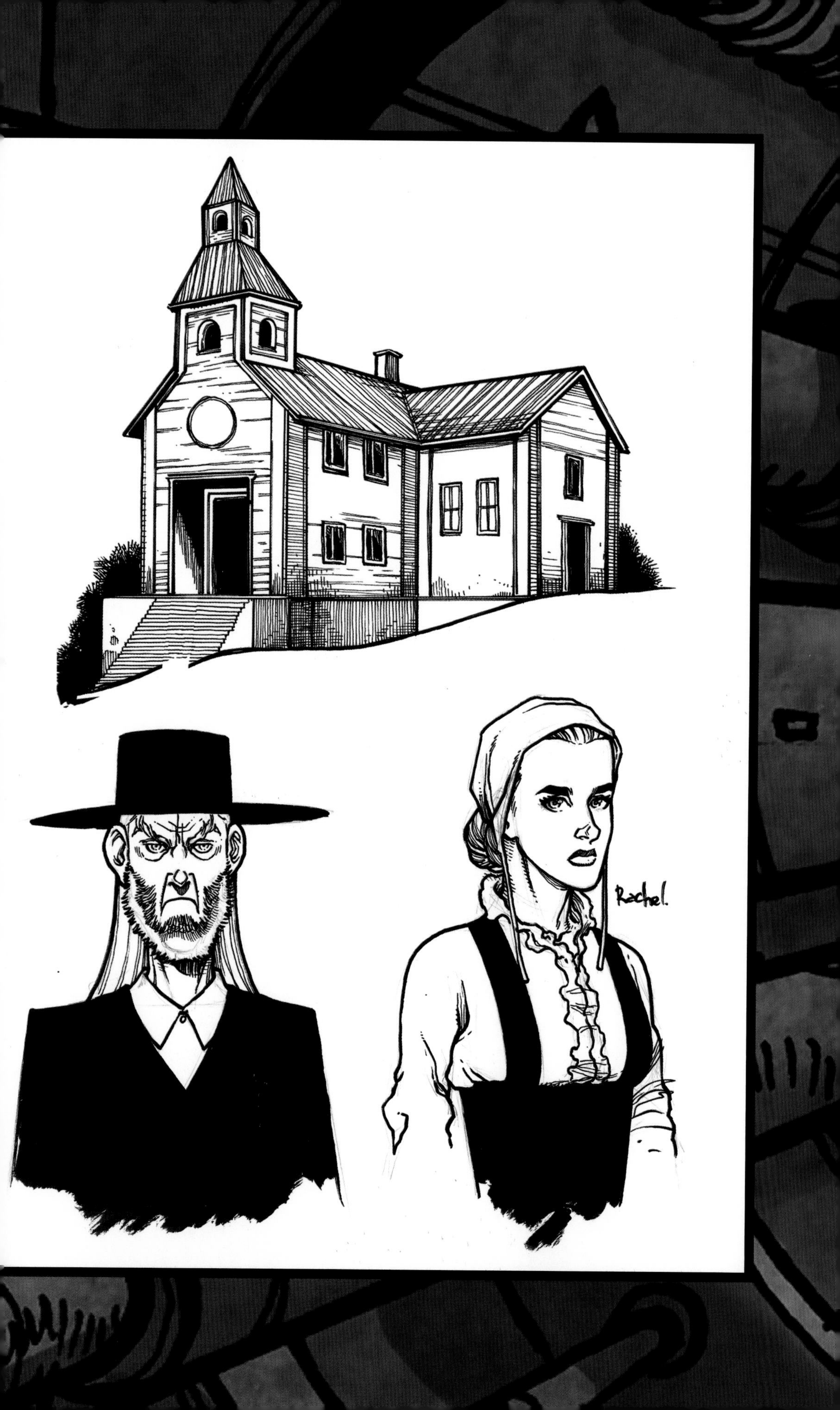
Rachel.

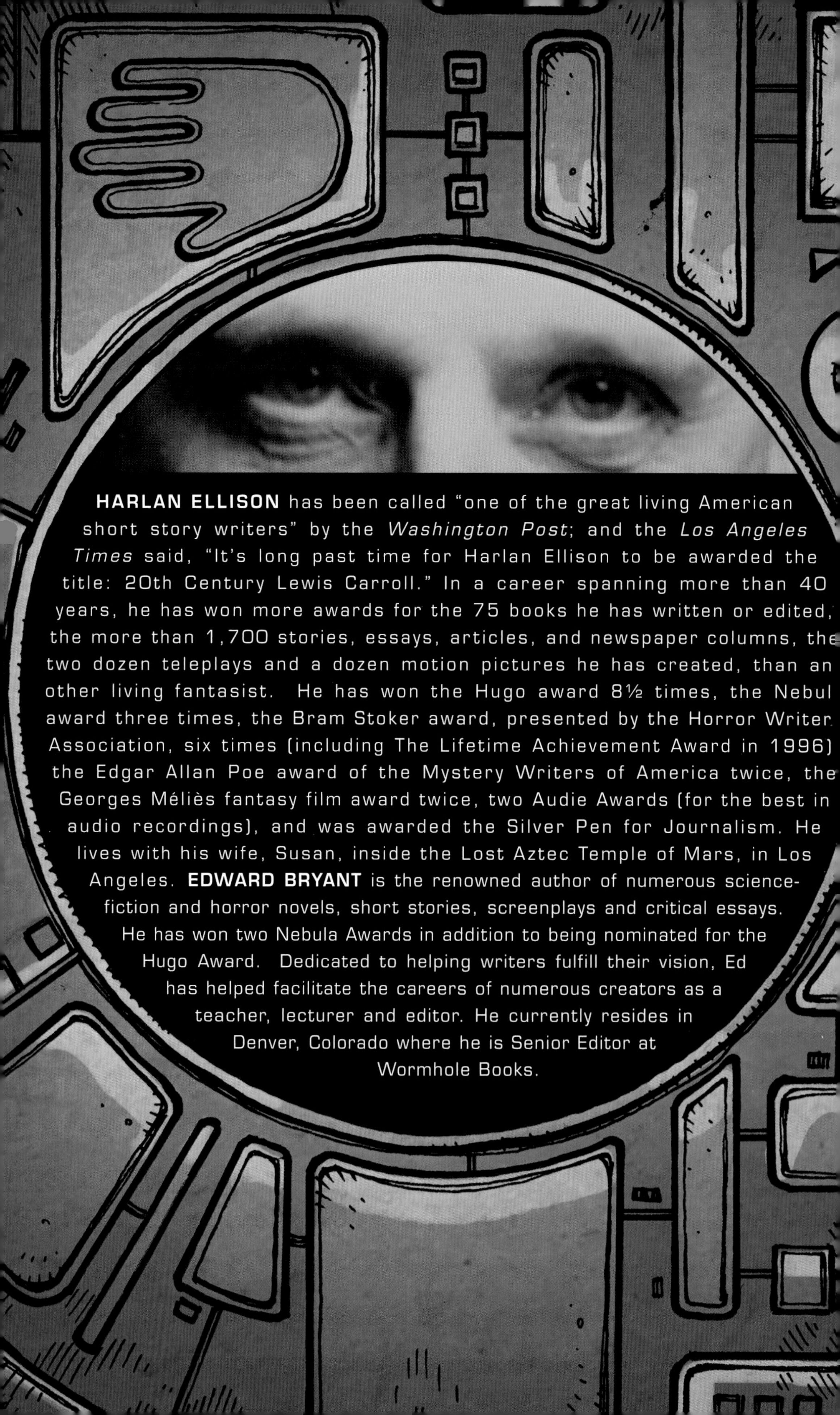

HARLAN ELLISON has been called "one of the great living American short story writers" by the *Washington Post*; and the *Los Angeles Times* said, "It's long past time for Harlan Ellison to be awarded the title: 20th Century Lewis Carroll." In a career spanning more than 40 years, he has won more awards for the 75 books he has written or edited, the more than 1,700 stories, essays, articles, and newspaper columns, the two dozen teleplays and a dozen motion pictures he has created, than an other living fantasist. He has won the Hugo award 8½ times, the Nebul award three times, the Bram Stoker award, presented by the Horror Writer Association, six times (including The Lifetime Achievement Award in 1996) the Edgar Allan Poe award of the Mystery Writers of America twice, the Georges Méliès fantasy film award twice, two Audie Awards (for the best in audio recordings), and was awarded the Silver Pen for Journalism. He lives with his wife, Susan, inside the Lost Aztec Temple of Mars, in Los Angeles. **EDWARD BRYANT** is the renowned author of numerous science-fiction and horror novels, short stories, screenplays and critical essays. He has won two Nebula Awards in addition to being nominated for the Hugo Award. Dedicated to helping writers fulfill their vision, Ed has helped facilitate the careers of numerous creators as a teacher, lecturer and editor. He currently resides in Denver, Colorado where he is Senior Editor at Wormhole Books.